Colorado's
Greenhorn Valley
Fact and Folklore

(1700 - 2000)

by

Gerald W. Crispin

Edited by Vera G. Crispin

Second edition revised and rewritten by Gerald W. Crispin

2003
Benchmark Book Craft
P. O. Box 19583
Colorado City, CO 81019

Second Edition
First Printing
February 2003

Laura Williams Halsy presents her Mount of the Holy Cross painting to Nat K. Mendelsohn, president of CCDC and developer of Colorado City.

(Courtesy of Pueblo Regional Library)

This second edition will be followed by a third edition reflecting new intelligence from reliable sources unknown at this time. If you, the reader, have valid knowledge or photographs not included in this text, please forward your name, address, and phone number to: Benchmark Book Craft, P.O. Box 19583, Colorado City, CO 81019. New enlightenment will not be published without a source. All materials will be returned to the enlightener in person, when possible.
On the other hand, all adverse criticisms and shallow sniveling should be mailed directly to the U. S. Government in Washington, D. C. Thank you.

ISBN 0-9744015-0-1
52281

Copyright 2003
by Gerald W. Crispin
All rights reserved

TABLE OF CONTENTS

Dedication	1
References	2
Preface	6
1. Greenhorn Valley	8
2. Natives and Possession	12
3. The Comanches	16
4. Chief Cuerno Verde	17
5. Zebulon Montgomery Pike	25
6. St. Vrain and the Bent Brothers	28
7. Frontier Conflict	39
8. Archibald Charles Metcalf	40
9. Luisa Sandoval Beckwourth Brown	45
10. Trapper John Brown	55
11. Mediumistic John Brown	66
12. Baca, Kinney, and Carson	75
13. Charlie Autobee	82
14. Edward G. Beckwith	86
15. Estefana Bent Hicklin	90
16. Alexander "Zan" Hicklin	97
17. George Sears	101
18. What Happened to the Indians?	104
19. Fossceco Family	105
20. Marion Mine	108
21. Rye Village	110
22. Rebirth of Colorado City	117
23. The First Ten Years	127
24. 1974-1990	154
25. Year 2000	175
Closing Comments	176
Index	181
Order Form	189

ILLUSTRATIONS

1. A general map of Colorado's historical Greenhorn Valley — 10
2. Don Juan Bautista de Anza and proper conquistador attire — 19
3. Captain Zebulon Montgomery Pike in formal uniform — 26
4. Ceran St. Vrain: French American called *Blackbeard* by the Indians — 29
5. William Bent in 1835 and the William Bent Fort in early 1840s — 31
6. Charles Bent: first U.S. Governor of New Mexico Territory — 36
7. Ceran St. Vrain: Frenchman who brought So. Colo. into the USA — 38
8. James P. Beckwourth: mulatto man who became a Crow chief — 48
9. Lucien B. Maxwell: sole owner of the Maxwell Land Grant — 54
10. George S. Simpson and Simpson's Rest in Trinidad, Colorado — 60
11. John D. Albert: Colorado resident who escaped the Taos Rebellion — 63
12. John Brown: pictured in his own book, ed. by J. S. Loveland in 1887 — 67
13. John Brown: medium & mystic with good friend James W. Waters — 71
14. Kit Carson: frontiersman, Indian agent, scout, & commander — 78
15. Charles Autobee, William Kroenig, & Joseph B. Doyle: frontiersmen — 85
16. Hicklin adobe ranch house & barn near Crow Village & Post Office — 92
17. Alexander Hicklin in 1850 and Estefana Bent Hicklin in 1927 — 94
18. Shady Greenhorn in 1949 and the Old Oaken Bucket at water well — 106
19. St. Vrain's grand daughters & *Birth Certificate of Colorado City* — 124
20. Mrs. Laura Williams Halsey with Mr. & Mrs. Ralph C. Taylor — 129
21. Mrs. Attie Provenzano: artist & great grand daughter of Carson — 132
22. Mrs. Laura Williams Halsey (Miss C-City) & Nat Mendelsohn — 134
23. Horse trail & pedestrian path between rows of trees at Colo. City — 139
24. Breaking ground for the Enco Service Center at Crow Village — 141
25. William M. White Jr. & Nathan K. Mendelsohn: C-City developers — 145
26. Lake Beckwith, Marina, Alpine Village, & Greenhorn Mountains — 153
27. Historical Crow Mercantile Building about 1980 before it collapsed — 160

ORDER FORM

Send to: Benchmark Book Craft   Date_____
           P. O. Box 19583
           Colorado City, CO 81019

Please ship <u>Colorado's Greenhorn Valley, Fact and Folklore, 1700-2000</u> by Gerald W. Crispin

Quantity	Unit Price	Shipping	Total Amount
1	$21.95	$3.00	$24.95
#____	_____	_____	_____

Sold to: Shipped to:

Customer   _____   _____
Street   _____   _____
City, State _____   _____
Zip   _____   _____

Received _____   Check Number _____

Preview

Television serials, movie theaters, and historical books dramatize the early American frontier as a place where eastern settlers hike into hostile western territories and clash with Indian warriors. The Greenhorn Valley (surrounding Colorado City) was exactly that kind of frontier. It was an arena of wild western conflict and killing.

Even the most conservative interpretation renders the Greenhorn Valley to have been a ruthless bush country. As early as the mid-1700s, a Comanche Chief named *Green Horn* (*Cuerno Verde* in Spanish) was assaulting early pueblos, butchering male homesteaders, and sacrificing their women and children.

Television and movie producers would be hard pressed to find better movie scripts for adventure, romance, suspense, survival, poverty, spiritualism, colonialism, patriotism, wealth, greed, theft, violence, murder, and sex – than written here in the fact and folklore of historic Greenhorn Valley.

The following historical sketch has five purposes: (1) to preserve the hefty history of the Valley; (2) to explore new meaning between the old teeth and mature noggins of early historians; (3) to prove guns did not "Win the West" but were instrumental in reducing both human and animal populations; (4) to demonstrate modern-day television has become today's pictorial gunslinger; and finally (5) to season the entire mix with a tiny touch of whimsical wit.

The 5th purpose is employed to keep readers from falling asleep; from becoming depressed over the many murders; and from mistaking this historical narration for some scholarly work of immutable importance.

Dedicated to

all residents of

Greenhorn Valley

Author's Note

All sources of information are hereby listed in chronological "disorder" giving those authors at the end of our alphabet a more prominent place of recognition long overdue.

Most sources of information are listed immediately below with the sole purpose of getting the reader's attention. In the same vein, pages 2-5 (representing two years of research) should be read out loud so buyers of this book might feel slightly better about exchanging their personal revenue for the following historical sketch.

References

Wilson, Elinor. *Jim Beckwourth, Black Mountain Man and War Chief of the Crows,* University of Oklahoma Press: Norman, OK, 1972.

Wilbar, Mrs. W. P. (daughter of Mr. Jacob Sayler who settled near Rye in 1874). Compiled by Mrs. Homer King. "Our Pioneers," by Arkansas Valley Chapter Daughters of the American Revolution, 1944.

Warner, Erin. *A Penny Earned, Story of the Pueblo Star-Journal and Chieftain,* by Johnson Publishing Co. of Denver, CO, 1992.

Thomas, Alfred B. and Ronald E. Kessler, *The San Luis Valley Historian (Juan Bautista de Anza Diary - a Messita Prairie Evening),* vol. xxvi, no. 1, 1994.

Thacker, Madelyne L. *The Past One Hundred Years in the Greenhorn Valley,* Published by the Bicentennial Committee, 11 pages, no date.

Taylor, Ralph C., ed. *The California City/Colorado City Sun,* monthly published by California City Development Co., Mar. 1964 - Feb. 1965.

Taylor, Ralph C., ed. *Colorado City Call,* Vol. 1, No. 1-5 monthly published by Colorado City Development Co., Oct. 1963 through Feb. 1964.

Taylor, Ralph C., ed. *The Colorado City Sun,* monthly published by Colorado City Development Co., Mar. 1965 through Nov. 1973.

Taylor, Ralph C. *Colorado South of the Border,* Sage Books, Denver, CO, 1963.

Taylor, Ralph C. *Galaxy,* Colorado Galaxy, 220 West Tenth St., Pueblo, Colo. 81003, 1878.

Taylor, Ralph C. *Pueblo,* Published for Pueblo Board of Education, 1979. *Star-Journal and The Pueblo Chieftain,* Pueblo, CO, 1963-1974.

Sprague, Marshall. *The Great Gates, the Story of the Rocky Mountain Passes,* Little, Brown and Company, 1964.

Sears, R. W. "The Pioneer Store at Greenhorn on the Santa Fe Trail," *The Colorado Magazine,* Published bimonthly by the State Historical Society of Colorado, vol. XXV, no. 6, Denver, CO, Nov. 1948.

San Luis Valley Historical Society, Inc. *The San Luis Valley Historian,* Volume II, Number 3, Summer, 1970.

San Luis Valley Historical Society, Inc. *The San Luis Valley Historian,* "Colorado's Oldest Wagon Road," Volume XXXII, 2000, Number 2.

Ruxton, George F. *Life in the Far West,* 1849.

Pueblo Chieftain and Star-Journal, Pueblo, CO, 1963 through 1974.

Prince, Bradford L. *Historical Sketches of New Mexico from the Earliest Records to the American Occupation,* Kansas City, MO, an appendix, 1883.

Monnett, John H. and Michael McCarthy, *Colorado Profiles, Men and Women Who Shaped the Centennial State,* Cordillera Press, Inc., 1987.

MacKell, Jan. *Greenhorn Rancho: A History of the Hicklins in Greenhorn Valley,* 1987.

Lecompte, Janet. *Pueblo, Hardscrabble, Greenhorn, the Upper Arkansas, 1832-1856,* University of Oklahoma Press: Norman, OK, 1978.

Laine, Barbara & Don. *Little Known Southwest,* Mountaineers Books, Seattle, WA, 2001.

Koch, Don. The Colorado Pass Book, *A Guide to Colorado's Backroad Mountain Passes,* First Pruett Publishing Paperback Edition, 1992.

Hyde, George E. (ed. by Savoie Lottinville). *Life of George Bent, Written From His Letters,* University of Oklahoma Press: Norman, OK, 1968.

Hollister, Ovando J. *The Mines of Colorado,* Springfield, Mass., 1867.

Hammond, George P. *The Adventures of Alexander Barclay Mountain Man,* Denver, CO, 1976.

Hafen, LeRoy R., ed. *The Mountain Men and the Fur Trade of the Far West,* Ten vols. Glendale, CA., 1965 -1972.

Hafen, LeRoy, R. "Pioneer Struggles for a Colorado Road Across the Rockies," *The Colorado Magazine,* Published by the State Historical and Natural History Society of Colorado, vol. III no. 1, Denver, CO, March, 1926.

Greenhorn Valley News, Colorado City-Rye-San-Isabel, CO, Vol. 1, No 1, April 1973 through Vol. 30, No.52, Dec. 2000, featuring several articles by Jan MacKell.

Garrard, Lewis H. *Wah-To-Tah and the Taos Trail,* Glendale, CA, 1938.

Farley, Mary M. *A Chronicle of Native Americans in Pueblo and Southeastern Colorado,* No publisher, No date (about 1984).

Eberhart, Perry. *Ghosts of the Colorado Plains,* 1986.

Denver Westerners (ed. by Numa L. James), *1957 Brand Book of Denver,* vol. 13, Johnson Publishing Co., Boulder, CO, 1957.

Denver Westerners (ed. by Arthur L. Campa), *The Denver Brand Book of 1965,* vol. 21, Johnson Publishing Co., Boulder, CO, 1965.

Dodds, Joanne West. *Pueblo, A Pictorial History,* by Donning Company/Publishers in Norfolk/Virginia Beach, 1982.

Crutchfield, James A. *Tragedy at Taos, the Revolt of 1847,* Republic of Texas Press, TX, 1995.

Cragin, F. W. "Notes of an Interview with Jose de Jesus Valdez, Walsenburg, Colo., Dec. 9, 1907, " *Cragin Collection,* Pioneers' Museum, Colorado Springs, CO, 1907.

Cragin, F. W. "Notes of an interview with Mrs. Felipe Ledoux," *Cragin Collection,* Pioneers' Museum, Colorado Springs, CO.

Cragin, F. W. "Notes of an interview with Jesse Nelson, Smith Canon Ranch Colo., July 9, 1908, *Cragin Collection.,* Pioneers' Museum, Colorado Springs, CO, 1908.

Cragin, F. W. "Notes of an interview with Tom Autobees," *Cragin Collection,* Avondale, Colo., Nov. 8 & 10, 1907.

Colorado City Sun, published by The Colorado City Development Company, Colorado City, CO, Nov. 1964 through Nov. 1973.

Colorado City Call, California City and Colorado City, Oct. 1963 through Oct. 1964.

Cheetham, Francis T. "Early Settlements of Southern Colorado," *The Colorado Magazine,* Published by the State Historical Society of Colorado, vol. V, Feb. 1928.

Chamblin, Thomas S., ed. *The Historical Encyclopedia of Colorado,* published by Colorado Historical Association, no date.

Carson, Phil. *Across the Northern Frontier, Spanish Exploration in Colorado,* 1998.

Campbell, Rosemae W. *From Trappers to Tourists, Fremont County 1830-1950,* no date.

Calhoun, W. C. *Colorado Gold Mines and Ghost Camps,* Frontier Book Co., Fort Davis, TX, 1969.

Brown, John Jr., and James Boyd. *History of San Bernardino and Riverside Counties,* 3 vols., Chicago, IL, 1922.

Brown, John Sr. *Mediumistic Experiences of John Brown the Medium of the*

Rockies, with Introduction by Prof. J. S. Loveland, Des Moines: Iowa Printing Company, 1887.

Brown, John. *Account Book,* copy in Geo. Beattie collection, Henry E. Huntington Library, San Marino, CA, no date.

Broadhead, Edward. "Fort Pueblo," Pueblo County Historical Society, Pueblo, CO, 1981.

Boyd and Carson, *Atlas of Colorado Ghost Towns,* 1984.

Bonner, T. D. *The Life and Adventures of James P. Beckwourth.* Reprint. Minneapolis, 1965.

Beulah Historical Society. *From Mace's Hole, the Way It Was, to Beulah, the Way It Is; a Comprehensive History of Beulah, Colorado,* Published by The Beulah Historical Society, 1979.

"Bent's Old Fort," National Historic Site publication, Superintendent, La Junta, CO., 1999.

Beckner, Raymond M., *Along Colorado Trails,* Beckner, 1975.

Barclay, Alexander. "Diary under date of Sept. 13, 1846," *Barclay Papers,* microfilm copy in Colorado State Archives, Denver, CO, 1846.

Autobees, Charles. "Testimony Jan.16, 1873, Colorado Private Land Claim no. 17, Records of the General Land Office, RG 49," *National Archives,* Washington, D.C., 1873.

Athearn, Frederic J. *Land of Contrast: a History of Southeast Colorado,* Bureau of Land Management, Denver, CO, 1985.

Ascherman, Arla. "Winds in the Cornfields of Early Pueblo County," Pueblo County Historical Society, Pueblo, CO, 1982.

Arbuthnot, Billie J., ed. *The Greenhorn Valley News,* published monthly by Graphic Arts Services, Inc. June 1973 through Dec. 1996.

* Interviews with Greenhorn Valley residents include Jim Cook, Jim Stewart, Bill DuPrez, and Herold (Cotton) Meredith.

Upon examining this piece of writing, serious critics will soon discover there are no footnote references to distract eye movement, reduce page size, and create unnecessary brain strain. <u>Most historical events are told in the present tense</u> to bring the reader closer to the past. Some direct quotations are noted allowing the reader to learn just exactly who is reporting, reflecting, talking, or down right lying through their teeth. And for those early writers who had no teeth, an untruth is often accompanied by a solid slurrr-p, which is more interesting than factual.

Colorado's Greenhorn Valley

Fact and Folklore (1700 – 2000)

Preface

Television serials, movie theaters, and history books dramatize the early American frontier as a place where eastern settlers hike into hostile western territories and clash with native Indian warriors. The Greenhorn Valley is exactly that kind of place, an arena of wild Western clashing and killing. Even the most conservative interpretation renders the Greenhorn Valley to have been a ruthless frontier. From the mid-1700s a Comanche Chief named Green Horn (*Cuerno Verde* in Spanish) is assaulting the early pueblos, butchering a large number of male settlers, and sacrificing women and children captives in cold blood.

Television and movie producers would be hard pressed to find better movie scripts for adventure, romance, suspense, poverty, survival, depression, spiritualism, colonialism, patriotism, commercialism, wealth, greed, theft, violence, massacre, and sex - than written here in the fact and folklore of Greenhorn Valley.

As one of many examples in *adventure*, Spanish Governor Juan de Anza (whose father has been killed by Indians) takes massive action to eliminate the murderous Chief Green Horn whose own father has been killed by Spaniards. Much like little David encountering the giant force of Goliath, their final clashing and killing occurs along a small creek, later named for the daring Chief Green Horn.

As one example in *romance*, mulatto trapper Jim Beckwourth (who adorns himself with gold chains, buttons, earrings, and never meets a woman he doesn't like) recreates himself as a Crow Indian Chief, acquires four Crow wives, and adopts several more attractive sisters. After the Crow affairs, he takes up with three different Hispanic ladies, the first being Luisa Sandoval, who becomes a legend in her own right. Luisa will establish the first trading post on Greenhorn Creek with her new lover, John Brown, while long-gone husband Jim Beckwourth is doing his business in California.

As one example in *suspense*, the great strength and courage of Luisa Sandoval Brown is documented in the following note taken from F. W. Cragin's interview with Mrs. Felipe Ledoux at Las Vegas, NM, on June 17, 1908. Mrs. Ledoux reports the following:

"On June 6, (1846), John Brown conducted a half-price sale of pants at this Greenhorn store, settled his account and closed his books. Then he started south with his wife Luisa, who was carrying their four-month-old son John Jr. in her arms. With them were Archibald Metcalf [Mrs. Felipe Ledoux's own husband] and Blackhawk, who were leading sixty horses and mules packed with deerskins traded from the Utes in the Wet Mountain Valley. Lucien Maxwell, his servant Indian George, and Charles Town, just arrived from the crossing of the Arkansas, joined them. Six or seven miles south of Greenhorn on Apache Creek the train was attacked by Jicarilla Apaches who drove off all the pack animals and their valuable burden. Some of the Indians took after Luisa Brown, who wheeled her horse, fastened her arm tightly about her baby's neck and dashed off toward Greenhorn. The men shouted at her to throw away the baby. Instead, with the Indians close behind her, she forced her horse to jump a deep arroyo and arrived at Greenhorn in safety. In this harrowing chase she wrenched young John's neck so that ever afterward he carried his head bent forward."

Two additional accounts of Luisa's harrowing escape from Apache warriors are documented a bit later when Mrs. Sandoval Beckwourth Brown is presented in more detail. I dare say, if too many examples are leaked out here in the beginning, there will be little or no story left to tell in the middle and at the end of this book.

Before reading events of the Greenhorn Valley between years 1700 and 2000, it is important to realize that fact and folklore about the Valley cannot be separated easily. No doubt, there were those who said much but were never recorded, those who knew much but said nothing, and those who knew little but said much. Consequently the following text is only as truthful as those persons who wagged their tongues and took pen in hand - right, wrong, or indifferent.

Since information about the Greenhorn is fairly limited, no regular person or key event has been left out because the information is of questionable origin. Since misinformation is frequently quoted over and over until it becomes truth among scholars, little effort is made to identify and evaluate the credibility of sources. In fact some undocumented sources of information (like journalists of the 1960s) appear quite credible, while other well-documented sources (written long after the fact) seem to suffer from memory loss, exaggeration, and commercial exploitation. On occasion, different accounts of the very same event are included for the reader's personal amusement or analysis.

The following story has five purposes: (1) to preserve the hefty history of Greenhorn Valley (past events are told in present tense); (2) explore new meaning between the old teeth and noggins of earlier authors; (3) prove that guns did not *win the West* but were a factor in eliminating various human and animal populations; (4) confirm that television has become a modern day gunman; and (5) season the whole mix with a tiny touch of whimsical wit, so that no reader will fall asleep from reading background, become depressed from the many murders, or mistake this historical sketch for some scholarly work of immutable importance.

The chronicle begins with a definition of Greenhorn Valley. It steps forward with a brief review of early people and how they struggled to possess the land. The story narrows to Comanche Indians and their infamous Chief Green Horn. It continues with a few well-known pioneers (like Captain Zebulon Pike and Ceran St. Vrain) who shape the Valley's destiny. Midway, storytelling focuses on a handful of not-so-well-known characters who trap, trade, farm, ranch, homestead, spiritualize, commercialize, and make love in the Valley. From the lives and deaths of these characters, Crow Village emerges as a creek-side settlement, then Rye takes shape as a small town. In the year 1963 Colorado City is re-created on the ruins of old Crow Village by California developers full of great expectations. The final pages reflect Greenhorn Valley in the year 2000, the same year this author and his wife bought land, built a house, and became citizens of this extraordinary valley.

Greenhorn Valley

From native residents until the present, Greenhorn Mountain has been a landmark towering 12,334 feet above sea level. Although not among the highest Rocky Mountain peaks, it compares well with two neighbors, *Pikes*

Peak and *Spanish Peaks*. Pikes Peak to the north of Greenhorn Valley is that tall, famous hill reaching to the clouds. Every July 4th automotive warriors (with money, power, and speed) scream their wheels to the summit on a dirt road, provoking the mountain spirit into a cloud of dust above Colorado Springs.

To the south of Colorado Springs (and Greenhorn Valley) two massive mountains dominate the horizon. Early Indians name these busty peaks *Huajatolla* (or *Breasts of the World* in English.) Consequently a few young children are heard to giggle while calling the mountains *Big Boobies of the Cosmos*. Slurrr'p.

This great lady of the land points one mountain breast 12,683 feet to the heavens; the other breast towers even higher at 13,623 feet. The Indian name, *Breasts of the World,* is probably uncomfortable for modest, Spanish Conquistadors, and the more acceptable *Spanish Peaks* name is substituted. As a result, *Spanish Peaks* can now be uttered by men, women, and children without choking on big breast embarrassment. Furthermore Indian names did not really count back in the early times, because the land was just being discovered by Spaniards and needed a real Spanish name to be properly discovered and recorded.

Because the Spanish Peaks stand alone and are not attached to any mountain chain, they appear higher than taller mountains within a group. Like Spanish Peaks, Greenhorn Mountain rises rapidly from its foothills and appears taller than its 12,334 feet elevation. Measuring from its base to its summit, Greenhorn Mountain is higher than Colorado's highest mountain rising out of the Continental Divide near Leadville, which is Mount Elbert at 14,431 feet. All hiking conditions being equal, it would take longer to climb the Greenhorn at 12,334 than Mount Elbert at 14,431.

Greenhorn Valley is a general area to the east of Greenhorn Mountain, but it does not appear on maps as such. However there is a depression in the Valley surrounding Greenhorn Creek. This depression originates high up in Greenhorn Mountain to the west of Rye Village and stretches out east to the plains. In the depression flowing west to east, Greenhorn Creek descends through Rye, into Colorado City, past I-25 and Groaners Flats, to Cedarwood Canyon, and then north-northeast toward Arkansas River. Up north, Greenhorn Valley reaches above Muddy Creek toward the St. Charles River and Valley. Down south, Greenhorn Valley reaches below Apache Creek toward the Huerfano River and Valley. The large picture places Greenhorn between the Arkansas River (which flows through Canon and Pueblo Cities) to the north and the Huerfano River (which flows through

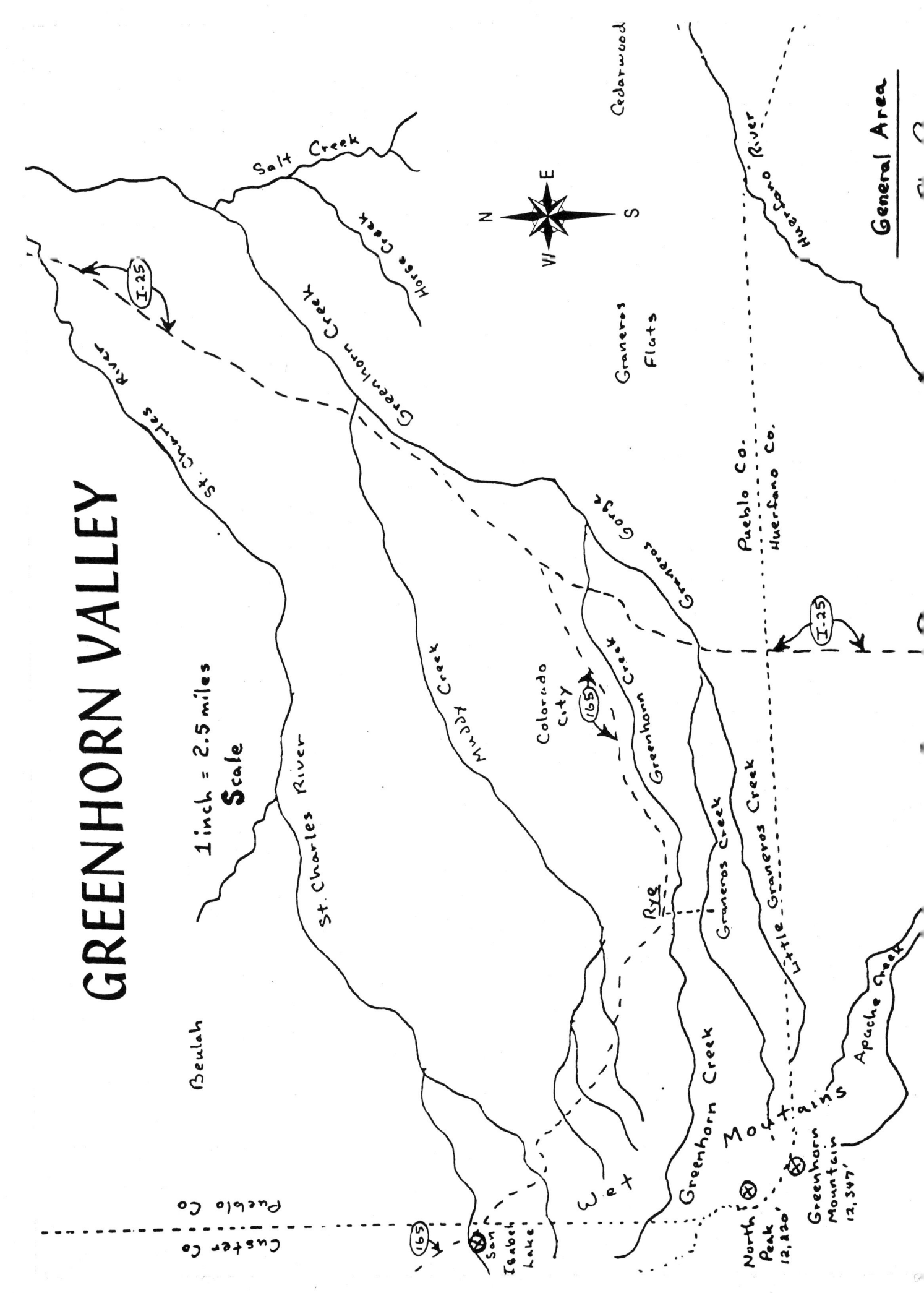

Malachite and Badito villages) to the south.

The name itself, *Greenhorn,* is taken from one bold and daring Chief Green Horn of the Comanches. It is on a small creek in a beautiful valley below a large mountain that Chief Green Horn (*Cuerno Verde*) is sent to the Happy Hunting Ground by Governor Juan Baptista de Anza in 1779. It is here, ten years before George Washington becomes the first president of the United States, Comanches suffer a major loss at the hands of pale-faced men. As Chief Green Horn becomes legendary in his courageous defeat, the small creek, beautiful valley, and large mountain come to bare his name. Some local seniors say Cuerno Verde's gaunt ghost still haunts the Valley. More on the Chief's life and death will follow.

Greenhorn, as a settlement, moved around over the years like diving birds in a lake - popping up on maps here and then over there. The John Brown camp (1845-1849) was located where the Taos Trail originally crossed Greenhorn Creek, a quarter mile east of Greenhorn Meadows Park and Cibola Drive. After the Browns joined the 1849 gold rush, old friends and traders remained at the Greenhorn Creek camp until 1853.

The second Greenhorn village was centered around the Hicklin Ranch House (1859-1874), located a quarter mile northeast of John Brown's store at the creek. More precisely, the adobe Ranch House stood on a hillside north of Greenhorn Creek (site of the current fire station) until the mid 1930s. The Hicklin village (called *Greenhorn* on early maps) spread over what is today's shopping plaza at the center of Colorado City.

The third Greenhorn was a stage stop and restaurant established in 1867. It was located five miles northeast of Hicklin Ranch where Muddy Creek joins Greenhorn Creek. The Greenhorn *Stage Stop* (also called *Muddy Creek Station*) included a post office from 1870-1885. Here the old Taos Trail came near to Greenhorn Creek but did not cross it. The stage-stop location mistakenly appears on early maps as the John Brown camp.

The fourth Greenhorn village (1874-1911) was located on Graneros Creek, a few miles southwest of the John Brown camp at Greenhorn Creek. Graneros village was designated *Greenhorn* on early maps and later became known as *Shady Greenhorn.* The old *Trapper's Trail* turned into the *Taos Trail*, crossed Greenhorn Creek; and ran south to the Graneros Greenhorn. The trail is currently posted as *Greenhorn Road* (or Hwy-181.)

Sometime after the Fossceco family arrives in 1916, their service station and store become known as the *Shady Greenhorn,* because of the many large oak trees edging the main road. As travel on the old Taos Trail dies out, the remaining two buildings at Shady Greenhorn are sealed up with boards over the windows and doors in 1947. The buildings currently stand at this rural location, where the last of the Fossceco family members still live, ranch cattle, and farm the land. Fossceco land extends east into the gorgeous Graneros Gorge. Because this heavenly wonder of nature itself is privately owned and clearly posted as such, it is advisable to increase one's life insurance prior to trespassing into the Graneros Gorge. A much wiser consideration and safer behavior would be to view the Gorge from on top of the north rim at the old gazebo ruins, which are owned by Colorado City and open to the public.

Finally there is a *Greenhorn D&RGW Railroad Station* about ten miles northeast of the Hicklin Ranch to be found on 1882-1897 maps.

Because the term *Greenhorn* appears in various locations on older maps (and a few newer maps), it is important to identify a particular location before entering into a discussion of any "Greenhorn settlement."

In recent years the settlement has become known as the Holland Duell Ranch, Duell-Stewart Ranch, Stewart Thoroughbreds, California City Development Company, and Colorado City Development Company. In 1963 the ranch estate becomes Colorado City of Pueblo County.

Today Colorado City spreads over the historical foundations of the Brown camp, Hicklin Ranch, Crow Ranch, Crow Junction, Greenhorn Creek, Crow Stage Stop, Crow Post Office, and Crow Mercantile Building.

With the coming of new Colorado City, *Crow Junction* remains a popular name for the region among seniors. Although fresh-as-paint citizens have tried to bury the historical name of *Crow*, the shrill cry of the cool, crow cock can still be heard on election days, when politicians propound their pretty promises. Slurrr-p.

Natives and Possession

The Aztecs and Toltecs occupy the region as early as 8,000 B.C. Greenhorn Valley is a natural food source. The mild climate, good soil, natural resources, wooded surroundings, lush grass, and nearness to the mountains present good hunting and living conditions. The earliest occupants are hunters and gatherers of wild game and plants, which the Valley has in abundance. Antelope, bison, elk, turkey, and small animals of the plains combine with bear, beaver, deer, fish, and small game of the mountains. Usable plants of the plains and foothills are juniper, pinion, yucca, and a wide variety of grasses. The stream beds offer up berries, chokecherries, currants, roses, cottonwood, and willow buds. Plants of the mountain regions include berries, clovers, grasses, juniper buds, and the inner bark of pines. In a sense the Greenhorn Valley is like a grocery store and meat market for the aboriginal Americans.

Following the Aztecs and Toltecs, the region is frequented by other natives who roam, camp, hunt, and fight in the Valley. These new visitors include Utes, Sioux, Shoshones, Pawnees, Pueblos, Navajos, Kiowas, Kiowa-Apaches, Comanches, Cheyennes, Blackfeet, Arikaras, Arapahoes, and Apaches. The network of old Indian trails will become Pueblo County.

The Utes are widespread and long lasting. Between 1300-1500 A.D. Ute Indians occupy most of what will become the State of Colorado, and there are seven Ute tribes: Yampa (Yamparika), Weeminuche, Uintah, Tabeguache (Uncompahgre), Parianuc (Grand River), Mouache, and Capote. Utes are among the first Indian groups to acquire horses and ride into the plains for buffalo hunts during the mid-1600s. Today Utes are the only Indian tribe still based in Colorado.

By the mid-1800s Greenhorn Valley has become a gathering place for both Native Americans and early pioneers. Cultural differences between the two groups create considerable conflict. While Indians believe Mother Earth belongs to everyone, the newcomers are on a material mission to trap the animals, conquer the enemy, and possess the land. Also as white men settle along the old Indian trails, they fight among themselves in order to defeat their brothers and take possession of the land.

Land-grabbing flag-planters arrive one after another, attempting to possess western territory like several high hawks diving down on a single wild prey. The Spanish claim Greenhorn Valley from 1492 to 1800. England's Virginia Colony demand the land in 1609 but are not taken seriously by Spain or others. In 1682 a French draft is rejected by Spain, a 1763 claim goes back to Spain, and in 1800 Spain returns the territory to France. The Louisiana Purchase of 1803 becomes the District of Louisiana in 1804 and the Louisiana Territory in 1805. Missouri claims the territory in 1812. South of Arkansas River becomes the Mexican Republic between 1821 and 1836. The Republic of Texas demands the area in 1836. Jeffersonians adopt the land in 1848. The United States conquest of Mexico and 1848 Treaty of Guadalupe Hidalgo end all foreign ownership in the territory. The Greenhorn Valley becomes New Mexican Territory between 1854 and 1861. A year later the Homestead Act is created. In August 1, 1876, the area becomes the State of Colorado.

The first business men to enter Colorado are French trappers arriving in the 1670s. They hike north from Louisiana, northwest along the Arkansas River, and into Greenhorn Valley. When Spanish officials stationed at Santa Fe hear of this most unpleasant migration into Spanish frontier lands, they mount horses and ride north to stop the invasion. In addition to stopping French trappers, the conquistadors harbor secondary motives. They want to explore the area for gold, trade with the native Indians, and convert their poor savage souls to a self-righteous form of Christianity. The theology of the Spanish Empire is simple: If you can't save Indian souls, enslave them. If you can't enslave them, then kill the braves, and sell the squaws and papooses for a handsome profit.

In 1706 General Juan Ulibarri with 40 Spanish soldiers from Santa Fe and 100 Indian allies from Christian missions enter the Greenhorn Valley looking for Indian slaves who have fled their owners. Like previous Spanish expeditions, Ulibarri sets foot into the Wet Mountain Valley through a pass between Sheep Mountains to the north and Veta Mountain to the south. Heading east, the trail follows down South Oak Creek to Badito Cone on the south end of Wet Mountains and turns northward. The Ulibarri party passes near Huerfano Butte and heads north across Greenhorn Creek. Continuing north on a trail now known as the 3-R and Siloam Roads, they cross San Carlos Creek (St. Charles Creek today.) San Carlos Creek features a north-side trail which takes them northeast to the Arkansas on the east side of what is currently the City of Pueblo. [Spanish-owned, Indian slaves of Santa Fe and Taos had a tradition of escaping NE to the Arkansas Valley. In 1664 Spanish leader Juan de Archuleta captured Taos Pueblo slaves near the Arkansas; in 1696 Spanish leader Don Diego de Vargas nabbed Taos and Picuris slaves near Pueblo.]

Runaway possessions are among the most difficult trappings, because they are subject to uncontrollable urges and demonstrations of escape. Some refer to this unacceptable, human condition as *free will*.

On Thursday, August 19, 1706, nine days after passing through Greenhorn Valley, the Ulibarri posse captures 62 Picuris slaves near the Arkansas (called *Napestle* by the Indians.) With human property in tow, they head to Santa Fe, once again parading south through Greenhorn Valley.

Thirteen years later (1719) the Spanish governor of New Mexico marches troops through Huerfano County (on the south side of Greenhorn) and punishes the local Indians for naughty behavior. A year later, conflict between French and Spanish heats to a boil. When a second unit of Spanish soldiers (commanded by Lieutenant Don Pedro di Villasur) marches into the Valley, the politically incorrect Indians are ready and waiting with a secret firepower. Pawnee Indians armed with guns are led into battle by French officers disguised as Indians, so testify the few who survived the battle. No doubt, the Pawnees enjoyed their first taste of gun power.

The French vs Spanish rivalry continues for another 100 years, but tempers are cooling. In May of 1816, as 24 French pioneers camp and trap beaver on Greenhorn Creek, they are arrested by Spanish officials and hauled off to Santa Fe as prisoners. After a brief confinement, the French trappers are released and sent home to St. Louis.

The conflict is cooling, but the Spanish have no intention of surrendering the land. Three years later (in 1819) Governor Don Facundo Malagres of New Mexico constructs a fort on the south side of Greenhorn Valley. His hilltop fort overlooks Oak Creek near Badito and is designed to safeguard the Valley. The fort commands a useful view of the mountain branch of Trapper's Trail leading to and from Sangre de Cristo Pass. Trapper's Trail will soon become known as the *Taos Trail.*

In 1821 when Mexico declares her independence, Huerfano County changes from Spanish Territory to Mexican Republic. This change creates new opportunities for United States Americans.

After its official founding in 1822, the Santa Fe Trail (including the *Mountain Branch* through Raton Pass) becomes the trail of choice leading to northern New Mexico. Among the first to use the Taos Trail (looping west off the Santa Fe), is the Glenn and Fowler expedition. Their travel party follows an established Indian path skirting the eastern side of the Greenhorn Mountains. Today Taos Trail is covered over with I-25 running south out of Pueblo. The *Greenhorn Mountains* to the west were first called *Wet Mountains* (or *Sierra Mojada*.) The name *Wet Mountains* is still used.

Aside from the hunting and trapping business, there is money to be plucked off tired and hungry travelers moving along the Santa Fe and Taos Trails. One of the first successful pioneers to set up shop is William Bent. In the early 1830s William establishes his first of several trading posts along the Arkansas River near today's city of Pueblo.

Heading west and southwest from Bent's Fort, the nearest settlement of whites (or Caucasians) is in northern New Mexico around the villages of Taos and Santa Fe. Here Spaniards and Mexicans alike raise grain and vegetable crops, sheep, horses, a few cows, and many children. Most likely the large number of children is a consequence of tired and lonely trappers seeking companionship during the long winter months.

Taos Trail soon emerges as a highway of merry matrimony for trappers and other travelers. From 1821 to the gold rush of 1849, Taos

Trail is widened and worn down by tired, lonely, mountain men going through the Greenhorn Valley and then south-southwest to the pleasant little town of Taos. In Taos they trade animal skins and marry Mexican girls, sometimes in a single deal. As a result, Hispanic influence dominates early settlements along the St. Charles, Greenhorn, and Huerfano creeks. For example, most early dwellings are constructed of Mexican adobe brick which is reinforced with wool and straw. The combination is most effective for insulating buildings against heat of summer and cold of winter. Other Mexican influences are fine foods, colorful clothing, and fun-loving social events like the *fandango*.

The Comanches

Apaches, Arapahoes, Cheyennes, Comanches, and Kiowas join the Utes in camping and hunting around Greenhorn Valley in the mid-1700s. They exist as migratory bands. When one group intrudes upon the immediate hunting grounds of another, the tribes fight with each other in order to defend their current living space.

The Comanche people are of medium height and well-built, with a tendency to be heavy-set. They have bronze-colored skin, black hair, dark eyes, eagle-beak noses, thin lips, and small beards. Polygamy is common and women are sold, traded, and sometimes stolen. The proud Comanches dominate other tribes and have not yet known defeat by the Spaniards.

At home with the land, Comanche braves appear from nowhere, come down on settlements, and disappear into the landscape. Because they know the land so well and are nomadic, the Spaniards can not keep track of them. The Comanches are mostly invisible unless they want to be seen.

Comanche tribes are particularly troublesome to the Spaniards in New Spain (or New Mexico). By the early 1770s Comanches begin to raid New Mexican villages and take everything they can get away with, horses and guns being the favorite booty. Comanches realize that in order to dominate others, the white man's horses and guns are needed. Also horses and guns give them superiority over rival Indians who are still traveling on foot, using arrows and lances to kill wild game and fellow Indians. The Comanches, like the Utes, are among the first tribes to acquire horses from the Spaniards, the difference being the Utes trade for steeds while Comanches borrow them. Personal wealth is measured by horse number.

These cunning Comanches grow bolder and more successful with each raid. They are greatly feared because of their stealing, killing, and carrying off women and children. In 1751 a party of 300 visit Taos to trade furs for food and trinkets. Upon departing, they can not resist the attractive settlement of Galisteo. After killing many of the settlers, the Comanches depart with numerous Galisteo possessions.

Governor Cachupin of New Mexico organizes Spanish troopers and charges after the cunning Comanches. The chase lasts several days and passes through the Greenhorn Valley. The race reaches a climax on the bank of Arkansas River. One hundred Comanches pay with their lives for their cruel crimes against the unsettled settlers. Conflict is growing.

During the next 25 years, the cunning Comanches headquarter in the general area of the Fountain and Arkansas Rivers at Pueblo. They continue to make frequent raids upon frontier settlements. Spanish villages become new hunting grounds filled with wonderful white wealth.

Chief Cuerno Verde

Spanish sources indicate senior members of the Comanche Council give *Cuerno Verde* his name. He is designated *Cuerno Verde* (*Green Horn* in English) because he is bold, daring, and fearless. He is like a young bull elk having new green horns, still young and growing. As Chief of the Comanches, Cuerno Verde destroys several pueblos, killing many settlers, and "sacrificing captives in cold blood."

Others sources attribute the name *Green Horn* to the chief's big leather cap to which he mounts *"green buffalo horns."* Governor Anza recognizes Chief Cuerno Verde at the final battle site by *"his insignia and devices."* Most likely the green-horn headdress is created to enhance the Chief's invincible, young-bull-elk image.

Cuerno Verde and his cunning Comanche tribe become fearless in theft, kidnapping, and murder. During the single year of 1774, there are several bloody attacks on New Mexican settlements, capturing livestock and hauling off women and children. In June warriors attack Picuris Pueblo and then Nambe. In July one thousand braves devastate Santa Cruz de la Canada. And in August one hundred Comanches assault Pecos.

Something has to be done to stop these fierce attacks on Spanish settlements. The current Governor Cachupin seems unable to handle the difficult situation. As a result, in 1777 Juan Bautista de Anza at the age of 42 replaces Cachupin. It is now one year after America's Declaration of

Independence and the beginning of the United States of America.

Juan Bautista de Anza's father and grandfather both fought against the Indians. From this childhood background, Juan de Anza has developed skills as an Indian fighter and military strategist. Now as governor, Juan Bautista de Anza has authority, power, and good reason to go after the cunning Comanches: the Indians killed his father.

Legend has it that Juan de Anza's father *"had been killed by the daring, arrogant young chieftain of the Comanches, called Cuerno Verde,"* and *"Cuerno Verde's father had been killed by Spaniards in an earlier campaign"* of 1768. The legend is colorful, but Cuerno Verde would have been a mere child and certainly not a chieftain when de Anza's father was killed. Another source claims Anza's *"father was killed by an Apache."* This account is far more likely.

The frequency and savagery of Comanche attacks demands Governor Anza's immediate attention and total commitment. To defeat Chief Cuerno Verde and check the Comanches, Gov. Anza makes full use of his countrymen's experience, knowledge, and maps. Spanish knowledge of the Comanche nation is reflected in a legend on Bernardo Miera y Pachico's map of 1778. It depicts lands stretching across northern New Mexico. The map clearly shows the Comanches are the dominant force.

After studying Spanish resources, Governor Anza chooses to take an offensive posture and attack his enemy in their own back yard, but he does not go to battle alone. Midsummer 1779, Gov. Anza organizes 90 soldiers, 200 militia (mainly settlers), and 250 Pueblo Indians. In total Anza has about 600 men in his army. Anza's transportation system or horse herd numbers *"more than one thousand."* The large horse herd creates maximum horse power, good horse sense, and a healthy amount of horseplay.

He outfits each soldier with three horses, various weapons, and food for 40 days. The men are *soldados de cueras*, (or *leather jackets*) armed with muskets, lances, and swords for general offense. They wear layered, leather jackets and carry shields for personal defense. The men are bold, courageous, and good marksmen who have grown up hunting on the frontier. Many are hardy, hybrid *mestizos* - a marvelous mixture of European and Indian ancestry.

In contrast to the *soldados de cueras*, the Spanish settlers and Pueblo Indians are a bit ragged as noted in Gov. Anza's personal journal:

"Because of their well-known poverty and wretchedness....I supplied the most needy, each with a good horse from the two hundred that I have

Juan Bautista de Anza
(Courtesy of Phil Carson &
New Nexico State Records
& Archives Center)

Don Diego de Vargas
in proper conquistador dress
led from 1692 to 1696

(Museum of New Mexico)

extra in the herd at the presidio and all of them with firearms with ten ball cartridge belts."

When Anza reaches the Conejos River north of Santa Fe, his party encounters 200 Apaches and Utes who have recently been humiliated by the Comanches near San Luis Lake. Wanting to avenge the defeat, these braves join Anza's party to seek and destroy their joint enemy.

Anza moves by night north up San Luis Valley. Some historians believe Anza comes east to the plains by Ute Pass. Others believe his army cuts south of Pikes Peak, crosses the not-yet-discovered gold fields of Cripple Creek, passes St. Peter's Dome, and descends Little Fountain Creek trail. Emerging undetected from the foothills to the edge of the plains, Anza surprises the Comanches in one of their base camps.

Early in the day (Aug. 31, 1779) scouts report to Anza the Comanches have become aware of their presence. As the Indians quickly break camp and flee east into the plains, Anza is *"resolved to attack without delay."* Parking his supplies and horse herd (guarded by 200 men), Anza mounts his steed and commands the soldiers to attack. His military troops try to surround the runaway Indians, but the attempt is unsuccessful. After a few miles of rough riding, Spanish soldiers catch up to the Comanches. A wild running battle continues another 12 miles along to the south, after which Anza's army prevails. Eighteen Indian men are killed and many more wounded. An additional 30 women, 34 children, and a large herd of 500 horses are captured near Wigwam (between Colorado Springs and Pueblo, just west of Fountain Creek.)

The puffed-up Governor records his great pleasure in seizing and distributing the Comanche estate:

"The Comanches lost all their goods; even the most necessary articles they abandoned. There was so much material that it could not be loaded on 100 horses. The spoil our people seized, dividing it equally. In this matter we had not the least unpleasantness."

With a party of 600, almost everyone receives one of the three: a horse, a woman, or a child. One can not help but speculate as to just who received a woman, who received a child, and who received a horse?

Included in the booty are many stolen horses and other goods once belonging to Spanish settlers. When Anza claims the stolen horses and other goods for his own party, isn't he himself then stealing the stolen possessions of his countrymen, the people he is protecting and defending?

Perhaps this is how the concept of *politician* was born. Grandpa Webster describes a politician as *"one versed in the art and science of government...scheming and maneuvering within a group...primarily interested in political offices from selfish or other narrow short-run interests."* The practice of focusing on the perpetrator and forgetting about the victim has become an American institution. Consequently today's American justice does little or nothing for the victims of crime.

Indian warriors, who survive the battle, dash south to warn Cuerno Verde of Anza's approach. Captives left behind are questioned regarding the whereabouts of their tribal leader. A few prisoners provide accurate information (under torture) regarding Chief Green Horn's return home from his latest raids upon Spanish settlements. Although Chief Green Horn is planning a victory party at his base camp just seized by Anza, a celebration will not be had.

Instead of waiting for Cuerno Verde to arrive, Anza marches his army south to meet the Chief as he returns from battle. Anza's diary reports the following day by day account in summary:

September 1, Wednesday: 21 miles of cautious travel is made to the south along what Anza refers to as the Sacramento River (or Fountain Creek) toward the Arkansas River. Some of the horses are tired and in need of rest after the previous day's running battle.

September 2, Thursday: Troops continue south nine miles to the Arkansas River where more Comanche horses are caught. Most of the Ute Indians, who have been traveling with Anza, depart (at Pueblo) without so much as a "good-bye." Another 18 miles are covered before evening. This movement departs the Arkansas heading southwest along the front range of the Greenhorn Mountains.

Late in the afternoon scouts, who normally ride ahead to find the best trail, return and report they have discovered the enemy coming in their direction. Anza hides the horse herd, and his troops take cover. Suddenly there is only a single gully separating Anza's army and the Comanche raiders. When Anza and his awesome army charge forward, the single gully is found to be filled with a *"wet boggy bottom."* Anza's attack is bungled in bog, and dusk turns to dark. Chief Green Horn and his weary warriors disappear into the nightfall.

Although some soldiers fear Cuerno Verde might return and attack under cover of darkness, there is no assault from either side during the long night. At daybreak Anza is anxious for the new day so he might confront the infamous Chief Cuerno Verde once again.

The new day brings Governor Anza and Cuerno Verde face to face beside a small creek. Firing off their guns, the Chief and 50 Comanche braves charge boldly into the midst of Anza's army. Green Horn has never been defeated and, true to his name, he is fearless - *but foolish!* Anza's 90 soldiers, 200 militia, and 250 Pueblo warriors have little difficulty crushing the greenhorn Chief, his son, four captains, a medicine man, and 10 others. Seeing their invincible leaders dropped and killed, the remaining Comanches assess their losses, turn tail, and flee the scene.

September 3, Friday: Anza's diary in translation (from Spanish to English) reads as follows:

"At the wood the enemy had already increased to more than forty, and they drew almost within gunshot, firing off their own muskets. In this way was recognized from his insignia and devices the famous Chief Cuerno Verde, who, his spirit proud and superior to all his followers, left them and came ahead, his horse curvetting spiritedly. Accordingly, I determined to have his life and his pride and arrogance precipitated him to this end.

"To accomplish this I ordered the vanguard on coming out of the woods which concealed their formation to join battle with two hundred lightly burdened men, that the cavalry and loaded animals with their guards should aid the vanguard for the purpose of forcing the enemy against this body if I succeeded in enclosing them as I planned with a half circle I was considering forming with the columns of the rear guard, and in order that the rear guard need not remain on watch over the horse herd and train while it was precipitating the enemy into the gully already mentioned. Thus should perish there those most important to us, that is, the party immediately behind the leader of the barbarians, cut off from their right and left flank.

"In order to execute both purposes and to fatigue as much as possible the horses of the enemy, in whose swiftness he placed his confidence for attacking and escaping, I withdrew swiftly apart from our Indian auxiliaries as though in retreat, but when my first plan was about to take effect the principal chieftain understood it and ordered all his men to retire. In view of this I proceeded to my second purpose and succeeded at once in cutting off from the larger body Cuerno Verde with his leading follower and they fell into the trap and the said gully. There without other recourse they sprang to the ground and entrenched behind their horse

made in this manner a defense as brave as it was glorious. Notwithstanding, the aforesaid Cuerno Verde perished with his first born son, the heir to his command, four of his most famous captains, a medicine man who preached that he was immortal, and ten more who were able to get in the place indicated.

"A larger number might have been killed, but I preferred the death of this chief even to more of those who escaped, because of his being constantly in this region the cruel scourge of this kingdom, and because he had exterminated many pueblos, killing hundreds and making as many prisoners whom he afterwards sacrificed in cold blood. His own nation accused him, ever since he took command, of forcing them to take up arms and volunteer against the Spaniards, a hatred of whom has dominated him because his father, who also held the same command and power, met death at our hands.

"I infer that his death was caused by his own intrepidity and the contempt that he wished to show for our people, being vaunted by the many successes that they have always obtained over us because of the irregularities with which they have always warred. He feared for the main body of his people who were defeated the afternoon before. This defeat had not been unknown to him for a musket lost in the battle by our Indian auxiliaries was in his possession, and withal, he had the temerity with fifty men of his daily and personal guard, to attack six hundred men in good formation. From this should be deduced the arrogance, presumption and pride which characterized this barbarian, and which he manifested until the last moment in various ways, disdaining even to load his own musket, which was done for him three times by another, while in the interval he was in danger.

"All of our people and the prisoners say that his death will be greatly lamented but I believe that their regret will not exceed the pleasure our people have had in it."

It is generally believed the Chief's "*spectacular headdress was claimed by Anza, and sent to Senior Governor Crouix with an account of the battle.*" In his letter to Crouix, Anza states the name *Green Horn* would be given to the local mountain and nearby stream.

Although Anza's diary gives a clear account of the actual killing of Chief Cuerno Verde and his guard, Monnett and McCarthy give their own account of the battle as they imagine it must have been. Most likely Monnett and McCarthy went on to become seasoned Hollywood writers:

"With frost breath, the chief shouted encouraging words to his young warriors as they mounted their swift ponies. His great medicine hat, fashioned from the hide of a mighty buffalo bull and gracefully winged by the beast's tremendous green-dyed horns, would protect them in battle. They were invincible! Seemingly at once, the painted war ponies attained full-gait. Astride their bare backs rode some of the greatest horsemen on the high plains. Screaming insults at the approaching troops, the confident warriors began releasing a barrage of deadly arrows from under the necks of their speeding ponies.

"Then within yards of the enemy, the fifty warriors heard the devastating sound of musketry. Blue puffs of smoke billowed rhythmically down a line of 300 guns, then rose lazily and dissipated into the early autumn air. Instantly, a lead ball struck the chief in the chest. He was thrown back so forcefully that he plunged head-first over the animal's flanks and hit the ground with such an impact that he rolled several yards before coming to rest face down at the edge of a snaking arroyo. The buffalo headdress, his divine assurance of immortality, had separated from his head upon impact. It now lay against a jutting boulder, one chartreuse horn cracked and broken at the tip. The great Comanche chief, Cuerno Verde ("Greenhorn"), was mortally wounded."

It is September 3, 1779, along side a small creek in a beautiful valley below a magnificent mountain, the great war Chief is put to rest by Gov. Juan Bautista de Anza and his party of 600 soldiers. The stream where Green Horn dies becomes known as Greenhorn Creek. The foothills surrounding Greenhorn Creek become known as Greenhorn Valley. The 12,334 foot mountain to the west bears the same name. The entire front range from Rye to Wetmore becomes known as the Greenhorn Mountains. Perhaps in time the entire State of Colorado will be called *The State of Greenhorn* as a tribute to the newer and younger politicians.

A Historical Society marker is erected in 1932 on the south side of new Hwy-181 as it crosses Greenhorn Creek. The marker is later moved east to I-25, and finally placed at the west end of Greenhorn Meadows Park. There is no "boggy gully" at any of these three sites and no solid evidence to establish the battle's actual location. However just south of Greenhorn Meadows Park, the creek splits and meanders a mile and a half east through South Park (now Meadowcreek.) Today Meadowcreek remains swampy even after nine beaver ponds were drained in the 1960s.

More significant than a battle location, this Comanche Chief with young horns protruding from his skull cap will long be remembered for his youthful courage and reckless aggression. The term *Greenhorn* has become a word used throughout the English speaking world reflecting a raw, simple, young, inexperienced, and unsophisticated person who does things the wiser persons would think about twice, or more.

After killing Chief Green Horn, Gov. Juan Bautista de Anza returns to Santa Fe via Sangre de Cristo Pass. It will take more devastating defeats in order to bring the Comanche nation to the white man's conference table.

Zebulon Montgomery Pike

In 1803 Jefferson of the United States pays Napoleon of France 15 million dollars for 909,130 square miles of new frontier land. This Louisiana Purchase doubles the size of the U. S. and transfers areas north and east of the Arkansas River to the U. S. The new land extends west of the Mississippi River to the Continental Divide and north of Spanish Texas to the Canadian border. Boundaries on the eastern slope of the Rockies are not well-defined, and this leads to ongoing conflict between the U. S. and her Spanish neighbor. Territory south of the Arkansas River will not be officially annexed until the end of the Mexican War in 1848.

Immediately after the Purchase of 1803, trappers expand west into Colorado to catch beaver needed for the making of fashionable hats back east. These early trappers trade with Indians and Spaniards alike. The trappers are government explorers and military officers caravanning west to examine and map the new American purchase. As Lewis and Clark return east from their trip across the Northwest frontier (1804-1806), Zebulon Pike is on his high horse and heading west along the Arkansas River to explore the new Southwest frontier.

Although President Jefferson and Congress do not authorize the Pike expedition, they probably have casual knowledge. Conceived by General James Wilkinson (governor of Upper Louisiana and Commander in Chief of the U. S. Army), the expedition is approved by his Secretary of War. Captain Zebulon Montgomery Pike marches west under Wilkinson's orders:

"...he was 27 years old - a small, compact, tactful, red-cheeked, blue-eyed young officer with wide swinging shoulders and a nose as straight as any Greek god's. He was army through and through."

Captain Zebulon Montgomery Pike, based on a portrait by Charles Wilson Peale which appeared in the 1810 edition of his journals

In July of 1806, Captain Zebulon Pike and party of 22 men (dressed in summer uniforms) launch a westward journey to the Rocky Mountains. Zebulon Pike is among the first American explorers to use a westward route that will become the Santa Fe and Taos Trails.

The Upper Arkansas River (flowing through Pueblo and Canon Cities) marks a vague boundary between the U. S. and Spain. Zealous Zebulon believes he has a legal right to explore south of the Upper Arkansas to the Red River. However Wilkinson advises him not to get caught exploring south of the Arkansas, because Spanish officials might not accept the French definition for land sold to the Americans. After all, Spaniards have been hanging around the area for 300 years and are somewhat attached.

As the expedition rolls west along the Arkansas River past present-day Pueblo and toward mesas northeast of Canon City, zealous Zeb is convinced that the *"grand peak"* to the north is by far the *"highest peak"* on American soil. Zeb estimates its height by triangulation to be 18,581 feet above sea level. Although he is 4,471 feet too high in his calculation, he still fails to comprehend the great height of this handsome peak.

Full of excitement, zealous Zebulon and 15 ill-clad, fellow flat-landers attempt to climb the tall mountain on the afternoon of November 24th, 1806. Surely this magnificent mountain will provide a good gander at their surroundings. The day hike lasts nearly a week, and they are unable to reach the summit because of deep snow. Zeb is well on his way to becoming another *"greenhorn"* of the Rocky Mountain Front Range.

A few days after the unsuccessful climb, zealous Zeb camps his party on the south bank of the Arkansas about 10 miles west of Pueblo and 20 miles north of Greenhorn. Zeb's camp site will become part of the Livesey Ranch, also known as *Settlement of Meadows.* The historical spot is now under water at Pueblo Lake State Park and visited regularly by a wide variety of fine, friendly fish.

During winter in the Rockies, zealous Zeb loses a number of his men from starvation and exposure to the cold. In late February, after crossing the magnificent Sangre de Cristo mountains and dropping a bit south into San Luis Valley, the winter struggle turns from bad to worse. Zeb and his remaining troops are captured and imprisoned - perhaps for their own good. First in Santa Fe and then in Chihuahua, they are held as spies trespassing onto Spanish land. One year after the expedition began, Zeb's hands are slapped, and he is sent home to Louisiana in July of 1807.

Here at home with nothing to do, he authors an account of his adventures in the Rockies. The book is published in 1810 and becomes a best-seller, both in English and in translation. The *"Grand Peak"* or *"Highest Peak"* in the Colorado Rockies (as Zeb Pike describes the mountain to later bear his name) creates great interest around the globe.

According to one source, zealous Zeb dies a hero's death at age 34 in the War of 1812 at the Battle of York when the U.S. attacks Toronto. Only seven years after leading his party west, the *"small, compact, tactful, red-cheeked, blue-eyed young officer"* is dead, but famous in death.

For those young Americans aspiring to have a tall mountain named after them - marching into winter wearing summer clothing, failing to climb a tall mountain, leading your men to a freezing-starving death, and then being captured by foreign troops in your own land is not enough for lasting notoriety. Instead, it is highly recommended that one write a bestselling book and have a heroic death at age 34.

Following Zebulon Montgomery Pike, other exploration parties travel through Pueblo County. The Stephen H. Long Expedition passes in 1820. Shortly after, Jacob Fowler and his party hike through Greenhorn Valley on route to Taos. Fowler's diary states that on January 31, 1822, he follows the north bank of the Rio San Carlos River (now the St. Charles) southwest from the Arkansas River at Pueblo. Departing the St. Charles (probably at Burnt Mill Rd.), he travels south along the foothills about ten miles where he crosses a stream (probably Greenhorn Creek.) From here he follows a fairly level wagon road another five miles south along the east slope of Greenhorn Mountains where he finds *"...the Remains of a Spanish fort to apperance ocepied about one year back...."* Most likely he finds the remains of a Spanish Fort built in 1819, used to defend Spanish Territory from Anglo-Americans moving along Trappers Trail.

After Jacob Fowler, Lieutenant John C. Fremont makes three visits to the area in 1843-44, 1845, and 1848. From spring of 1846 until spring of 1847 about 300 Mormons build *"Mormon Town."* Half mile east of El Pueblo and south of the Arkansas a meeting hall is added for regular church services. All but two Mormon families move on to Utah by May of 1847. Six years later in 1853, Captain John W. Gunnison passes through the Greenhorn Valley leaving a provocative mark on the area (to be discussed later.)

St. Vrain and the Bent Brothers

One of the most memorable men to carry the American flag into the Southwest is trapper Ceran de Hault de Lassus de St. Vrain. Ceran's

29

Ceran St. Vrain

(Courtesy of Kit Carson Home
and Museum of New Mexico)

adventures between 1824 and 1870 spell out the conflict of cultures in frontier borderlands. As merchant, freighter, soldier, politician, and flour miller; he leaves his name and influence on the dusty prairies and wet foothills of Greenhorn Mountain.

Ceran St. Vrain (second of ten children) is born to Jacques Marcellin Ceran de Hault de Lassus de St. Vrain and Marie Felicite Dubreuil St. Vrain on May 5, 1802, at Spanish Lake near what is today St. Louis, MO.

Ceran (1802-1870) develops into a quick-witted extrovert with stocky build, dark eyes, and heavy black beard. In the summer of 1824, Ceran puts his French nobility in a back pocket and hires on with an early trading caravan going to Santa Fe. The party is supervised by William Becknell who has already opened trade between New Mexico and Missouri. The Trapper's Trail is becoming better known as the *Taos Trail,* as it passes through Greenhorn Valley en route to Taos.

The Greenhorn is now a crossroad and resting place along the Taos Trail, which loops west off the Santa Fe Trail and skirts the south end of the Wet Mountains. As Taos trail comes into the Greenhorn Valley from the northeast (now I-25 out of Pueblo), the left fork turns south to Walsenburg, and the right fork swings southwest through the mountains into the San Luis Valley. A third trail heads northwest along the front range to Canon City, and a fourth points southeast to the Huerfano valley.

Although Ceran St. Vrain's first impression of the Greenhorn Valley is less than wonderful, he learns Spanish, dabbles in politics, and becomes a trapper. While he traps beaver from Wyoming to Mexico, his greatest catch will later be the land along the Front Range of the Rocky Mountains.

Charles and William Bent (French-Canadian trappers) are working for the American Fur Company in 1826. The brothers build their first stockade on Turkey Creek near Saddle Horn Buttes northwest of Pueblo. In 1829 Ceran St. Vrain joins the Bent brothers in hauling a caravan of supplies to Santa Fe. A year later they form a partnership and engage other trappers. They erect a small "picket post" stockade on the Arkansas nine miles east of Fountain Creek in December of 1832. The fort measures 137' x 178' with walls 14,' and it is named *Fort William* for the younger Bent. Fort William Trading Post is the first true settlement and trading store near Greenhorn Valley to the south. Pueblo as a town will be laid out 30 years later (1860) around 4th Street and Santa Fe Avenue.

The St. Vrain/Bent camps at the Pueblo site are among the first of various trading posts established along the Upper Arkansas. These small forts become the closest thing to home for many early trappers who

William Bent's Fort 1841 to 1842

William Bent in 1835 (Courtesy of Pioneers' Museum, Colo. Spgs., CO)

venture into the untamed west. Nowhere else can a mangy, mountain man dance with a real wild-Western, Indian girl.

Fort William is abandoned a few years later after the Bents kill three Shosoni Indians who are thought to have stolen mules. A new, larger fort is built 70 miles down stream where the Santa Fe and Taos Trails split. The new fort is called *Bent's Fort*, and later *Bent's Old Fort*. This fort is still close enough to draw trappers from the mountains; yet nearer to the Cheyenne, Arapahoe, and Kiowa hunting grounds. Bent's Fort will become the single most important factor in developing Greenhorn Valley.

In 1847 William, now the fort manager, is dealing with a variety of problems: A large flow of new settlers along the Trail is disrupting the delicate Indian trade. Water holes surrounding the fort are becoming polluted. Neighboring cottonwood groves are being cut down, and the essential buffalo herds are disappearing from the Plains. As many Cheyennes move away in 1848, William tries unsuccessfully to sell the fort to the U.S. military. To make matters worse, the U.S. Government is signing treaties with the Indians and then breaking them at will. In 1849 a cholera epidemic breaks out among the remaining Cheyennes, killing the Indians and ending trade. William chooses to abandon Bent's Old Fort.

Some sources say worthy William tried to burn (or blow up) the fort before leaving in 1852. Damaged but not destroyed, operations at the badly burnt fort are carried on by a few other traders. The damaged fort continues as a stage station and becomes home base for cattle ranchers. By the early 1900s the fort is totally abandoned, and many of its building materials have been carried off by local settlers. In 1926 the site is given to the Daughters of the American Revolution, who pass it to the Colorado Historical Society, who then pass it to the National Park Service.

In 1853, after abandoning Bent's Old Fort, worthy William builds a New Fort 40 miles down river at Big Timbers, so named for its large cottonwood trees between Las Animas and Lamar. In his final years, William moves back near the Old Fort location. The fact that William Bent has forts in several locations (just as Greenhorn settlements moved around) makes for some great confusion among historians.

During the Old Fort days, the St. Vrain/Bent party meet local Indian tribes and make friends with them. Although the Indians have buffalo skins to trade, the Bents are mostly interested in acquiring beaver skins to sell back east. Thousands of beaver pelts pass through the fort.

With an eye to the future, business-minded William Bent marries Owl Woman (daughter of a Cheyenne medicine man) about 1835, and he becomes a member of her Cheyenne tribe. William sometimes lives with Owl Woman in her village; he is referred to as *Little White Man.* Four children are born to the marriage: Mary, Robert, George, and Julia. George will later publish a book about his life as a half-breed, Cheyenne warrior.

Owl Woman dies at Julia's birth, and William takes her younger sister, Yellow Woman, as a second wife. His close relationship with Cheyenne Indians ensures many tribes will trade at the fort - as opposed to attacking it. Staying married into the Cheyenne nation proves to be an excellent life insurance policy for William who survives 45 long years on the frontier.

Ceran St. Vrain is a major factor during the first five years of trading on the Arkansas. Ceran, the trapper and business man, pulls French nobility from his rear pocket and forms several partnerships with Missouri merchants. As a growing entrepreneur, he makes the 800-mile trip between the Missouri River suppliers and Santa Fe buyers each and every year. Between trips Ceran marries the daughter of influential Carlos Beaubien, a connection leading to the huge land grant.

The St. Vrain/Bent trading post becomes an ongoing success. When the beaver trade dies in the East, it is replaced with an abundance of Indian trade in the West. At certain times of the year Ute, Snake, Sioux, Pawnee, Kiowa, Crow, Comanche, Cheyenne, Arapahoe, and Prairie Apaches camp around the Fort. During the heaviest period of trading (1832-1855), Indians number in the thousands while frontier white men number only a few hundred. In the 1840s the St. Vrain/Bent Company is doing more business than any other American company, except Astor's Fur Company.

William's Cheyenne son, George, records the following:

"The trade room was full of Indian men and women all day long; others came just to visit and talk, and there was often a circle of chiefs sitting with my father or his partners, smoking and talking. Wagons came in from New Mexico loaded with gaudy striped Mexican blankets, silver dollars, silver in bars, and other strange things. We could go out and play with the Indian children, or go to the corral back of the fort and watch One-eyed Juan and his men riding and breaking the wild horses."

When Indians come to Fort Bent, they bring moccasins, deerskins, buffalo robes, bows & arrows, and stolen horses taken in raids (no questions are asked.) They trade for American and Navajo blankets, iron wares, brass rings, axes, guns, flour, coffee, tobacco, bracelets, beads, and whiskey - but not in that order. Whiskey is the most popular and profitable item a trader has to sell an Indian. One Cheyenne Indian tells Colonel Dodge in 1835 at Bent's Fort that *"...in arranging the good things of this world in order of rank...whiskey should stand first; then tobacco; third, guns; fourth, horses; and fifth, women."* Some Indian tribes give, trade, and sell their women as property, much the same as women were treated and traded in Old Testament Bible times.

Most of the whiskey for trade comes from the Taos distillery of Simeon Turley (1806-1847.) Simeon has learned the basic skill of distilling whiskey during his frontier childhood. In 1836 Charles Autobee, an ex-trapper from St. Louis, comes to work for him as a traveling salesman. Soon everyone with something to trade has the opportunity to become *filled with spirits*. This is not the same as becoming *spiritual*, although some at the time may have thought so.

Charles Bent (1799-1847) stays at Old Bent's Fort occasionally, but he maintains a home in Taos from the mid-1830s. He marries into a prominent family and uses his growing influence to increase the flow of American trade. Charles spends a much of his time on the Santa Fe Trail moving merchandise between Missouri suppliers and western settlements.

While Charles Bent is moving goods across the land, Alexander Barclay (1810-1855) is managing the Old Fort from 1838 to 1842. After 1842, the well-educated Englishman becomes an independent trader at El Pueblo, then establishes his *Barclay's Houses* two miles to the west.

Sometime after 1840, two more Bent brothers, Robert and George, come to live and help out at Old Fort. Normally, the sizable trading post has from 40 to 60 workers. At its peak of trade, the fort employs about 100 workers, many Indian women from a dozen different tribes. In addition to the workers, there are many children. Casual association among employees leads to easy mixing in the workplace and at social events. Intermarriage is normal. However the billiard room (where drinking and gambling take place) is not open to Indian and Mexican laborers. Following late night dances, fort supervisors, trappers, and hunters go to their own private quarters. Craftsmen sleep in their work rooms. Indians are sent outside the fort to camp for the night.

The newly arrived Bent brothers, Robert and George, are probably not partners in the business, but George looks after the fort when brother William takes his annual wagon train (1832-1852) to Westport, MO (now Kansas City.) He exchanges furs for a new stock of saleable goods. Worthy William leaves the fort each spring and returns in fall. Brother

Robert dies of tuberculosis at the fort in 1847, and brother George is killed the following year by Indians just outside the fort. After 1852, William makes the long trip to Missouri twice each year.

All of the Bent forts are built on the north side of the Arkansas because south of the river is Mexican territory. In the early 1840's, Governor Manuel Armijo of the Mexican government offers free land (in what is today Southern Colorado) to dependable citizens who will build a house, grow crops, and breed cattle. The Mexican government wants to colonize quickly with Mexican residents before French trappers (like St. Vrain and the Bent Brothers) dominated the area.

However Mexican citizens are very much afraid of the Indians, and few want to risk the consequence of claiming Indian territory as their own. As the French-Americans will soon learn, Indian territories are not like pretty pieces of cake to be gobbled up at will.

When the Mexican government starts the big land giveaway, there are not many Frenchmen around. But most of the Mexican Land Grants end up in the hands of three Frenchmen: Ceran St. Vrain, Gervacio Nolan, and Charles H. Beaubien. To acquire free Mexican land these Frenchmen wisely become naturalized citizens of Mexico.

Nine million acres are divided into 197 parcels and given away. The largest of the 197 parcels is the Ceran St. Vrain and Cornelio Vigil parcel, covering more than four million acres, and it includes the Greenhorn. On December 8, 1843, St. Vrain and Vigil petition Governor Armijo for the large parcel, and the land is granted to them on January 2, 1844.

The vast land grant includes the river valleys (north to south) of St. Charles, Greenhorn, Huerfano, Apishapa, Cuchara, and Purgatoire. Today these valleys include the towns of Rye, Colorado City, Walsenburg, La Veta, Aguilar, Trinidad, La Junta, Las Animas, Rocky Ford, Fowler, and others falling within this Southern Colorado circle.

While the great land giveaway is going on, the once reliable beaver trade begins to fade. From 1841-1844, P. Chouteau Jr. & Co. buys all of the "pale fur" trappers can collect. In the spring of 1844, the Bent business sends only four packs of beaver to St. Louis, which signals significant suffering in the beaver trade.

As the demand for beaver slowly dies out back East, Charles Bent is thinking about his future in the West, and he establishes a permanent residence in Taos. Charles is named the first governor of New Mexico, and Kit Carson becomes the first Lieutenant Governor. Charles then acquires a one-sixth interest in Ceran St. Vrain's land grant. His new purchase

Charles Bent

Charles Bent, elder brother of William & first U.S. governor of New Mexico

(from The History of the Military Occupation of the Territory of New Mexico from 1846 to 1851 by the Government of the United States, by Ralph Emerson Twitchell) includes Greenhorn Valley. Although he will not live long enough to enjoy the land, daughter Estefana will homestead the Greenhorn legacy in 1859.

After Charles' untimely death at Taos in 1847, Ceran St. Vrain and William Bent continue as partners for several years. Ceran eventually sells his share of the Arkansas River business to William. Ceran moves permanently to the Santa Fe/Taos area where he has other trading posts.

The town of Taos is nestled in a mountain valley north of Santa Fe and features an Indian Pueblo. Near to the Taos Pueblo is a Mexican village known as *San Fernando de Taos*, where a number of displaced fur trappers have established residents. Among the displaced trappers frequently visiting Taos are Kit Carson, Jim Waters, Bill New, Levin Mitchell, Maurice Le Duc, Rube Herring, John Hawkins, Asa Estes, John Burroughs, John Brown, Calvin Briggs, Jim Beckwourth, and Marcelino Baca. Some of these legendary characters will be discussed in greater detail.

Only William Becknell and a few Delaware Indians (Jim Dickey, Jim Swanock, Little Beaver, and *"Big Nigger"*) continue trapping after 1842. Becknell and the Delawares continue trading at places like Fort Bent, Alexander Barclay's, The Pueblo, Hardscrabble, and John Brown's store on Greenhorn Creek. *Big Nigger*'s name appears as a December 28, 1846, entry in John Brown's account book. Shortly after trading at the Brown camp, Big Nigger travels to Taos where he visits his Indian wife who lives among the women of Taos Pueblo. As he arrives at the pueblo, the *"Taos Rebellion"* (against American occupation of New Mexico) is about to happen. When violence breaks out on January 20, 1847, Big chooses to join the rebellion with his wife's people.

When Governor Bent is murdered, American troops under Colonel Sterling Price and a volunteer company of mountain men under Colonel Ceran St. Vrain march into Taos. They are halted by Big Nigger and the rebels. Next day, when the attack resumes, Big is one of several rebels cornered in the back room of an adobe church. After a furious fight against overwhelming odds, Big is generally believed to perish in the church. Yet Big's final defenses are so spectacular some friends believe he has escaped from the church and fled to the Wet Mountain Valley on the west side of Greenhorn Mountains. Here in the favorite hunting ground of Delaware trappers, Big is said to have lived out his days as an outlaw.

Three years after the Taos Rebellion Ceran St. Vrain is one of the largest landowners in a two-state area. In 1855 he celebrates Fourth of July from the top of Greenhorn Mountain overlooking the Valley.

In 1870 at the age of 68, Ceran dies quietly at his mansion in Mora.

Ceran St. Vrain

(Western History Department
Denver Public Library)

Governors, statesmen, dignitaries, and more than 2,000 persons pay their final respects to Colonel of Volunteers at his full military funeral.

This French American (called *Blackbeard* by the Indians) played a large role in bringing Southern Colorado into the U.S., and the name *St. Vrain* has been given to towns, businesses, streets, streams, glaciers, a fort, mountain peaks, and a nuclear power plant.

Frontier Conflict

America's Declaration of Independence makes the possession of land by an individual a most attractive right for all citizens. Nearly all early Americans wish to have a parcel of land (small, medium, or large) they can call their own. Unfortunately many of the land transactions among frontier settlers are handshake deals with no record or legal title to the land and its improvements. Mexican land grants, homesteading practices, Indian treaties, mining claims, squatters' rights, and awkward surveys produce legal confusions requiring years, decades, and sometimes generations to resolve. Out of these conflicts (and the common practice of squatting on the land for ownership) comes the legal practice of - *"possession is nine-tenths of the law."* Physical possession of a parcel of land not only gives the squatter an immediate advantage, but *"it places upon other contestants the long-range legal burden of proving their own right to the same parcel of land."*

Many frontier murders are a direct result of lawless land disputes. Guns are not only a means of acquiring food for the family but an awful offense in taking land and a dreadful defense in keeping it.

Unlike early settlers who are preoccupied with planting a flag and claiming the land, American Indians are migratory. They move with the seasons and food sources. Their mobile lodges are made of buffalo hides sewn together and stretched over lodge poles in the shape of a cone. These lodges are easy to transport and good for any season. Many of the basic tepees are about ten feet in diameter at the bottom; they rise twelve feet high; and they are secured to the ground with pickets.

One sad element about the Indian lodge is that American natives fail to copyright their tent design. Eventually, tepee lodges are found along the highways and byways of modern man. These roadside motels are built of stucco and concrete instead of buffalo hides, because Western gunslingers have exterminated all herds of free roaming buffalo.

In contrast one rather positive element emerges from tent usage. Brave campers are now seen as temporary dwellers in designated campgrounds, occasionally peering out of their wigwam machines, the RV. Some campers search for seasonal wildlife and natural environment, which is a good food source for spiritual awakening. Others miss the twinkle of TV and go home to their Lazy Boy chairs and chips.

There is one final conflict. Arapahoe Indians utilize dog houses made of wicker works and covered with skins. Like the Arapahoes, U.S. Americans utilize wood and shingle dog houses for their beastly, barking, biting, best friends. But unlike the U.S. Americans, Arapahoe Americans make humans their best friends. They raise dogs as delicate meat to be eaten with those good friends on special occasions.

Archibald Charles Metcalf

Archibald Charles Metcalf is a six-foot-tall, handsome, heavily built, lively character from New York. He traps and trades in frontier societies beginning about 1841. Archibald rises to wealth and prominence; he mysteriously disappears ten years later; and he leaves behind an attractive young wife and some unhappy creditors.

Archibald is born in 1815, the son of Thomas and Mary Jane Metcalf. In late 1840 at the age of 25, he meanders west to the Arkansas and drifts into the Greenhorn Valley. Here he hooks up with three other mountaineer trappers: Marcelino Baca, John Brown, and William New. They hunt, trap, and hangout along Greenhorn Creek in the early 1840s.

Like other trappers, Archibald makes periodic trips to Taos. During his first few visits, he notices the growing whiskey trade. By the summer of 1843, *"Archa"* is a frequent visitor to the liquor store at Fort Pueblo Trading Post (1842-1854.) During the following year, Archa becomes quite active in the liquor business, and by the end of 1844 he is an important part of Fort Pueblo liquor trade. Fort Pueblo (called El Pueblo and The Pueblo) was located where the Pueblo City Ice Arena stands today.

While on a business trip to Taos, Archa falls in love with good-looking Maria de la *"Luz"* Trujillo, 15-year-old daughter of Jose Francisco Trujillo and Maria Natividad Sandoval. Archa's love for Luz is so transcending, he renounces his Episcopal faith to join the Catholic Church. Archa and Maria marry in Taos on October 30, 1845, where Archa *"paid a large marriage fee normally reserved for foreigners."* Perhaps the

Church wanted Archa to demonstrate the sincerity of his new religious convictions through material means.

The newlyweds depart Taos and travel to the small village of The Pueblo which is to become their home. At The Pueblo the couple emerge as socialites. Alexander Barclay writes in his diary: Archa is *"the soul of fun"* at dance parties. Other stories make further reference to Archa's *"fine-featured appearance and dynamic personality."* And Luz is no wallflower. When Kearny's troops arrive at Bent's Fort on the Arkansas in August of 1846, Luz parades herself down to the fort and entertains the Missouri officers at a frontier *fandango* (Spanish dance party.)

Lady Luz is often left behind at The Pueblo for long periods while fun-loving Archa goes about his trade with Utes in the western mountains and Arapahoes/Cheyennes on the eastern plains. While doing his traveling and trading business, Archa hears about the terrible Taos Rebellion.

After four months of new-owner control by the United States, the natives of Taos (Indians and Mexicans) have risen up against the new foreign control and have murdered many Americans, including the first governor (Charles Bent); his young brother-in-law (Pablo Jaramillo); the circuit attorney (James White Leal); prefect officers (Narciso Beaubien and Cornelio Vigil); and the local sheriff (Steve Lee.)

George Bent, son of William Bent, records the grim details of his Uncle Charles' murder at Taos:

"On January 19, 1847, a mob of Indians entered San Fernando and made a rush toward the calabozo. Vigil, the town prefect, met them alone and attempted to disperse them, but they kill him and cut his body to pieces. This was early in the morning. They broke into the calabozo next and released the Indian prisoners, then the whole mob of them rushed to my uncle's house, a flat-roofed, one story adobe building. The doors and windows were heavily barred, so some of the Indians got upon the flat roof and began to cut a hole. My uncle went to a window and spoke to the Indians, reminding them of their old friendship for him, that he had lived among them for years and had helped nearly all of them out of trouble at different times; but they jeered him and fired in at him. His wife brought his pistols but he would not touch them, as he knew that if he fired a shot the Indians would kill his wife and children. By this time the Indians on the roof had cut a large hole and they now leaped down into the room and shot my uncle down at the feet of his wife and children. They shot his body full of arrows, a chief ran up and fired a pistol in my uncle's face;

then they tore off his scalp. The mob now went through the whole town, breaking into houses and killing every American they could find....While these bands of murderers were breaking into houses, one of the Indians stretched my uncle's scalp on a small piece of board, fastening it with brass-headed tacks, and paraded it through the streets."

When local officials are killed by the rebels on January 19 of 1847, San Fernando de Taos remains precariously in the hands of surviving colonels, clerks, Indian agents, and wild dogs.

As news of the Taos Rebellion reaches Santa Fe, Colonel Ceran St. Vrain forms a company of rough and rugged *Mountain Volunteers* to aid Colonel Sterling Price in putting an end to the rebels. Second in command of St. Vrain's volunteer company is (none other than) First Lieutenant Archibald Charles Metcalf. The rough and rugged Mountain Volunteers arrive at Taos and soon round up the rebels.

Fun-loving Archa remains at Taos to participate in the trial of rebel leaders. On March 1 of 1847, Archa is hired to be sheriff of Taos County. As Sheriff, he is responsible for jailing the prisoners, erecting the gallows, and hanging those found guilty of leading the revolt.

Hanging the rebel leaders seems to be a great pleasure for fun-loving Archa. According to adventurer Lewis Garrard, who is at the scene, Archa borrows lariats from the Mountain Volunteers and makes nifty neck nooses. As he lubricates the nooses with soft soap, he is heard to say, *"This'll make em slip easy - a long ways too easy for them, I 'spect."*

With nooses hung around their necks, fun-loving Archa places the convicted rebels in a wagon beneath the gallows. After driving the wagon out from under their feet and watching them wiggle to death, he cuts the bodies down and presents them to the weeping widows. Without further delay, Archa strolls off to his father-in-law's tavern. He drinks egg nog with other Americans until they are all thoroughly drunk.

The ritual of getting drunk celebrates a job well-done: as in *"an eye for an eye, a tooth for a tooth,"* and a murder for a murder. The Americans have avenged the murder of U. S. citizens and taught the rebels a lesson. Unfortunately the rebels who opposed the new government are a bit too much dead to learn from the lesson.

Tavern owner and father-in-law Asa Estes is an old trapper who married Archa's mother-in-law, Maria Natividad Sandoval. Natividad's own father, Francisco Trujillo, was murdered by the Utes at Robidoux's Fort Uncompahgre in 1844.

After the hangings, the drinking, and the hangovers, fun-loving Archa buys 65 *fanegas* of wheat (8 gallons or a bushel) from the estate of Simeon Turleya. Once again he marches off to trade with Ute Indians. When he fails to appear in a Taos court hearing on September 6 of 1847, his office of sheriff is rendered vacant. Vicente St. Vrain is appointed to take over the position.

In October Archa returns home to The Pueblo from his trading trip with the Utes. Apparently trading with the Indians was quite good, because a month later he buys out Alexander Barclay's store at The Pueblo Trading Post.

Along with Taos traders named Charles Town, Lucien Maxwell, Blackhawk (or Pascual Riviere), and others, Archa meets with Utes camped on the west side of Greenhorn Mountain. The Taos traders exchange a large amount of flour and beans for 600 Ute deerskins.

Shorty after the trade, Archa and his men load the same 600 deerskins upon 30 mules and 50 horses at the John Brown store on Greenhorn Creek. They plan to trade the deerskins in Taos. Since the travel party has made many purchases at the John Brown store on credit, John, his wife, and infant child join the caravan to Taos. Most likely the Browns plan to keep a close eye on their investment, get paid in Taos, and then do some serious shopping on the plaza.

Only a few miles into the trip, just south of Greenhorn at the well-named Apache Creek, the caravan is attacked by a band of Apache Indians. According to Charles Town, a member of the caravan, they successfully resist the attack and kill three Apache braves. Unsettled by the ambush and near death of John's wife and son, John Brown and Archa Metcalf are concerned about more attacks. Archa, John, Luisa, and little John withdraw from the caravan and return to the Greenhorn camp.

All other members of the party continue south toward Taos. On June 20th Apaches again attack the caravan from rocks overlooking the Manco de Buro Pass in the Raton Mountains. All members of the party are murdered except Lucien Maxwell and George Galvez. Lucien is shot in the back of his head trying to escape, and he falls unconscious. George is himself wounded but still able to save Lucien:

"George, known as Indian George who had been ransomed from captivity among the Indians by William Bent, was devoted to Maxwell and brought Lucien water in his hat, revived him, and despite a wound of his own, got Lucien away safely."

The entire pack of 600 deerskins, 50 horses, and 30 mules is taken by the Apaches. Not bad for a day's work. It was certainly easier than breeding a large herd of horses and mules, then hunting down a ton of mule dear. This timesaving device of leeching from the work of others, instead of doing the work oneself, is still popular today among pathetic parasites.

On August 23 of 1848, a year after becoming sheriff of Taos, fun-loving Archa is back in Taos trying to collect his annual income from the County of Taos. Archa not only fails to collect back pay, but the County of Taos has determined that he owes money to them.

Early in 1849, fun-loving Archa takes a business trip east on the Arkansas to trade with Kiowa Indians near today's Dodge City, KS. Next he visits Barclay's new trading post in northeastern New Mexico. After making a few more trips to Santa Fe, the last reference to Archa is found in Barclay's diary dated "July 19, 1849." Archa leaves Fort Barclay to join up with Kit Carson, who is on route to the upper trail crossing of the North Platte River near today's Casper, WY. Carson plans to help build a bridge. What happens to Archa at this point is uncertain.

Archa's wife (Luz Metcalf) says her husband died of cholera at Fort Laramie in "1848." However it was not until 1849-1850 that the cholera epidemic hit Fort Laramie, and Archa was still alive at Barclay's in July of 1849. Perhaps cholera did take him while working on the bridge. If so, Luz is right about his death but wrong about the date. Another source states Archa was killed while trading with Kiowas on the Santa Fe Trail at Pawnee Rock (or Walnut Fork.)

Since fun-loving Archa owes John Brown $230 from the June 1848 Apache ambush, maybe Archa disappears to avoid the debt. In the 1840s the sum of $230 is more than just pocket change. In a plea written as late as June 1849, Brown begs Archa for payment of his debt, because he and his family are about to leave for California. Also it appears Charles Barclay lost money to Archa in connection with the bridge building event.

As early as October of 1848, lonely Luz returns to Taos and takes up with Lieutenant Joseph H. Whittlesey who has come to Taos with a cavalry regiment. Perhaps Luz moves the death of husband Archa from 1849-1850 back to 1848 in order to create a bit more time between the old Archa and the new Joseph. Then again, since Archa was gone for long periods of time, Luz may have given up on her marriage long before Archa disappears at age 35.

During the time she lives with Lieutenant Whittlesey, Luz bares a daughter named Fannie. Still attractive in 1855, Luz marries Felipe

Ledoux, the son of well-known trapper Abraham Ledoux. Luz will live with Felipe Ledoux, who is five years her junior, for another 55 years until her final exit from Las Vegas, NM, on July 5, 1910.

Luisa Sandoval Beckwourth Brown

Luisa Sandoval, a young Spanish woman from Taos, will become the first woman to settle on Greenhorn Creek. Although little is known about Luisa's early life, her first husband (James Pierson Beckwourth) publishes a wild and crazy autobiography in 1856. From James P. Beckwourth's life story we learn about Luisa indirectly as a young woman.

Mr. James Beckwourth publishes an extensive autobiography, but he is not real big on telling his story accurately. James misstates dates, places, people, and events. He provides plenty of information but not particularly accurate material. Beckwourth's life story reads like a sizzling soap opera rather than a personal history.

In 1798 Jim Beckwourth is born in Virginia and later moves to St. Louis with his wealthy father and 22 Negro slaves. Beckwourth fails to mention that he and his Negro mother are among the slaves.

Mulatto Jim is fathered by Sir Jennings *Beckwith*, grandson of Sir Marmaduke *Beckwith* of Richmond County, VA. Jim grows up six feet tall, muscular, and strong. He has great potential to become a mountain man.

Mulatto Jim has a few years of schooling and can write somewhat legibly. He speaks English well. He will learn to speak French with ease, understand Spanish, and know several Indian dialects.
Spelling, however, is his weakness, even to the point of signing his own name *Beckwourth* instead of *Beckwith*. Honoring his own signature, *Beckwourth* is used hereafter in place of his given name, *Beckwith*.

As a young adult in St. Louis, Jim is freed from slavery by his Irish father, and he apprentices in Casner's blacksmith shop. Jim's interest in a young girl leads to the breaking of his boss's rules and the end of his apprenticeship. As Jim's life unfolds, he will rarely meet a woman he does not like. Luisa will become his seventh wife.

Not far from St. Louis the Indians at Fever River are becoming troublesome. While most settlers gather in *"companies"* for protection, curious Jim visits Fever River and gets better acquainted with his Indian neighbors: *"The Indians soon became very friendly to me, and I was indebted to them for showing me their choicest hunting grounds."* In time

Jim will not only recreate himself as an Indian, but a Crow Indian Chief.

In the fall of 1824, General William H. Ashley is assembling a frontier expedition and needs recruits. Curious Jim has a burning desire to visit the much-talked-about Western wilderness. He joins the travel party in the summer of 1825.

Two years later while under the supervision of William L. Sublette (who has acquired General Ashley's fur trade), curious Jim is presented with a Blackfoot Indian woman as a gift for his hard work in opening a new trading post in Blackfoot territory. Jim accepts the Indian woman as his wife. Rising further in popularity, he is presented with the younger sister of the first wife. Jim is now a man in need of higher ground. Having two more wives than he cares to have, Jim casually leaves the camp and his two Blackfoot wives behind.

Under the wonderful wits and cool courage of Jedediah Smith and James Clyman, curious Jim proves to be a worthy student. He learns well the skill of hand-to-hand combat. He learns to launch the lance, wield the war club, shoot the bow and arrow, and gear the grisly gun.

With these useful skills under his belt, curious Jim recreates himself as an American Indian. To become an Indian he invents some personal history to be shared with the Crow nation in South Park, CO. He tells the Crow tribe that as a small child, he was ripped from the arms of his Crow family by Cheyenne warriors and sold to white people. Thus:

"...having been captured years before by the Cheyennes and sold by them to the whites, with whom he had lived ever since. Much excitement and rejoicing greeted this astonishing news, followed by demands that Jim be turned over to the tribe forthwith."

Creative Jim takes his new Indian status seriously. He acquires four Crow wives and adopts several Crow sisters, all *"very pretty"* and *"intelligent."* Although serious about being an Indian, Jim wears his marital commitments like seasonal clothing. He casually puts on wives and takes them off as the seasons change. Besides, casual marriages are common among the Crows.

Jim weds like a Crow, walks like a Crow, talks like a Crow, and dresses like a Crow. Therefore he must be a Crow:

"Jim Beckwourth took to Indian costume as thought born to wear it. On occasion he dressed in elaborately beaded and embroidered buckskin,

braided his hair into long rolls, or tied it at the neck with a gaudy ribbon, He loved personal ornaments: gold chains, buttons, even earrings - his ears were pierced in several places."

Creative Jim emerges as a romancer, bareback rider, expert shooter, and gifted liar. He uses his storytelling skills to build a reputation as successful merchant and Crow Indian Chief. As Crow Chief, his leadership role is to acquire needed guns, ammunition, beads, and cloth - in exchange for elk skins, beaver pelts, and buffalo robes. With weapons in hand, it is now necessary for Jim to sound like a warrior:

"No, hold! Warriors, listen! If these old men can not fight, let them retire with the women and children. We can kill every one of these Black Feet: then let us do it. If we attempt to run from here, we shall be shot in the back, and lose more warriors than to fight and kill them all. If we get killed, our friends who love us here will mourn our loss, while those in the spirit land will sing and rejoice to welcome us there, if we ascend to them dying like braves. The Great Spirit has sent these enemies here for us to slay; if we do not slay them, he will be angry with us, and will never suffer us to conquer our enemies again....Come, follow me, and I will show you how the braves of the great white chief fight their enemies."

After ten years in the Wild West, creative Jim departs the Crow nation and makes his way to Florida. Here he embraces adventure in the Seminole Wars (1835 to 1842.) He joins in the fun as express rider, master teamster, sub-conductor, muleteer, and wagon master. In 1839, failing to find enough excitement in the war, Jim returns to St. Louis where he searches for other employment.

A year later creative Jim is back in the Rockies, this time with a trading company pedaling booze to the Indians. When his firm sells out, he joins the Bent/St. Vrain Company. Soon bored at Bent's Fort, Jim forms a partnership with an old acquaintance named Lee, and they move to Taos. As the newest local merchants, they set up a trading post for Indians.

It is here in the village of Taos creative Jim meets and marries Luisa Sandoval who will become the first woman to live and trade on Greenhorn Creek. Jim refers to *"Senorita Louisa Sandeville"* (notice the spelling problem) as his wife and by her has a daughter named Matilda. Since churches in Taos record no such marriage, Jim probably took up with Luisa Sandoval in the same informal way he married six Indian women.

James P. Beckwourth
(Courtesy of the Historical Society of Colo.)

Creative Jim leaves his Taos store behind and moves Luisa Sandoval back to where the Fountain and Arkansas Rivers converge. According to Jim, they arrive in October of 1842 and are soon joined by more trappers who have families. Together they build an adobe fort and trading post *"60 yards square."*

Other sources indicate El Pueblo was already established by October of 1842, and the original builders and owners were Francisco Conn; Robert Fisher; Mathew Kinkead; Joseph Mantz; and George Simpson. Jim and Luisa Beckwourth are numbered among those associated with El Pueblo which has a trading room, storage rooms, and sleeping rooms.

During the spring and summer of 1843, many of the families are successful in raising crops, *"such as wheat, corn, oats, potatoes and abundance of almost all kinds of vegetables."* In addition to Jim and Luisa Beckwourth, early residents of The Pueblo include Dick Wootton; Simeon Turley; Bill Tharp; Teresita Suaso; David Spaulding; George Simpson; Archa Metcalf; William Kroenig; Bill Garey (Guerrier); Robert Fisher; Joseph Doyle; Marcelino Baca; Alexander Barclay; and Charles Autobee.

Taken from her home in Taos, Luisa Sandoval Beckwourth is now living at The Pueblo which is getting the reputation of *"a collecting pot of the scum of the mountains."*

Down stream at their new location, the Bents view The Pueblo as bad competition, uncontrolled liquor trade, and the arrival of undesirable Mexican traders. The Bents try to get a military post established in the area to control The Pueblo, but they are unsuccessful. In 1843 Luisa's husband is in good favor with the Indians, but he is disliked by both the Bents and some Mexicans. After less than a year at The Pueblo, creative Jim departs for California and does not return for three years. Leaving wife Luisa and baby Matilda behind, Jim takes 15 men and various trading goods to what is now Los Angeles. They arrive January of 1844.

Long-gone Jim conducts his usual trade business until Californians rebel against Mexican control in 1845. When war is declared between United States and Mexico in 1846, Jim chooses a side. With about 1,800 stray horses found roaming Californian ranches, Jim disappears from Pueblo de Angeles and heads home to The Pueblo. As to the stolen horses, Jim says, *"This was a fair capture and our morals justified it, for it was war-time."* Arriving home with many horses, Jim plans to continue his business career at The Pueblo, but the trading post is not the same home Jim left three years earlier. While long-gone Jim was away, life at The Pueblo continued in high style, and Luisa Sandoval has remarried.

Why does Luisa remarry while her husband is absent? According to Jim Beckwourth's autobiography, trapper John Brown gives Jim's wife (Luisa) a forged letter stating that he (husband Jim) no longer cares for her and releases her from all marital obligation. Rejected and dejected, Luisa hooks up with John Brown, the very messenger of bad news.

Long-gone Jim recalls: when he arrived at Pueblo, Luisa came forward, regretted her new relationship, and offered herself back to him. In response, Jim stepped aside and gallantly declined to take back his slightly used wife. Jim made no mention of his daughter, Matilda.

Long-gone Jim is extremely independent, follows opportunity, thrives on adventure, and seeks personal fame. There is little room in his life for close family relations, except as a convenience. His various wives are good for sexual gratification, cooking meals, scraping hides, sewing bead work, and light conversation. Casting off Luisa and Matilda gives Jim the ongoing freedom he normally enjoys. After giving up his relationship with Luisa, Jim will marry twice more.

Later the same year, long-gone Jim gets caught up in the Taos rebellion of 1846. *"He carried dispatches for the army and acted as guide and interpreter."* After the rebellion, Jim operates a hotel in Santa Fe; he is present at the hangings of Taos rebels; he sets up trade stores in Monterey and Sacramento; he prospects for gold along the American River; he creates a new mountain pass; he lays out a road through the pass; and he establishes a hotel in a pleasant valley leading to the pass. In October 1854 Jim meets Thomas D. Bonner who agrees to write his life story.

Thomas D. Bonner (called *Squire* by some) is equally as peculiar as Jim Beckwourth. Mr. T. D. Bonner manages to get himself elected as Justice of the Peace, because it pays well. The Squire misuses his authority to acquire handsome profits; he sets up his own newspaper as a *"violent temperance reformer;"* then he writes sensational prose and poetry to attract readers.

During the long cold winter of 1854-55, the squirrelly Squire settles in at Beckwourth's hotel. Bonner and Beckwourth draw up a contract to share equally in the profits. Together they create Jim's life story which introduces us to Luisa Sandoval.

After the book is published, there is no evidence long-gone Jim receives any of the profits. Six years after writing the book, Bonner is accused of *"shop-breaking and theft"* of rum. Eventually T. D. dies of alcoholism. The Squire's misuse of authority has made a terrible tight turn back to him. The great evil he has done to others has returned to terminate his own life.

Jim Beckwourth dies on October 30 of 1866 in the heart of Crow hunting grounds where he has spent much of his life. He expires in the lodge of Iron Bull and is buried by his Crow host. Beckwourth's pleasant valley, ranch, trail, and mountain pass still bare his name.

Beckwourth's book containing the odd story of his return home and finding his wife married to another is published in 1856. By this time Luisa Sandoval and John Brown have been living in California for six years with Jim's daughter, Matilda, and more children of their own.

In direct contrast to the Beckwourth book, family members of Luisa Sandoval and John Brown tell a different story while long-gone Jim was away from home for three years:

"Louisa convinced authorities that she had been deserted and she married John Brown on May 1, 1845. They moved to Greenhorn Valley, taking with them Beckwourth's daughter, Matilda, whom they reared."

If the Brown family story is correct, Luisa and John marry about two years after Jim Beckwourth took a long hike to the West Coast. When lady Luisa shifts into second gear, she and John Brown leave The Pueblo and set up a small trading post on Greenhorn Creek. Luisa is an essential business partner actively running the store when John is away. Luisa sells merchandise to visitors, purchases goods from peons, handles the expenses at *fandangos,* provides tobacco, and bar tends whiskey at the social events. She is becoming a wonder woman of the wild west.

To help Luisa keep Spanish dances rolling at the Greenhorn camp, the Browns employ harmonious Jose, locally known as *"Jose the Fiddler."* Jose earns about eight dollars a month with his skill on the twanger, as reported by George Ruxton (English traveler, army officer, and writer) in the late 1840s. Luisa gives birth to John Jr. on October 3 of 1847.

In addition to being a business woman, Luisa Sandoval Beckwourth Brown is a lady of great strength and courage. The following notes are taken from F. W. Cragin's interview with Mrs. Felipe Ledoux (former wife of Archa Metcalf) at Las Vegas, NM, on June 17, 1908:

"On June 6...John Brown conducted a half-price sale of pants at this Greenhorn store, settled his account and closed his books. Then he started south with his wife Luisa, who was carrying their four-month-old son John Jr. in her arms. With them were Archibald Metcalf [Mrs. Felipe

Ledoux's early husband] and Blackhawk, who were leading sixty horses and mules packed with deerskins traded from the Utes in the Wet Mountain Valley. Lucien Maxwell, his servant Indian George, and Charles Town, just arrived from the crossing of the Arkansas, joined them. Six or seven miles south of Greenhorn on Apache Creek the train was attacked by Jicarilla Apaches who drove off all the pack animals and their valuable burden. Some of the Indians took after Luisa Brown, who wheeled her horse, fastened her arm tightly about her baby's neck and dashed off toward Greenhorn. The men shouted at her to throw away the baby. Instead, with the Indians close behind her, she forced her horse to jump a deep arroyo and arrived at Greenhorn in safety. In this harrowing chase she wrenched young John's neck so that ever afterward he carried his head bent forward."

A second account of the same event is penned by longtime journalist and Colorado historian, Ralph C. Taylor, who writes without sources. His source of information is propably Mrs. Dorothy Price Shaw:

"In the 1840s a little party consisting of Lucien Maxwell, Charles Towne, James [Archibald] Metcalf and Mr. and Mrs. John Brown and their small son, John, were traveling the Taos Trail from Greenhorn to New Mexico when the Indians attacked them near Apache Creek. The Indians tried to capture Mrs. Brown, who was riding on a horse with little John. The men in the party had out-distanced Mrs. Brown and shouted to her to try and make her horse jump an arroyo to join them. They intended to shoot her if necessary to keep her from being captured alive by the Apaches. At the last moment the horse jumped the gulch. Mrs. Brown clutched the baby's neck so tightly that his spine was wrenched and the child grew up with his head bent forward."

A third account of the escape (occuring in 1848) is told by none other than John Brown Jr. himself, who grows up to become a school teacher and biographer in California. Most likely John Jr. has heard this tale told many times around the dinner table, until the story has stretched itself into a family legend. At age 73, two decades after his father's death, biographer John Jr. recalls the miraculous escape in third person:

"When about a year old he [John, Jr.] experienced an almost miraculous escape from the Apache Indians, and owes his life to the

sublime courage of his devoted mother....His father and fellow mountaineers, having accumulated a large quantity of buffalo robes and beaver pelts, concluded to send a pack train to Taos, Mew Mexico, their trading post at that time, from whence, after selling their peltries, they would return with provisions. Mrs. Brown, with her baby boy, accompanied this expedition, and on the way through the mountains they were attacked by a band of Apache Indians, who captured the whole pack train and killed some of the hunters. While fleeing on horseback from these pursuing and desperate warriors, some of the men shouted at Mrs. Brown, 'Throw that child away or the Indians will get you,' but the faithful mother indignantly exclaimed while endeavoring to escape as fast as the fleet horse could run with her, 'Never; when that baby boy is thrown away, I will go with him.' Fortunately, the pursued cavalcade soon reached a deep ravine, where the hunters were safe from the arrows and bullets of the Indians....These hunters with Mrs. Brown and her baby, were glad to reach Taos, the trading post, alive."

Of these three stories, the first portrays Luisa as the courageous woman with infant child dashing away from the attack and returning home to Greenhorn Creek. The second features her as a skilled rider jumping over a deep ditch to join the caravan party. The third pictures her as a devoted mother willing to die with her son rather than increase her own chances for escape to a deep ravine with others. Luisa Brown is no doubt all three: brave woman, skilled rider, and devoted mother.

Of the three stories, John Brown Jr.'s account appears to have some silly errors. First, little John is only a few months old and not a year, according to Metcalf's wife. Second, the trappers transport deerskins and not buffalo robes and beaver pelts. Third, they are traveling near Apache Creek in the foothills and not yet in the mountains. Fourth, no members of the party are killed on this first attack but later on the second attack 80 miles south of Apache Creek. Fifth, the caravan did not reach Taos safe and happy, because all members of the party were murdered except Lucien Maxwell and his Indian servant. Remember, Archa Metcalf who was at the scene reported he, John, Luisa, and their infant returned to the Greenhorn in fear of more Apache attacks. The remaining caravan of men, horses, and deerskins went on to be ambushed in the Raton Mountains.

Perhaps infant John's memory is consciously clouded at the time of his neck-wrenching, which may have twisted things in his little noggin. Then again, 73 years is a great distance from the actual event. Most likely

Lucien B. Maxwell (from *Uncle Dick* by H. L. Conard & Courtesy of Denver Public Library Western Collection)

John Jr. is merely penning the family legend. Junior's story is most noteworthy in that (as a loving tribute to mother Luisa) he alone chooses not to mention his spine-wrenching trauma and life long consequence.

Under *"Claims for Indian Depredation in New Mexico,"* Lucien Maxwell claims a loss of 30 mules, 50 horses, 600 deerskins stolen by Jicarilla Apaches on June 12, 1848. Lucien does not file the claim until 1854, and the claim goes unpaid, probably because of the six year delay.

It is of some small interest that Archa Metcalf's wife gives the date of June 6, 1846, for the attack on Luisa, which is two years earlier than the actual attack and loss (of June 12, 1848) reported by Lucien Maxwell.

As an early trader in the Greenhorn Valley, Lucien Bonaparte Maxwell has good reason to do business with Luisa Sandoval Beckwourth Brown on Greenhorn Creek. Maxwell is a marvelous story all by himself. In brief he drifts West, acquires a number of Indian languages; travels with John C. Fremont in 1842; develops a close friendship with Kit Carson; becomes sole owner of the Beaubien and Miranda Land Grant (later the Maxwell Land Grant); founds the town of Rayado; and establishes his own bank (with his picture engraved on the currency.) Then, he loses it all to generosity with friends, high living, gambling, and bad investments.

Trapper John Brown

In the 1800s there are no less than three John Browns who locate in the Huerfano and Greenhorn Valleys. First and foremost, there is the John Brown, trapper and storekeeper at Greenhorn Creek, who with lady Luisa pioneers the Valley in the mid 1840s. Second, there is John M. Brown, who is murdered with his wife Sarah at La Veta in 1876. Third, there is John Henry Brown, early pioneer on the Huerfano, who is interviewed by historian F. W. Cragin at Walsenburg in 1907.

Trapper John Brown, who will become storekeeper with Luisa, is born in Worchester, MA, on December 22 of 1817. As a young man, he rafts on the Mississippi River, becomes shipwrecked off Galveston, fights at the battle of San Jacinto, and spends two years at Fort Leavenworth. Following Leavenworth, John embarks on a western adventure as trapper, hunter, trader, lover, storekeeper, writer, father of ten children, Justice of the Peace, and marvelous medium of heavenly spirits.

Psychic John is no run-of-the-mill medium; he has a personal *"spirit guide"* to caution and direct his actions. In his book entitled *Mediumistic*

Experiences of John Brown, the Medium of the Rockies, John recalls many events which reflect spiritual associations. The following dream foretells the outcome of a hunting trip that will take place the next day:

"It was in those early days when the buffalo, elk, bear, deer, antelope and mountain sheep (big horn, as the Indian called them), mixed with occasional bands of wild horses...that Estes, Stone and myself spread our robes for the night beneath a tall fir tree...so well constructed that no rain could wet this natural bed. It was in this solitary place, in the dead of the night, when all was still except the howling of the buffalo wolf, in the distance, that my spirit guide, my angel friend, with whom, I am waiting to go and live, came to me and said: 'John, come with me.' We had not gone far before we came to a lone depression, or deep ravine whose sides were covered with small oak trees or brush, with an occasional pine tree. Right there, my guide seemed to disappear, or rather I thought he was close behind me, and I was mounted on my horse, with Estes and Stone on either side of me, when the following conversation was had. As we looked across the ravine I saw a huge grizzly bear moving rapidly up the steep mountain side....We then discovered another large grizzly, on the opposite side of the ravine, among the oaks, eating acorns....I had no sooner fired than I heard a hideous growl and the cracking of brush behind me; for I assure you I did not wait to see what effect my shot had. I ran by Estes, who, seeing no bear coming, accompanied me to a safe retreat from the scene of our adventure. I then saw Stone, standing where I had left him, making signs that all was safe, that I had killed the bear....On reaching the place where the bear stood when I shot, we found he had rolled several rods down the gorge, tearing and biting off limbs from small trees as large as a man's arm. In his dying struggles he had cleared off a place sufficiently large for us to work in skinning him. He was a monster, the king of the forest, weighing nearly twelve hundred pounds....Here all seemed to vanish, all seemed to fade out; and, only on awakening in the morning did I realize what I had seen and what I had passed through."

[Next day before the hunt] "I related all to my companions, who declared that nothing of the kind should take place...."

[At the end of the hunt] "But the time came, and we all three, stood beside the monster, who lay upon his back, with our knives in hand, when all of a sudden Estes dropped his knife and declared he would not take any of that meat....The great mystery to me, was the taking from me all knowledge of what I had passed through and made known."

For three years during his Greenhorn days, John's spirit guide is with him like a guardian angel, making special visits at night and revealing detailed events that will occur in the near future:

"Although my guide did not look nor act as I did, yet so closely were we connected that at times I thought that we were one person. I could not separate myself from him nor could he from me, neither did either of us wish to do so. There seemed to be a complete oneness, and this close connection lasted over three years, without the intermission of a single day or night.

"During this time he would, by word, gesture, or by a writing already prepared, make known to me future occurrences. If in writing, he handed me a roll or manuscript, and by unrolling it I appeared to be instantaneously impressed with every word there written, and could repeat it on the following day, but after the events, set forth, had transpired, it soon passed from my memory...."

Not all happenings pass from John's memory. In his collection of *Mediumistic Experiences*, he reports several events rather seriously without so much as a trace of humor.

By contrast, the residents of The Pueblo are probably having many a chuckle over the pious Brown and his invisible friends. As a form of amusement, they gamble on John's mystical predictions. When it finally comes to John's attention, his companions are making bets on his foreshadowings. Although John takes offense, it does not stop one enterprising associate from trying to cut a deal with the mystic himself:

"Finally, Timothy Goodale, one of the company, proposed to me to give the information to him exclusively, and that he would divide, equally with me, the money he could win. I refused, and resented the offer.

"I shall never forget the indignant look my guide gave when next I saw him, as, pointing his finger at Goodale, he said: 'John, gambling is an abomination in the sight of angels and all good men. Have nothing to do with that man.' I obeyed his instructions, but his power to give me information seemed to have departed....Since that time he has visited me only at long intervals, being apparently under the restraint of some one superior to himself."

Even though mystical John obeys the spirit's warning to stay away from enterprising Goodale (spelled Goodall and Goodell), John looses regular contact with his angelic friend shortly after the episode. Apparently even spirit guides can get angry and hold a grudge.

John Brown helps build The Pueblo in the winter of 1841-42. About this time according to Tom Tobin, John kills a Frenchman in a fight over a beautiful Mexican girl named Nicolasa. The gun duel takes place on the Greenhorn ranch of Jose Meis. A year and a half later on July 4 of 1843, Rube Herring supposedly kills Henry Beer at Fort Lupton in a fight over the same Nicolasa. Afterward, Rube Herring takes Nicolasa to The Pueblo and lives with her until Jim Waters causes her to stray his way. In the habit of competing for another man's wife, Jim Waters does in fact kill Ed Tharp in a quarrel over Ed's wife, Candelara. This grim story will come later.

John Brown and Timothy Goodale reconcile their differences. When mystical John writes about his spiritual experiences, he frequently names Tim among other companions such as Jim Waters; Dick Owens; John Burrows; and Calvin Briggs. John recalls life in an Indian lodge with John Burrows and Calvin Briggs from 1843 to 1844 on the Arkansas River near The Pueblo. It was here at The Pueblo in the spring of 1843 Jim Beckwourth left wife Luisa and child Matilda behind.

One night John's spirit guide comes to him in a dream and says when he and Calvin go out to check traps and hunt deer the next day, he should stay with Calvin or else something terrible will happen. The next morning he and Calvin march off hunting together, but they separate at the junction of the Arkansas and St. Charles Rivers. Since John has apparently forgotten the dream, he receives a second strong warning to go back and find Calvin. When John returns to the St. Charles, he finds Calvin face down on the river ice with his hand caught beneath the cold water in one of his beaver traps, and the hole in the ice is too narrow to withdraw the trap on his hand. In this condition Calvin would have quickly frozen in the ice if it had not been for John and his spirit guide.

In relating another experience, mystical John gives a description of the traditional *"trapper's oath."* John shares his vision of friend Jim Waters arriving at The Pueblo with a white woman and her two children. In the vision Jim is transporting trade goods of shirts, hats, knives, powder, tobacco, a box of small white clay pipes, and a fine iron-gray horse. Jim has brought the horse for Tim Goodale, the gambler. Although most of John's friends are skeptical, Tim Goodale (potential beneficiary) saddles up his mule tied by the door and is about to depart for The Pueblo.

"All right," says Dick Owens, *"I will administer the oath,"* and Tim receives the muzzle of Dick's loaded rifle into his mouth. Gun in mouth Tim mumbles the trappers oath: *"to return the next day, dead or alive."* Soon Tim is on his mule, down the road, and out of sight. The next day he returns to camp wearing a new shirt, carrying a plug of tobacco, smoking a white clay pipe, and towing his new, iron-gray mare.

From the time she first arrived in 1844 until she left in 1846, Mrs. Felipe Ledoux recalls trapper John living near The Pueblo. By the time Mrs. Ledoux departs, John Brown has given up (or lost) the fair Nicolasa and has taken up with Luisa Sandoval Beckwourth. By 1846 John and Luisa have left The Pueblo and set up a small trading camp on Greenhorn Creek 25 miles away. The location is John Brown's old trapping ground.

Taos Trail leaves The Pueblo and heads southwest along the foothills of the Wet Mountains. This 25-mile-stretch leading to Greenhorn Creek was first known as *Trappers Trail*. Taos Trail branches south from the Old Crow Ranch House crossing the creek just south of today's Cibola Drive. From here the Trail skirts the southeast side of Greenhorn Mountain, dips through Wet Mountain Valley, rises across the Sangre de Cristo Mountains into San Luis Valley, and follows the Rio Grande River south to Taos. A second branch of Trappers' Trail leaves Greenhorn and points south to what is now Walsenburg and Trinidad. It crosses over the Raton Mountains and continues south over hill and dale to Santa Fe.

The Greenhorn Creek crossing is an ideal place for a trading post. In 1845 John and Luisa Brown begin a detailed account book with names and dates of all business transactions. The store trades whiskey, tobacco, thread, skins, rope, pans, horses, corn, cookware, clothing, buffalo robes, and beans. Whiskey is not only the most popular but the most profitable trade item. John buys whiskey for $2.25 a gallon and sells it for $1.00 (or one buffalo robe) per pint. His biggest transaction the first year is with Blackhawk, a half-Indian trader also known as Pascual Riviere. Blackhawk trades seven gallons of whiskey for 112 pounds of iron.

The first year and a half John Brown's business is a primitive affair, perhaps no more than a *"camp,"* as Alexander Barclay describes it in his diary of March 1846. Alexander Barclay and Joseph Doyle have come to the Brown camp from Hardscrabble to rent yokes and harnesses for farming.

Another early settler on Greenhorn Creek is George Simpson (1818-1885) whose hunting skills are limited to rounding up stray cattle for John. Barclay refers to George as one hunting lost cattle, *"cutting ice on the river all day,...playing cards and doing the loafer,...and returning from*

Mountain top called *Simpson's Rest* on the northwest edge of Trinidad, CO, where George S. Simpson is buried

George S. Simpson

Pueblo and having been there all night drinking."

In the spring of 1846, John hires a few Mexican peons to farm, herd stock, make adobe brick, and dig irrigation ditches. Water is diverted from Greenhorn Creek and channeled northeast across open fields for farming. During summer and fall, the irrigated fields produce good crops of corn, pumpkin, watermelon, and wheat. John acquires more cattle and horses, requiring additional workers. By the fall of 1847, the John Brown camp includes 20 peons, their families, and a new grist mill on the creek.

Another arrival to the settlement is Maurice Pierre LeDuc who is listed as *"Morace"* in Brown's account book. French born Maurice remains at the Brown camp during the summer and fall of 1846. In 1830 Maurice had built his own *Fort Le Duc* (or *Old Maurice's Fort*) eight miles south of Florence near Wetmore. In 1843 Joseph Doyle, Alexander Barclay, and George Simpson opened a trading post at a nearby location.

The Brown store is actually very white. It serves white travelers, white traders, and white farmers, but not red skins. Not wanting to be left out, Jicarilla Apaches conduct their own style of business in June of 1846. Apaches raid the Brown camp and ride off with 20 horses belonging to *"Mais Leduke [Maurice LeDuc], Browne [John Brown] and Murray."*

In his 1847 writing, George Frederick Ruxton describes the Brown camp as one adobe hovel and several Indian lodges. Mountain men and their squaws farm using irrigation ditches built by Spanish settlers in 1840. If this is indeed the case, what became of the Spanish settlers of 1840?

In addition to building new adobe houses, Brown constructs a grist mill to grind wheat into flour. The mill is costly and difficult. Dick Lacy Wootton remembers the mill as *"a building of logs, the machinery crude, the burr stones hewn out of granite."* Twelve years after John and family have relocated to California, John Brown of Walsenburg (no relation to the grist mill builder) recalls *"the millstones were still down by Greenhorn Creek in 1860, long after the building had fallen apart and disappeared."*

By 1848 jolly John has hired 37 men to look after his cattle, horses and farm fields. According to John's account book, three men are hired in 1845, twenty-four in 1846, eight in 1847, and two more in 1848. Of these workers, three can be considered faithful peons: Charno, Tucksender, and Scapoolar. They stay for more than a few months at a time. Transient laborers are provided room and board in exchange for their work, while his more dependable peons are paid in cold cash. Also the faithful are given extra money for more difficult chores like making bricks, building houses, and collecting salt. Because salt is heavy and has to be transported from the saline beds of South Park (100 miles to the northwest), salt is a valuable luxury on the Greenhorn.

Luxuries aside, one can live a simple life in the Valley with little or no expense by gathering wild plants, hunting game, growing crops, and sleeping under a buffalo robe. To make life in the Valley a bit more comfortable, a lucky male might acquire an Indian squaw and sleep in her Indian lodge with a natural heat-exchange system. But make no mistake, a warm wife, solid effort, and simple living does not eliminate frontier dangers. One must be on guard at all times.

At dusk on January 23 of 1847 (just south of Greenhorn Creek) a hunter from Mormon Town sees something coming toward him that looks half man and half animal. The hunter raises up in his stirrups to get a better look. At that very moment, the wild thing motions to him and lumbers forward. Terrified, the hunter turns tail and gallops north toward his home near The Pueblo. The creature beneath the animal skin is totally exhausted. He is a little fellow named John D. Albert (1806-1899.)

On the east side of Sangre de Cristo Pass, John Albert shot a deer, cleaned out the gut, and wrapped the skin around him to keep from freezing in the cold. After failing to flag down the Mormon hunter, Albert staggers north to Greenhorn Creek. The eagle eye of Blackhawk sees a desperate man wrapped in deerskin and carries Albert into the Greenhorn store. During Albert's recovery period, he tells the following story:

"He and eight or ten other Americans had been employed by Simeon Turley at the mill and distillery on Rio Hondo twelve miles north of Taos. On January 19, 1847, Charles Town arrived at Turley's from Taos and hastily informed Turley that the Taos Indians, joined with Mexicans, had risen in a mob at Taos and killed Governor Charles Bent and every American they could lay hands on. After Charles Town had left for Santa Fe, the mob appeared at sunrise at Turley's gate with a flag of truce. Turley indignantly refused to surrender, and the mob opened fire, keeping up a rain of bullets which shattered every window and rattled against the thick mud walls like hail. As night fell, the mob set fire to the mill. John Albert and a companion opened the back door leading to a fenced garden and dashed out, firing wildly into the crowd. Albert's friend was killed, but Albert reached the log fence and lay concealed underneath it as the mob rushed into the burning buildings and killed the remaining defenders. Turley, William LeBlanc and Tom Autobees had escaped into the night by digging a hole through the back adobe wall. Tom made it to Santa Fe and

John D. Albert
(from the *Denver Post* in 1901 &
Courtesy of the Historical Society of Colorado)

LeBlanc to Greenhorn, but Turley, who was lame, was caught and killed."

Another witness at the Taos Rebellion recalls at sunrise on January 20th, 500 Indians and Mexicans appear at Simeon Turley's front gate demanding his house, mill, and men. They promise to spare Simeon's life. Simeon, who has never been a mountain man but is fond of money and comfort, indignantly replies that he will not surrender. If they want his property and men, *"...they must take them."*

The mob opens fire. The men in the mill grab their rifles, take aim, and return fire. The gunfire continues all day, into the night, and through the next day. As the sun sets on January 21st, the rebels charge the mill, gain entrance, and set the building on fire. Simeon and men have no choice but to try an escape: some charge directly at the mob, some dig through the floor into the granary, and some club a hole through a wall in back. It is Simeon Turley, Antoine LeBlanc, and Tom Tobin (Autobee) who break through the rear wall of the mill and slip into the darkness. Tobin makes it to Santa Fe and LeBlanc to Greenhorn, but Turley's lameness prevents him from traveling more than a few miles. In the hills behind the blazing mill, Turley meets a Mexican on horseback to whom he offers his fine gold watch for the man's horse. The Mexican refuses, telling Turley to hide in a certain place, and he will send aid. Unable to travel farther, Turley hides in the designated place. The Mexican returns to the mill and informs the rebels of Turley's situation. Rebels go in search of Simeon, locate the mill owner, and shoot him dead. Turley's home is looted of gold, then burned to the ground. Turley and business are finished. After ten years of taking animal skins from the Indians in trade for his booze, Simeon (well-known for his *Taos Lightning*) dies one of the richest men in New Mexico.

Leaders of the rebellion are rounded up, tried, and hung at Taos in April of 1847, three months after the rebellion. Many of the jurors are part-time residents of the Arkansas Valley: including Charles Town, Lucien Maxwell, John L. Hatcher, Robert Fisher, Asa Estes, Jean-Baptiste Charlefou, Charles Autobee, and Archibald Metcalf. Fun loving Archa Metcalf is appointed sheriff of Taos.

Two months after the necktie party, Kit Carson, Jesse Hodges Nelson, and ten others leave Taos and head for the United States. Traveling from Taos to Greenhorn, they have an escort of trigger-happy soldiers, *"more dangerous than Indians,"* reported Jesse Nelson. Upon arriving at Greenhorn camp, they meet Bill New, Calvin Jones, and some Mexican hired hands. Where is John Brown and his family?

The Kit Carson troop proceeds north to the trail crossing of the St. Charles where it finds John Brown and his family, Charles White, Rube Herring, and probably Jim Waters. These residents are described as occupying old houses in various stages of repair and using old fields with irrigation ditches. Since the Greenhorn and St. Charles settlements are only 18 miles apart, jolly John may have had business operations at both locations. No doubt John's main place of trade was at Greenhorn Creek. The following event gives further evidence to the fact.

On Wednesday, February 2nd of 1848, Ed Tharp (just two months shy of his 24th birthday) and Jim Waters (often pursuing another man's wife) get into an argument at Louis Tharp's store in El Pueblo. The fight has to do with Ed's wife, Candelara who is a dark, attractive, half-Indian woman. During the argument and ensuing fight, Jim Waters kills Ed Tharp. The argument and killing are generally considered to be Jim Water's fault. The following day Alexander Barclay helps bury young Ed on Tenderfoot Hill.

After the incident, killer Jim hides out on Fountain Creek for a few days while his friends from The Pueblo bring him meat, coffee, and bread. Since banishment is the normal punishment for murder in early frontier settlements, Jim makes his way to Greenhorn Creek and hires a wagon team to fetch his belongings from The Pueblo. He remains at the Greenhorn under the watchful wing of jolly John Brown. Murderer though he is, no one at either The Pueblo or Greenhorn wish to give killer Jim up to harsh American justice. Jim grinds flower and herds cattle for John until they both join the gold rush to California a year later.

In the spring of 1849, many residents of Greenhorn Valley contract gold fever. The first of June, a wagon train departs with John Brown, wife Luisa, and their three children. Joining them are John Burroughs and Calvin T. Briggs, with their Shoshone (or Snake) wives and children. Also joining the caravan to California are Lancaster Lupton; his Cheyenne wife and four children; Rube Herring (without his Nicolasa); Charles White; Alexis Godey; and Jim Waters (with his recently-widowed Candelara.)

During the summer of 1849, Bill New is still raising cattle in Greenhorn Valley and doing business as usual with reds and whites alike. One visitor reports:

"...a Trading Post occupied by several white Hunters and a number of Indians of various Tribes, many of whom had Huts outside the post. The Fort was packed with valuable furs, which the Hunters carried on Pack Mules and sold to the Santa Fe Traders."

In addition to Bill New raising cattle, there are others still carrying on trade at Greenhorn Creek such as Seth Ward, Ben Ryder, Dick Owens, Archibald Metcalf, Charles Kinney, Calvin Jones, William Guerrier, Joe Dennis, Marcelino Baca, Jim Dickey and Jim Swanock (the Delawares), and Tesson (the half-Cheyenne.)

In summary the legendary John Brown came to Greenhorn Valley as a simple trapper, and he emerged as general store owner; irrigation ditch builder; farmer and rancher; popular psychic; and *"Medium of the Rockies."* Having done all this, the life story of jolly John is far from over.

Now in San Bernardino, CA, John will become a wealthy spiritualist; writer of letters; preacher of sermons; healer of the sick; and, at his pinnacle, a self-proclaimed prophet raising people up from death itself. This last feat is not to be taken lightly because raising the dead is not an easy thing to do, even under the best of conditions.

Mediumistic John Brown

On the frontier John Brown became an outstanding storyteller which was a valuable skill and popular pastime. Now in California John's mystical messages gradually appear in publications of his time: *Spiritual Offering, Foundation Principles, Western Watchman, Golden Gate, Mind and Matter.* In 1887, 38 years after departing the Greenhorn, a book is published containing newspaper articles, letters, and essays written by John himself. The legacy is not an autobiography or even a biography; it is a reflection of the mediumistic experiences of John Brown.

Longtime friend and scholar J. S. Loveland edits John's personal experiences into a collection of short stories to make them more *"readable and comprehensible."* The anthology is published under the title *The Mediumistic Experiences of John Brown the Medium of the Rockies.* Professor Loveland says he wants his mystical friend to become known beyond a small circle of mutual friends. The friends are W. A. Conn, Jim Waters, Dr. Peacock, Dr. Hickey, Dr. Oliver, and Dr. Herrold.

The Mediumistic Experiences of John Brown is a book worth exploring in some depth. Mystical John is stranger than wild and crazy fiction. Also his 1887 publication is quite old and hard to access for the general reader. Perhaps impossible.

The book begins with John's editor and longtime friend, Professor J.

THE MEDIUMISTIC EXPERIENCES

—OF—

JOHN BROWN,

—THE—

MEDIUM OF THE ROCKIES,

WITH AN INTRODUCTION BY

PROF. J. S. LOVELAND.

DES MOINES:
MOSES HULL & CO.
1887.

John Brown as pictured in his own book, edited by J. S. Loveland in 1887

S. Loveland. Loveland introduces the text by explaining just how spirit guides appear to John and put messages into his hand:

"This writing is executed, to a great extent, while he is asleep - or apparently so, as he finds the writing in the morning; and either the spirits executed it themselves; or, what is more probable, they induce a somnambulic condition and impress him to write in that condition....

"Years before the 'mystic rap' was heard at Hydesville, John Brown, in the weird fastnesses of the Rocky Mountains, living in a lodge, built like the Indian's was nightly visited by his spirit teacher and informed of the more important events to transpire in the ensuing day. Without exception, the predictions of the prophet were fulfilled."

While still living in Greenhorn Valley, mystical John losses touch with his spirit guide. Upon moving to California in 1849, he settles at a place called San Juan Bautista. During his residence in San Juan; Brown, Waters, and Godey open St. John Hotel, a store, and livery station. John gets himself elected as Justice of the Peace and reconnects with his spirit guide. The guide brings various visions and a new power to heal:

"I seldom went voluntarily to treat the sick, but was usually taken by my guide, without knowing where I was going, thus proving that it was the spirit and not myself that performed the cure. I could always tell when there was work, my control desired me to do. The first symptom was a prickling sensation commencing at my feet, which worked gradually upward until it penetrated my whole system, and I became subject to and obeyed the mandates of the controlling spirit....

"Spirit hands pushed me along as I walked. I can never forget the feeling that came over me as I entered the sick room. My flesh lay in wrinkles and my clothing was wet with perspiration. Most of the young man's friends, believing that his time had come to die, had left him to pass in quiet to his spirit home, only his father and mother remaining to close his eyes. As I approached the bedside, my right hand, moved by spirit agency, was laid upon his head, where it remained a short time, when it was taken away, and in a moment was again placed upon his head being gradually moved over and around the head. The young man, when I entered, was motionless and apparently dying, but he soon turned his head and his dry and wrinkled eye stared me in the face....

"I knew the recovery would take place as I had stated, and that so

sudden a cure, without the use of other remedy than the touch of my hand would cause talk and excitement, and not wishing to be known in the matter, I went to a store close by and procured a bottle of lime juice, and put a little in the boy's mouth, saying to his father, 'that will restore your son to health....' All I stated to the father and mother proved true...."

Mystical John describes himself as no great writer or scholar but rather *"a student in search of good teachers."* He sees the earth as a school house where spirit guides transport him back to important information he has missed earlier in life. Editor J. S. Loveland explains:

"A career was now opening of which he little dreamed. Instead of a few trappers and hunters, he was to meet with thousands of men and women, ignorant of immortality, and by various forms of spirit power, show them the light of life. To the 'spirit of prophecy' was to be added a wondrous power of healing - at times - seeming to raise the very dead."

By the late 1850s, mystical John has moved to San Bernardino where he meets regularly with *"spiritual fraternities, circles and seances."* Demonstrating his powers of *"clairvoyance and spirit perception,"* John can become entranced; make predictions; perform clairvoyant medical examinations; and (on special occasions) raise the dead to live again. D. S. Smith (M. D. and friend) writes the following:

"Another time a child in the place was pronounced dead by the attending physician, Brown says 'no it is not dead it only sleepeth, I will go and awaken it;' accordingly he went to the child, made a few passes over it, when the child began to show signs of life. 'There,' says Brown, 'it is alive and in a little while will call for food,' which also proved true; and it goes now that Brown raised the dead....Seeing is believing, so you will have samples of his powers if he remains long with you. He has much need of confidence in himself; having been always in the mountains and on the frontier, he does not know his own ability, and the natural refinement he possesses...."

Some clients come to miracle John for guidance regarding business matters; other folks come to acquire messages from departed friends and family members. On one occasion, lifelong friend and cohort from the Greenhorn Valley, Jim Waters, is bitten by a mad cow which tears the flesh and infects his arm:

> "He became so affected that he employed two strong men to watch him, lest in an unguarded moment he might be taken with some uncontrollable spasmodical affection and injure some of his family....
>
> "I mentally asked my spirit guide to procure some medical aid that would cure Mr. W. of his malady, stating at the same time, that he could use me for one of his instruments. After a few moments my hand and arm were moved by spirit agency, and the first finger on my right hand was placed on the center of his forehead, and I was compelled to say; 'Mr. Waters, from this moment you are healed, you will never again feel any effects of hydrophobia. That is all. We are done.
>
> "Mr. Waters exclaimed, 'My God! what in the world are you about? I never felt better in my life. I feel perfectly well in body and in mind.'
>
> "He has never felt the least effect of canine madness from that day till this."

A few years later, miracle John is standing on a street corner unaware the daughter of Jim Waters has fallen ill and dropped dead. A strong urge comes over John, and he is compelled to follow the direction of his spirit guide. Shortly after being guided to Jim Water's house, John saves his friend's daughter from a ghastly grip of the grim reaper:

> "My legs carried me along without exertion on my part till I got half a mile out of town. I had no idea where I was going, or what I was going for, till I got in front of Mr. Waters' house, I did not think of stopping there, but my legs made a right angle to the left, I went through the gate, rang the bell, and Mr. Waters met me at the door. As he opened the door he was weeping, and said to me, 'John, you have come too late, our little girl has just died. She is dead.'
>
> "I made no reply. Before I reached the door, I felt as though some one had laid over me a cloak or mantle that gave me great power. Up to that time I had no knowledge of any one being sick at this place, but as I had often been affected in this way, I knew just what was to be done. I walked in, laid off my hat, and attempted to lay off my cloak; it felt and seemed so natural; for me to do so, but I could not see it, neither could any one else, yet I thought I had it on. The little dead child was in the arms of old lady Parrish, who lives here now. Her mother, Mrs. Waters, was in an adjoining room, preparing its burial clothes....My hand went, without my

James W. Waters in 1874

(from L. A. Ingersoll of
San Bernardino County,
L. A., 1904, & Courtesy
of Berkeley Library)

John Brown

(portrait on the cover of
his book published in 1897)

help, to the head of (I might say) the deceased, and there for a moment became fixed; directly it was loosened.... I then looked up into Mr. W's face, his eyes seemed to impart to me a knowledge that he had faith. I said to him: 'Sit down with me, all will be well soon.' I could see doubt, fear and hope sparkling in his eyes.

"I told him to rest easy, that in fifteen minutes his little girl would be nursing her mother's breast in perfectly good health. It seemed to cheer, yet it was astonishing to him. By this time I was moved to go again and touch the dead child with my hand. I could see by the color in the face that life was returning. I took hold of its little hands, shook them, and talked to it as though it had been living; I took hold of its feet, moved them, and told it to wake up and see grandpa. Shortly it began to move its hands and arms; it gasped and stretched, and looked up at me and was in perfect health....Reader, who did this? Was it I? No; I was only an instrument in the hands of those who stood right behind; for there ne're was a painter that drew a design, but a greater than he stood behind him. The cloak or mantle I wore into that room I did not bring away, it gradually went from me till it was gone."

Bringing the deceased daughter of a friend back to life is rather remarkable. Miracle John can do even more as a result of his strong connection to *"spiritualism."* On one occasion, it became necessary for John to bring *"himself"* back from the dead:

"I heard the doctors say, 'that is the last; he will not move again; he is dead.' ...I knew that I had left my body....I heard Dr. Dickey say to one he met on the stairs: 'You are too late; he is dead." ...all at once I was raised by a power, unseen by me, and moved directly over my body....I then lowered down and seemed to soak back into the body which all had pronounced dead....My eyes could see, and I was alive in the same body I now inhabit. As soon as life was visible the doctors were recalled, but said they could do nothing for me, as they knew not the cause of my illness and had never seen or heard of a case of the kind before."

There seems to be no limit to the sensational spiritualism of miracle John. At one Sunday gathering of *"San Bernardino Spiritualist,"* John is taken up by *"good angels"* and shown their home in the heavens. Beginning on a low plane, John is lifted up through departments until he arrives at the highest department. Here angels from heaven speak to miracle John about their commitment to restore the rights of men and the equality of women:

"...we, the spirits of men, residents of the celestial sphere, do pledge ourselves to aid and assist our brothers, residents of earth, by all honorable means to prevent farther encroachments upon their rights, and to remove those already made by legislative enactments; and to further help in this good work, by assisting all good souls, at the ballot to rebuke, with their votes, all further efforts to infringe upon the rights guaranteed to men. And, in furtherance of these rights, we join hands with our brethren on earth to place woman where she justly belongs, in that position which makes her equal with man in all political and religious rights, that she may no longer be the property of man."

With a direct connection to the angels of heaven, miracle John is not a man to keep spiritual secrets to himself. John shares his spiritual knowledge and experience by giving helpful hints regarding the methods used by his own spirit guides. At one point he opens the door and instructs others how to form and conduct their own super circles:

"We should set our houses in order by purifying our bodies from alcoholic beverages, tobacco and whatever evil there may be lurking about us....Then let us choose a few friends, say six, most congenial; appoint one of their number as spokesman, who should do all the talking with the spirits; the balance of the circle may tell him to ask whatever they please. I have known a spokesman of this kind to soon become a medium; and I have seen spirits shower magnetic influence on them till they would speak and say: 'Oh, do you feel that wind?'

"...the worst feature of all, is, when the spirit manifests a readiness to communicate, for some one of the circle to say: 'Well, go on now, give us anything you please; just suit yourselves, etc.' The spirits of all classes who are present accept this as a general invitation, and all make a rush, which ends in general confusion by moving and throwing things around. It may not be thus in all cases, I am only telling what I have seen."

Among the miscellaneous articles written by miracle John, there is one in particular that explains the perplexing mystery of how giant stones were moved and put in to perfect places on the Egyptian pyramids. John's spirit guide takes him back in time to ancient Egypt and demonstrates the secret of mastering a massive rock:

> *"I saw at a short distance from me, a stone of prodigious size many feet in length and width; this stone, my guide said, marked the history of a race of people unknown to human thought of the present day. To one end of this monster was fastened a string, a mere thread, about five feet in length, close by it stood a little girl, apparently about eight years of age. I saw her stoop down and take the end of this thread in her hand, at the same time this immense rock seemed to assume the weight of a feather. As she moved forward, this huge mass would follow her, not leaving a trace of it on the ground. It rather seemed to float a little above the ground and followed this young lady as a faithful servant would follow its master. She was its master, but whence this power? In this I fail to answer. I know, and yet I cannot tell...."*

Miracle John continues to have sensational experiences in his final three years (1883-1886.) Periodically he vacates his own body and visits dead relatives. At one point he locates the first break in the Atlantic cable, but no one of importance listens to him.

Near to the end of his time, miracle John lives and preaches for the coming of what he calls *Modern Spiritualism*. This is a skill which must be performed by outstanding mediums like himself. Aside from himself, John acknowledges mediums of various talents: some who hide their gifts; some who become popular; some who remain faithful workers; and some who actually become angels on Earth.

In sharp contrast to angels on Earth, John reflects strong dislikes for the Bible; the "Christian Church;" Christians in general; and the Jesuits in particular. Despite his dislike for the Bible and Christians, miracle John is quite capable of preaching Christian principles:

> *"May you be endowed with wisdom to help banish the dark cloud that is constantly gathering at the door of the poor.*
>
> *"...let me say to you, my brothers and sister, be not selfish; remember that the great secret about heaven here and hereafter is in doing good to others. Soon the cold blast of winter will spread her white mantle over the land and then it will be time to remember the poor. If we ever find a heaven it will be just such a one as we have made for ourselves."*
>
> *"Love is the great key that opens nature's arcana to view, and*

introduces us to the All-Father; then His children become united; thus the oneness....

"It is a pleasure to know that I have done some good, during my earthly existence. It has always been my great desire to give ease instead of pain, comfort instead of sorrow, joy instead of grief, happiness instead of misery."

Miracle John sees himself as both prophet of the new age and the target of hateful attacks. He sees himself as *"hero and martyr,"* trying to fulfill his designated mission. John's life attempts to emulate his personal heroes - Garrison, Phillips, Greeley, and Lincoln. As miracle worker and *Medium of the Rockies*, John Brown concludes his book of personal experiences on page 167 with a farewell poem of guidance:

"Raise the standard high above you,
    Let no traitor cast it down;
Then, when life on earth is ended
    You will gain your heavenly crown.

Bid defiance to old error,
    Let the golden rule prevail,
Then we'll meet beyond the river,
    Just beyond the shadowy vale."

Significant time has been devoted to miracle John, not because he was a prophet, a hero, or a martyr; but because he was among the first to trap along Greenhorn Creek. He was the first to set up trading on the Greenhorn, and he was a colorful kaleidoscope of behavior.

Baca, Kinney, and Carson

John is not the only character of Greenhorn Valley. There are other trappers and traders of the Rocky Mountain Front Range who make a living by trading animal skins for basic supplies. They live alone and survive by their wits, reflexes, rifles, and traps. Marcelino Baca is another of the early rough and tough mountain men to trap in Greenhorn Valley. Englishman George F. Ruxton (1821-1848) describes Marcelino as one:

"...who, though a Mexican, despised his people and adjured his blood, having been all his life in the mountains with the white hunters - looked down easily upon six feet and odd inches. In form a Hercules, he had the symmetry of an Apollo; with strikingly handsome features, and masses of long black hair hanging from his slouching beaver over the shoulders of his buckskin hunting shirt."

Marcelino Baca brags. He has spent nine years in the Rocky Mountains, living exclusively on meat and tasting neither salt nor bread during that time. Perhaps his meat diet produces an independent trader who is rough and tough. For sure, his cholesterol count is on the rise.

Marcelino begins his mountain man life as a trapper about 1832, establishing himself as *"the best trapper and hunter in the mountains and ever first in the fight."* George Ruxton tells stories about Marcelino escaping from Indians and killing them when necessary. Like storyteller Ruxton, historian F. W. Cragin records the following incident:

"Around the end of 1838, Marcelino blundered into Pawnee land on the Platte River. The Pawnees took him captive and prepared him for a peculiarly unpleasant ritual sacrifice: After tying the captive to a post, the Indians would build a fire nearby and dance; as they danced, they would approach the victim, cut off a strip of flesh, roast it in the fire and eat it, the captive perishing miserably in the meantime. While the handsome trapper was being fattened for such a feast, the chief's daughter fell in love with him and begged her father to spare his life. Her wish was granted and Marcelino was released. He took his Pawnee Pocahontas to wife, giving her his mother's name of Tomasa or Tomacita."

From his companionship with Tomasa, Marcelino's first son, Jose, is born near South Platte River in 1839. A second son, Luis, is born at Fort Laramie in 1841. A third child and first daughter, Elena, is born at the Hardscrabble settlement where he is successful in farming. Marcelino is called *Rico* (or *Rich Man*) by the Mexicans. When Elena blossoms into womanhood, she will marry the son of Charles Autobee.

After the birth of daughter Elena in 1846, Marcelino takes his wife and three children to Taos for the official family sacraments of marriage and baptism. The Baca family returns to the handsome Greenhorn Valley where Marcelino has frequently hunted. Neighboring the John Brown store, the Baca's ranch cattle and farm vegetables. Beans, corn, watermelon, and wheat are grown for personal use and to trade with locals.

The Marcelino family, the John Brown family, and their employees are expanding into a settlement. In 1847 Charles Kinney purchases *"sundries"* at the Greenhorn in trade for his cow and 33 pounds of flour. Mr. Kinney will return and become part of the village in two years.

By the summer of 1848, Bill New joins the community. Along with Bill comes his 23-year-old bride who becomes the stepmother of his two half-Indian children, Nancy and Jane. Mary is the first Anglo woman to live on the Greenhorn, and it is here she gives birth to their third child, Gethro. Two years later Bill moves his family to Lucien Maxwell's settlement at Rayado (near Taos) where Bill will be killed by Indians.

In the summer of 1849, most of the travelers passing through Greenhorn Valley are gold seekers on route to California. One large group of 50 men venture west to explore for gold on the western slope of Sangre de Cristo Pass. When little gold is found, the men return disappointed.

Six others with dubious destinies stop at Greenhorn camp to sell their wagons and reorganize into smaller units. For two days they unload their wagons and make up horse packs. Residents of the Greenhorn derive benefit from the discarded *"comforts."*

A Delaware Indian guide is hired for $50 and a *good horse*. The Delaware leads them successfully to Salt Lake City. On the other side of Salt Lake, he gallops off on his good horse. Having been deserted in some obscure desert location, the perplexed party of six drift far to the south. They are not heard from again.

In the meantime Charles Kinney has returned to the Greenhorn and is living *"among the Indians, with a very ladylike little white woman, fair-complexioned and modest in her appearance."* His wife is the second Anglo woman (rare on the frontier) to reside at Greenhorn Creek. Mountain men of marriageable mind have three choices: a Mexican from Taos, an Indian from a dozen neighboring tribes, or some mixture of both.

In place of the well-known Kit Carson, the lesser-known Charles Kinney is hired as guide for a troop of *"mule men."* Kinney charges the mule men $77 which includes their choice of three mules and two wagons. Charles will guide them safely to Salt Lake City.

Kit Carson and Tim Goodale are busy driving 50 horses and mules to Fort Laramie for trade with northern emigrants. After the trading, Tim Goodale heads west to California, and Kit Carson is on his way home south to Rayado. When Kit reaches the Greenhorn with only one Mexican boy at his side, he learns that Apache braves are ahead on the trail. Apparently

Kit Carson

(sketched with his horse, Apache)

General Christopher Carson

(frontiersman, Indian agent, scout, & commander of troops at Fort Garland

Kit Carson

(shortly before he died at Fort Lyon in 1868, Courtesy of the Historical Society of Colorado)

during the summer of 1849, heavy traffic along the Taos Trail attracted the attention of Indians, and by the spring of 1850 Apaches are ambushing travelers to the south of Greenhorn.

When Carson arrives at Greenhorn camp and learns of the ill-tempered Apaches ahead on the trail, he asks the men of Greenhorn for assistance. Charles Kinney is the only man to step forward. Kit persuades Charles to ride shotgun as they journey south through dangerous territory. Although Carson and Kinney make a safe trip to Rayado, Kit is unpleasantly surprised to find that Apaches have run off with horses from his ranch. Carson takes the stealing of his horses rather seriously, in contrast to Indians who steal horses regularly as part of their everyday exercise. During March of 1850, Kit and his patrol chase after nine Indians who have stolen his horses. They catch up with the Apaches and kill five.

In the summer of 1852 at the Greenhorn settlement, a mixed party of Navajoes, Jicarilla Apaches, and Utes kill a man. They steal horses, cattle, and destroy grain. Marcelino's losses are considerable. Eighteen miles to the northeast, Indians raid St. Charles camp and carry off provisions, animals, and money. They kidnap one person. The conflict is growing grim.

Late in 1852 only a couple of vacant shanties remain at St. Charles, and only two other settlements are still in operation. There is William Bent's log trading houses at Big Timber, which remains the winter camps for Cheyenne and Arapahoe Indians. And there is Marcelino Baca's small business at Greenhorn Creek, where he and his friend Montoya have been living with their Indian wives and children.

Marcelino travels to Taos late in the year and returns home to the Greenhorn in February of 1853 with a party of merchants led by Charles Autobee. Charles is developing a camp where the Huerfano River joins the Arkansas. The merchants from Rio Colorado (north of Taos) travel east to Big Timber where they trade merchandise with Arapahoes and Cheyennes. On their way home after trading, they stop at Greenhorn where Marcelino and Montoya urge them to spend the summer farming. As a matter of convenience, the land is fairly flat; the ditches are already in place; the houses and corrals are still livable.

Two members of the Rio party, William Kroenig and William LeBlanc, accept the invitation. In late May LeBlanc returns to Rio Colorado, NM, while Kroenig finishes planting beans, corn, and wheat with his six Mexican peons. The Mexicans build adobe houses with yards enclosed by poles stuck in the ground. Montoya is the meat market; he supplies the workers with deer and antelope for one dollar per animal.

While Kroenig and Montoya look after things, manly Marcelino moves his family back to the deserted Pueblo. They reside in the old abandoned fort near Fountain Creek where they build a four-room log cabin and dig irrigation ditches. After planting a cornfield in the early spring of 1853, a flash flood washes away the young corn. Once again the Bacas return to the Greenhorn where the irrigated fields are being farmed by Kroenig and his workers. Here Marcelino accepts temporary employment to guide Captain J. W. Gunnison and his party over Sangre de Cristo Pass to Fort Massachusetts. Come fall, Kroenig transports his harvest north where he sells it on the Oregon Trail. From the profits he purchases cattle and sheep, then joins Autobee where the Huerfano River joins the Arkansas.

In the fall of 1853, manly Marcelino returns to his large log house and irrigation ditches on the Fountain River near The Pueblo (in recent years the site of Walter's Brewery & Pueblo Union Stock Yards.) More determined than ever, he constructs 13 more cabins for his workers and corrals for the horses and cattle. By the end of the year, a number of new people have been drawn to the area by Autobee's effort on the Huerfano, The effort is supported by Ceran St. Vrain, co-owner of the land grant.

A year later on Christmas, Marcelino suffers another major loss in livestock, but he gets off much better than his neighbors:

"At the end of the year, early Christmas morning of December 25, 1854, Chief Blanco and his men, apparently friendly as usual, paid Marcelino's ranch a visit, asking to come inside the house. Marcelino would have let the Utes in, but an old man named Barela strongly objected, and his wise advice prevailed. As the Indians went away, crossing the Fountain towards Pueblo, they drove off all Marcelino's cattle and horses that had not been secured in the corrals. Marcelino's loss of 73 head of cattle, 13 horses, and 2 mules amounted to over $4,000."

Marcelino loses cattle, horses, and mules. Across the river, the renovated Pueblo (originally Fort Pueblo and El Pueblo) will lose much more on this Christmas day. The Old Pueblo is about to meet its bloody end, because there is no Barela to send Chief Tierra Blanco with his Ute and Apache braves away. With evil intent, Blanco and his Indian warriors are allowed into the fort:

"On Christmas Day 1854, a band of Utes led by Blanco massacred the occupants of the fort. Jose Ignacio Valencia, Juan Rafael Medina,

Guadalupe Vigil, Francisco Mestas, Juan Blas Martin, Benito Sandoval, Juan Aragon, Tanislado de Luna, and Manuel Lucero were killed. Chepita Miera, Felix and Juan Isidro Sandoval were taken captives. Felix and Juan were later returned to their families, but Chepita was killed."

Prominent residents like Dick Wootton, Joseph Doyle, and George Simpson are lucky to be away from El Pueblo during Christmas. Although these three will return to Greenhorn Valley for one more season of farming, Marcelino's ranch across the river (and other settlements on the Arkansas and Huerfano) become abandoned. Exceptions include the Charles Autobee and Dick Wootton families with their faithful employees. *"Uncle Dick"* Wootton (1816-1893) remains because his wife is well along with her pregnancy. It is feared she and child will not survive a long trip to Taos. Even in taking the risky delay, Dolores Wootton dies on May 6, 1855, after giving birth to their child.

While the Indian situation grows worse, New Mexican authorities do little or nothing to investigate reports about Utes terrorizing settlements on the Arkansas, St. Charles, and Greenhorn. New Mexican authorities, who first gave land away to bring settlers, now believe the pioneers have no business settling in these valleys. As evidence of the change, the terms of a 1849 treaty are carefully spelled out to the Utes by Superintendent James Calhoun. He says the treaty is designed to protect Utes from unlicensed traders and white settlers who trespass onto their sacred lands. Consequently native Americans come to believe it is their legal right to attack travelers; steal horses, guns, and supplies; and drive unwanted settlers off sacred lands. The white man is trespassing and in violation of this 1849 treaty.

During these early years, New Mexican authorities are crazy-makers; they make everyone crazy, settlers and Indians alike. They invite pioneers to come settle the land; promise land grants; give the land grants; ignore the Indian aggression fail to protect the settlers; and give the land back to the Indians in an 1849 treaty. As usual, the treaty will soon be broken.

When the Utes return to the Pueblo region and kill Marcelino's brother, Benito, Marcelino has had enough. Losing his brother on top of his wealth, he moves his family south to the small frontier village of Rio Colorado, NM. Marcelino Baca spends the rest of his civilian years in Rio just north of Taos. The town is now called *Red River*.

On February 21, 1862, seven years after moving to Rio, Marcelino is killed by a shot in the forehead at the Battle of Valverde. He is serving with the New Mexico Volunteers in battle against Confederate invaders. His wife, Tomasa, will survive him by nine years.

Six years before Marcelino's death, Indian aggression has turned the Greenhorn into a ghost valley. It seems like the 25-year-struggle by early settlers to develop the Greenhorn Valley has come to a solid halt. Yet in just two more years, new permanent settlements will reappear in large numbers along railroad lines.

During the peace-treaty period, longtime white friends of the Indians advise them to be friendly, exercise patience, and remain calm. The wonderful, wise, White Father of Washington will create something marvelous for them if they will only remain patient. While the Indians wait, their lands are consumed by a large wave of settlers who roll in via the steam engine. The patiently waiting Indians are then rounded up, disarmed, humiliated, and marched off to reservations. The wonderful, wise, white Father of Washington had spoken.

Charlie Autobee

Autobee is the spelling used by the family today, but *Autobees* is generally found in older documents and will be used from now on. As trapper, guide, and pioneer, Charlie Autobees starts his farm on the west bank of the Huerfano River. It extends two miles south of the Arkansas. His farm is one of the first settlements along the Huerfano. He farms most every year after 1852, and the ranch becomes his permanent home.

In 1834 Charlie Autobees first hooks up with Simeon Turley of Taos as a freighter transporting flour and *Taos Lightning* booze by burro. He works for Simeon off and on until 1847. After starting to work at Arroyo Hondo, Charlie takes up with Serafina Avila. They become legally married in 1842, and four of their five children grow to adulthood.

During Charlie Autobees' business travels around the West, he collects a few informal wives, which include six Indian women. He marrys a Cheyenne, Flathead, Navajo, Sioux, Ute, and an Arapaho named Siccamo (or Sycamore.) Siccamo will play an important role in his life.

In the spring of 1846, chancy Charlie tries his hand at part-time farming where the Taos Trail crosses St. Charles Creek (nine miles south of Pueblo now exit #88 on I-25.) This early location is known as *San Carlos*, named after the local creek. The location will later be known as *St. Charles Creek* and then *Lime*. The San Carlos camp is 18 miles north of the John Brown store on the Greenhorn. Brown's account book shows a small amount of business transacted during the summer of 1847 with people from San Carlos, including Autobees' squaw, Siccamo.

Charlie's half-brother, Tom Tate Tobin (known as Tom Autobees), joins Charlie in farming. *"They built a house for themselves and their hired hands, Salvador Avila and Antonio Chavez. Red-haired Levin 'Colorado' Mitchell and a hired man named Truillo join them, and two or three others."* In an effort to stop others from settling in the area, Utes drive Charlie and his associates out of San Carlos camp. By late 1848 San Carlos is deserted. Charlie moves to Mora in 1850 and on to Rio in 1852.

Twenty years later, as stage stations are established on streams south of Pueblo, the *San Carlos* becomes a stage stop. A postal service is listed at San Carlos from 1866 to 1876 (perhaps to 1881), and it is called *St. Charles Post Office*. Hemmed in with limestone bluffs, the St. Charles stop will eventually become known as *Lime* with a P.O. from 1898-1943.

The business association between Charlie Autobees and Simeon Turley ends when Simeon is murdered during the Taos uprising of 1847. Charlie is most fortunate to be away from Turley's mill while the uprising takes place. Four days after the massacre, Charlie Autobees and Tom Tobin join Captain Ceran St. Vrain and his company of Mountain Volunteers in Santa Fe. Charlie will sit on the jury condemning the rebels to death.

In 1852 chancy Charlie joins with Dick Wootton, William Kroenig, Joseph Doyle, and others in an effort to farm the south side of the Arkansas, a mile west of where the Huerfano branches southwest. During the 1852-54 growing seasons, while living at the Wootton-Doyle plaza, Charlie grows corn along the Huerfano two miles south of the Arkansas.

Following the Christmas Day massacre at El Pueblo in 1854, Charlie and his eldest son, Mariano, with a group of other men go to The Pueblo. They bury all the bludgeoned bodies in a common grave. Son Mariano will later marry Elena Baca, the daughter of Marcelino and Tomasa Baca.

When the Wootten-Doyle plaza is abandoned a year later, chancy Charlie and four-dozen associates (William Kroenig, Joseph Barnoy, and Juan Chiquito) build a placita at Autobees' farming site.

William Kroenig, George Simpson, and Alexander Barclay are all related to Joseph Bainbridge Doyle through Teresita, the common-law wife of Alexander Barclay and mother-in-law of the other men. Before moving in with Barclay, Teresita has had four children with Manuel Suaso and one with Mathew Kinkead.

Joseph B. Doyle works for the Bent Brothers from 1838-1842. After having unprofitable partnerships with William Kroenig, George Simpson, and Dick Wootton, he relocates 16 miles southwest of Autobees on the west bank of the Huerfano. Here Doyle purchases two square miles from the St. Vrain-Vigil grant. In 1859 he establishes an eastern-styled home, a Mexican placita, irrigation ditches, and a flour mill.

Chancy Charlie endures a series of personal injuries in 1856. He is first wounded by Utes while he and his Arapaho wife, Siccamo, return from a trading trip near the present town of Boggsville:

"He continued to fire his rifle while Siccamo loaded for him. Juan Chiquite and his son became frighten and hid in a wagon until Charlie pulled them out and threatened to turn them over to the Utes. This made them brave fighters again. The battle continued all day, but the Utes were unable to kill or capture the party. Finally, after the sun went down, the Indians retreated and Charlie was able to withdraw. His small party hurried on to the Huerfano and arrived without further mishap."

Later the same year, chancy Charlie puts his eldest son, Mariano (married to Marcelino Baca's daughter) in charge of their village, and he goes off to work for government officials in Fort Garland. Here at Fort Garland Charlie is stabbed in the chest by a Mexican named Juan Pineda. Although his wound is thought to be near fatal by some, Charlie recovers in only one month. As longtime friends, Charlie and Marcelino will stage a mock duel featuring swords on horseback in 1859 at Rio Colorado, NM, to *"create a sensation."*

In the same year Charlie is stabbed in the back by a Mexican at Fort Union. Much like the first stabbing, the second has little lingering effect. His three injuries during the same year are taken in stride.

No doubt Charlie presents one terribly, tough target, as the 44-year-old warrior has a commanding presence. At six-foot and well-built, his face is deeply lined with scars and framed in long black hair streaked with gray. He has a stern face with deep piercing eyes.

Although uneducated, Charlie is a persuasive man with leadership ability who can gather around him a colony of four dozen people. *"Mexicans and half-breeds looked up to him as their ruler and guide."*

After recovering from his three injuries, chancy Charlie gathers all family members, including wives Serafina and Siccamo, to his new ranch. Siccamo lives at the ranch and is treated well. When she dies in 1864, Siccamo is buried in the same family cemetery at the Huerfano riverside

Charles Autobees. *State Historical Society of Colorado photo.*

One of Colorado's first commercial vegetable growers was William Kroenig, who farmed on the Huerfano.

Joseph B. Doyle was one of the first operators of American flour mills in the Southwest. He farmed in the Huerfano Valley and operated stores in Pueblo and Denver.

where Serafina will be laid to rest seven years later.

June 7, 1859, on route to the gold fields of Colorado, Texan H. M. Gass stops at Charlie's ranch and makes the following note in his Diary:

"Today we came to Auteby's [Autobees'] ranch, situated on the west side of Huerfano River. The ranch consists of some four or five square cabins, built of cottonwood logs, and covered with poles and mud-flat roofs. The owner, himself, is an old French trapper; his wife is Mexican. They are farming on a small scale. There are, I presume, some fifty persons here at Auteby's. They are farming by irrigation. They raise fine corn and pumpkins, and very fine garden vegetables. They sell their corn for five dollars a bushel."

In addition to corn and pumpkins, Charlie farms potatoes, beets, and rutabagas. He will also build a costly grist mill at the riverside.

Chancy Charlie claims title to 97,000 acres on the Huerfano in 1860, but he is down-sized to 686 acres by the Surveyor General in 1869. Charlie mortgages his 686 acre estate for $1,200 in 1875. He can not pay off the loan, and two years later he is forced to sell the land at public auction. He maintains the right to live in his house. In 1879 the Colorado General Assembly allots him a small pension as pioneer guide and scout. By 1880 Charlie is 68 years old and nearly broke. Two years later he dies and is buried on his ranch.

Charlie has lived a full and worthwhile life as a pioneer, trapper, mountain man, scout and guide in the Civil War, and a Colorado Volunteer soldier. He has served at Fort Garland, guided Colonel John M. Chivington to Sand Creek, and established his own colony where he farmed and ranched. He had several wives. And he had two towns named after him.

Edward G. Beckwith

Captain J. W. Gunnison is chosen by the United States Congress (over John C. Fremont) to lead an expedition west in search of a satisfactory train trail through the Rocky Mountains. Capt. Gunnison is a good-looking, 40-year-old, New Hampshire native, a West Pointer, and veteran of the Florida Seminole wars. Second in Command is Lieutenant Edward G. Beckwith, who is not to be confused with Jim Beckwourth.

Gunnison starts his expedition from St. Louis in June. Traveling members included, *"eight engineers, a group of teamsters and employees, 16 six-mule wagons of supplies, an instrument carriage hauled by four mules, a four-mule ambulance, and an escort of 32 mounted riflemen."*

The search party follows Santa Fe Trail along the Arkansas River until it reaches Bent's Fort, near today's La Junta. The fort is abandoned; only some adobe walls and towers are standing. The group leaders follow what they believe to be the Huerfano River flowing southwest to the south side of Greenhorn Valley. As Capt. Gunnison and his party of brilliant topographical engineers survey along the creek for a railroad route to the Pacific, it becomes increasingly apparent - they are lost. At this point it is determined they are not on the Huerfano River but on Apishapa Creek. The Apishaps branches southwest some miles east of the Huerfano. Gunnison has become another greenhorn, and he scratches his good-looking, 40-year-old, New Hampshire, West Point braincase.

After a good scratch, Capt. Gunnison sends Lt. Beckwith and five other men to scout for and find the well-known Greenhorn settlement. Upon locating the settlement, Gunnison hopes to find a jolly good guide who can successfully lead his survey team through the mountains.

Lt. E. G. Beckwith records his hike through Greenhorn Valley in 1853, leaving behind a most accurate description of the region. Edward Beckwith's account describes wildlife, wild horses, ground cover, neighborhood creeks, farm fields, irrigation ditches, corrals, and six families who remain at the village. Beckwith is visiting Greenhorn camp four years after John Brown and family have moved on to California.

Beckwith describes Greenhorn Valley and the settlement with great detail. His description on August 6th is worth examining. The following word-picture may have caused Beckwith's own name to be given to the 70-acre lake, now known as Lake Beckwith. Lake Beckwith will be enhanced by the main irrigation ditch diverted from Greenhorn Creek:

"August 6. - ...accompanied by five men, I started at an early hour of the morning in search of the Greenhorn settlement, on a stream of the same name rising in a range of mountains to the east of the Wet river valley, to obtain information of the country, and, if possible, procure a guide well acquainted with it and with the mountain passes we were about to explore.

"Our course from camp was W.N.W., in a direct line for the Wet mountains, crossing the Cuchara....we passed innumerable prairie dog towns, herds of deer and antelope, and several bands of beautiful wild

horses, which came circling round us in all the pride of their native freedom, at a distance of fifty or eighty yards, and at the report of a rifle dashing wildly away over prairie, hill, and valley, exciting our admiration....

"We next came to the Apache creek, whose sources in the Wet mountains had been visible during our morning ride. It is a small mountain stream, with water at this time only in pools. Willow, plum, thorn, and cherry bushes, with a few cotton-wood trees, grow densely thick on its borders, and we were detained an hour in making a passage through them.

"Following this trail we rose over a hill and descended into a rough narrow ravine, which we followed in a northeast direction for a mile and a half, and then passed over a high ridge - a spur of the Wet mountains - covered with oak bushes, to another ravine, on the sides of which we were gladdened by the sight of a herd of cattle and horses feeding, and were soon in the camp of a trader from New Mexico returning from Fort Laramie. From him we learned that the two streams and ravines are called the Graneros, by the Spaniards.

"Passing over another sharp ridge, we descended in two miles to the fine little valley of the Greenhorn, a stream of two feet in width and three or four inches in depth, which is now entirely diverted from its natural channel and employed in irrigating the lands of the six New Mexican families who reside at and constitute the present population of the place.

"They plant a few acres of corn and of wheat, of beans and of watermelons - in all, an area equal to that of the farm of a small eastern farmer, who cultivates his own fields. Two hundred fanegas of wheat and fifty of corn, with the requisite amount of beans and melons, constitute the largest total crop of this valley. They have a few cattle and horses - the latter very poor.

"The houses are built of adobe or sun-dried brick, without windows or other openings than a single door, in entering which a man of six feet in stature must bow very low. In front of each house is enclosed a small space of ground, twenty yards in width, by poles planted in the earth and lashed to horizontal strips by rawhide thongs. These picketed yards are intended as a protection against Indians - the Utes having killed some of their cattle last year, destroyed their grain, and stolen their horses.

"Corrals are attached to the backs of their houses, built in all respects like the front enclosures. With one exception all the houses of this settlement are joined, and a tall man can reach to the roof, on which the whole population, not absent in the fields, assembled on the approach *of my party, not knowing whether to expect friends or foes.*

"I enjoyed the hospitality of the smaller mansion, being invited to a seat on the only article of furniture in the room, a bench against the wall, spread with a blanket and furnished with a pillow. On the earthen floor, at the sides of the room, were two or three narrow beds on wool mattresses.

"I soon found the guide I wanted, and engaged his services hence to Fort Massachusetts, in the San Luis valley of New Mexico. Massalino [Marcelino] is, by birth, of the Spanish New Mexican race, of about forty-five years of age; and having spent it entire in the wild life of a mountaineer - by turns a hunter, a trapper, a trader, a voyager, a fighter, a farmer, and a guide - he is familiar with the country westward to the Pacific...."

Although Marcelino Baca has already been discussed is some detail, it is rare to get the actual talk of a manly mountain man. Lieutenant Beckwith records Marcelino's personal style of talking about himself:

" 'I have lived nine years on meat alone, at one time,' said he, 'in these mountains, without tasting bread or salt; and I can now live well enough for me with coffee and the little meat I can kill....I never see a grizzly bear but I give him a shot. I try to hit in the right spot; but if I miss it, I have to run. We will have a fine chance for fun....' and his dark liquid eyes flashed as he looked towards the mountains, and visions of his grizzly friends appeared to his imagination....

"The mistress of the house very courteously inquired where I would have my bed prepared, which I preferred leaving to her own convenience. I should, however, have been a little surprised, had this been my first visit to a New Mexican residence, at the place selected - in the yard, just in front of the door, under the broad, bright, blue canopy of heaven, brilliant with stars. I enjoyed the matronly grace and dignity of the mistress as she brought forth the pallet and spread the necessary blankets to exclude the chilly night winds from the mountains. There, too, were spread the beds for the family, the open air being preferred to the house during pleasant weather...."

After a single overnight on the Greenhorn, Lieutenant Beckwith takes manly Marcelino to the expedition camp of green Gunnison. Before long, the entire party caravans west toward Sangre de Cristo Pass. As the old Spanish trail climbs South Oak Creek near the ruins of Governor Melgares'

1819 fort, the trail is found to be too rough and not suitable for a train track. Manly Marcelino directs Capt. Gunnison to a neighboring ravine where the engineers, teamsters, and employees cut a six-mile path to the summit of Sangre de Cristo Pass. When the survey party reaches Fort Massachusetts on the other side, Marcelino concludes his temporary employment and returns home to the Greenhorn camp.

On October 26, 1853, Gunnison and seven of his men are exploring the Sevier River near Sevier Desert. An emigrant caravan has recently passed through the area and shot dead a Paiute chief's father. The Paiutes are filled with anger and decide to kill the next white man they meet.

The next white man happens to be green Gunnison and seven of his men. The angry Paiutes raid the Gunnison camp at dawn and pump 15 arrows into Captain J. W. Gunnison. Besides Gunnison, the Paiutes kill botanist F. Creutzfeldt, artist Richard Kern, and five others. Consequently it becomes necessary for Lt. Edward Beckwith to step forward and take over what is left of the Gunnison expedition. After spending the winter in Salt Lake City, the Beckwith party continues west to California.

Estefana Bent Hicklin

Maria Ignacia Jaramillo is from a wealthy Spanish-Mexican family. Maria's sister, Josefa (or Josephana) Jaramillo, is *"of high ranking Spanish heritage"* and married to Kit Carson. Maria Ignacia marries Charles Bent in 1836, and seven years later Dona Estefana is born to them. While Estefana is the youngest of three children, her sister Teresina is three years older and brother Alfredo is eight years her senior.

Since the mid-1830s, Charles Bent has had a home at Don Fernando de Taos. Estefana's father is appointed Territorial Governor by General Stephen W. Kearny on September 22 of 1846, but the Governor will serve only four months. Although his official residence and duties are in Santa Fe, Gov. Charles Bent is visiting his family in Taos when the rebellion breaks out. Dona Estefana is only three years old when her father is scalped in her presence on January 19 of 1847. After the massacre, three-year-old Estefana and her elder sister, Teresina, are taken to Mrs. Carson at Uncle Carson's ranch. Longtime friend and business partner Ceran St. Vrain transports the two nieces of Kit Carson to Santa Fe where they are placed in a convent with the Sisters of Loretto.

By the age of 12, Estefana has blossomed well, and a number of men are trying to court her into marriage, as was the custom. At age 13 Dona Estefana meets Alexander *"Zan"* Hicklin at the home of Uncle Kit Carson. The degree of attraction is uncertain. On the down side, Estefana is a young teenager, has no father, and has a mother who is unable to care for her. On the up side, Estefana is attractive, of marriageable age, and heir to the Charles Bent estate. It is a mystery as to why she is the only heir.

Born in Worcester, MA, in 1819 Alexander Hicklin comes to Taos about 1846 in a wagon train consigned to the store of Ceran St. Vrain. Alexander is a large, rugged teamster (driver of horse teams) for Ceran. He drives cargo to California and back. He has lived in Taos off and on as a sheep breeder for a decade before meeting Estefana. Zan probably finds Estefana and her assets attractive - especially the inheritance.

Dona Estefana Bent marries Alexander Hicklin at the Catholic Church in Taos on October 20 of 1856, nine years after her father was murdered in the same town. At age 16, when Estefana Bent Hicklin gives birth to Alexander Hicklin Jr, husband Alexander is a veteran of travel and trade at age 37. He is 21 years her senior.

At the time of Dona Estefana's marriage, gold is being discovered in Colorado. While many gamblers are dreaming of gold, Alexander Hicklin is dreaming of Estefana Bent's inheritance. As heir to the Charles Bent estate, Estefana may have been obliged to acquire the Greenhorn Valley for herself and her new family.

In order to take title through the Surveyor General, Estefana must live on the land and farm the soil for a certain period of time. She will be among the first women of Greenhorn Valley to own land.

In 1859 Dona Estefana and husband depart Taos with their infant son, and they travel to the Greenhorn Valley. Here they construct a Spanish-style ranch house on a hill side overlooking the Taos Trail crossing of Greenhorn Creek. The adobe house is composed of four rooms side by side, each with its own fireplace. The motel-style rooms open south onto a veranda overlooking the creek. Colorado City Fire Station and Medical Center will eventually be erected on the ranch house location.

Exploring the area as a girl bride, Dona Estefana recalls finding an *"old stone fort."* Most likely the old stone fort is the remains of John Brown's water-powered grist mill, built and used a dozen years earlier.

The Hicklins have property rights to three irrigation ditches originally built by the Browns. Near to the ditches they cultivate the land and raise livestock. As time passes, they will serve meals, accommodate overnight guests, and manage an underground railroad for Confederates.

Hicklin ranch house prior to being removed in the 1930s
(Courtesy of Pueblo Library District)

The adobe ranch house and barn of Alexander and Estefana Hicklin stood on a knoll above Greenhorn Creek near Crow Post Office and Crow Village

Life on the Greenhorn is an adventure full of surprises. During such events, Estefana appears to be a strong woman capable of speaking her mind. When Ute Indians barge into her ranch house unexpectedly, she is pretty much alone except for her infant son and another young child. Journalist Jan MacKell tells the following story:

"The Utes and their chief were not accustomed to the white man's ways and entered the adobe without bothering to knock. Estefana was obligated to give the men anything they wanted. With a stock of bacon, flour, coffee, salt, and a copper kettle from the stove the Indians were seemingly satisfied and on their way - until the Ute chief spied some cattle in a nearby corral. Legend has it that when the chief ordered some braves to take the cattle, Estefana had had enough. She bravely stood between the Indians and her cattle, demanding to be left alone. Somehow during this encounter, the chief recognized Estefana as the daughter of Charles Bent. He then presented her with a silver and turquoise bracelet, and told her to wear it always. Should future Indian marauders visit the house, he said, she was to show the bracelet. It would be an automatic safeguard against harm. The chief apparently kept his promise, since the Hicklin's were never bothered by Indians again."

A second example of Dona Estefana's courage in the face of danger is reported by longtime journalist Ralph C. Taylor:

"Beaubois, a Frenchman who lived near Huerfano Butte for several years, moved to Greenhorn where he lived with the Alexander Hicklin family. Within a few months an American who had cultivated crops for Beaubois on a share basis, rode over to the Hicklin place and shot Beaubois as he stood talking to Hicklin. The wounded Frenchman ran into the Hicklin kitchen. As Mrs. Hicklin tried to protect Beaubois, the irate share cropper burst into the house and shot his former landlord through the head as he lay on the floor. Beaubois' burial was the beginning of a little cemetery on the Greenhorn, where several of the Hicklins later were interned."

With courage in her backbones, Dona Estefana spends many years trying to acquire title to her five-thousand-acre ranch estate from the U.S. government and trying to defend it from pompous poachers. Although she petitions for the land when she arrives in 1859, dispute over the Mexican title drags through U.S. courts for many years. The testimonies of

 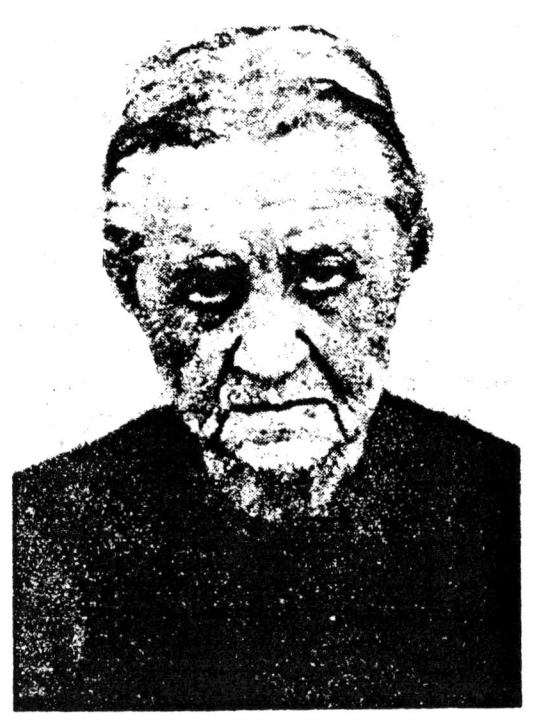

Alexander Hicklin in the 1850s before marrying Dona Estefana and moving to the Greenhorn

Dona Estefana Bent Hicklin about three years before her death in 1927

(Courtesy of Pueblo Library District)

Alexander Hicklin (Dec. 26, 1871), Thomas Oliver Boggs (Jan. 11, 1873), and others demonstrate Ceran St. Vrain believed to his dying day Greenhorn Valley was part of his grant.

Although 5,119 acres are granted to the Hicklins in 1874, Estefana's husband does not live to see the land become their own. Zan dies at age 55, ten days before title is granted. The American justice system was slow then, as it is slow now. Sometimes it moves not at all.

Now at age 34 Dona Estefana is still a young, attractive woman with three children to raise, a ranch to run, and farm fields to maintain. After Zan's death, Estefana will stay and struggle on her Greenhorn Valley estate for another 17 years.

Two years after her husband's death, Estefana joins the local school board. She often loans her silk gowns and jewelry to neighborhood girls for school dances.

Though title is granted in 1874, President Grant does not sign the paperwork until 1877. Even so, the Hicklin estate is determined by some authorities to be outside the boundaries of Ceran St. Vrain's land grant. Consequently Estefana continues to face squatters who trespass on her irrigated fields and Greenhorn Creek.

During the late 1870s and early 1880s, the Hicklins are constantly harassed by individuals who move on to the land and squat themselves down in fields or along the creek. Among these square squatters is Richard L. Phillips who has been a U.S. marshal. Being a bit full of himself, the 43-year-old Phillips claims to have settled on the land prior to the Vigil-St. Vrain Grant of January 2, 1844. This date would make Phillips nine years of age at the time Governor Armijo granted the land to Ceran St. Vain and Cornellio Vigil. Phillips would have been the first Boy Scout to settle on Greenhorn Creek, and it would place him there about the same time John and Luisa Brown set up business. The Browns made no mention of any Richard L. Phillips during their residence in the 1840s.

Richard Phillips now drops anchor in one of the Hicklin meadows and refuses to move his big squat. On September 21 of 1878, Alex (or Alec) Hicklin Jr. at age 19 and Thomas (Tom) Hicklin at age 16 visit the meadow and gather a load of hay which Phillips has already bundled. Phillips becomes enraged, and both boys are gunned down. Alex Jr. dies within a few minutes; Tom lives another 19 years but never fully recovers from his gunshot wounds. Tom will later marry Emma Shaw and have a daughter.

Alex and Tom are buried beside their father (and Mr. Beabuois) in a small family cemetery at the back of the Hicklin ranch house. This family cemetery will be moved up the hill a half mile west of the ranch house. It will be moved as a publicity stunt performed by California developers.

Following the killings, felonious Phillips is *"found drunk near the shooting by neighboring ranchers John Warner and John Williams."* At the trial Phillips states he was indeed drunk at the time. Consequently he is convicted of manslaughter (perhaps boy-slaughter) and sentenced to a ten-year prison term. He is let out early for good behavior. Many other drunks have come to realize being smashed is a valid excuse for doing most any illegal behavior.

Alex Jr., himself, had a dream of dying shortly before his murder. As a result of the crime, Alex's wife (Janie Frink) becomes a widow and his mother looses her eldest son. Alex has been sentenced to death, and he remains dead after Phillips is released from Canon City Penitentiary.

In addition to Alex Jr. and Tom, Dona Estefana has a third son named Alfred who is born Dec. 21, 1871, at Greenhorn. Alfred is only seven years old when felonious Phillips kills brother Alex and wounds brother Tom. Upon reaching adulthood, Alfred moves away from the Valley and locates in the small mining town of Victor, CO.

In the late 1870s local businessman George Sears leases land from Dona Estefana. By 1881 George and Estefana have a friendship. They visit each other periodically, and George loans Estefana $1,200. In 1884 the association turns sour. Jan MacKill, feature writer of the *Greenhorn Valley News*, shares the following:

"The friendship ceased abruptly in 1884, however, when Estefana sued Sears over a business deal. She may have appeared ignorant, but Estefana did know to settle her disputes in court. Her claim was that she sold Sears some land in 1882 for $3,000, but got only $925 instead. Five years later, in 1889, the court determined that Estefana's limited knowledge of English rendered the sale invalid. Sears appealed to the court in 1893 for the $1,200 Estefana owed him, but she was released from debt under the statute of limitations law."

Limited by a second language and not experienced in business matters, Spanish born Estefana sells her land about 1891 to pay off debts. The Hicklin estate is passed through various owners and becomes known as the *Hayden Ranch*, then later the *Crow Ranch*. Mr. and Mrs. Holland Duell Jr. will purchase the estate in 1947.

Without a place to live Dona Estefana is forced to move in with her neighbors. Eventually she moves to Walsenburg and lives with Mrs. Julia Rice and family until her death in 1927 at age 84. Estefana Bent Hicklin is buried in Walsenburg Cemetery at a grave marked by the Daughters of the American Revolution. She outlived Zan Hicklin by half a century, but of course Zan had robbed the cradle of the Charles Bent estate.

Estefana's adobe ranch house remained on a knoll overlooking the Old Crow Village and P.O. which operated 1885-91 and 1896-1907. The adobe ranch house was removed in the late 1930s or early 1940s. But for sure, the historical ranch house *"ain't there no more."* As a memorial, there is a fire station and medical building where Dona Estefana Bent Hicklin stood her ground for 17 years after the loss of husband Zan.

Alexander "Zan" Hicklin

Six-foot-tall Alexander Hicklin marries the 13-year-old daughter of Gov. Charles and Maria Ignacia Bent. *Zan,* short for *Alexander,* is a good friend of *Kit,* short for Carson. Zan has worked for Charles Bent, Ceran St. Vrain, and other *"notables of the time."* For anyone to be a notable of the time, it is quite necessary to have a short, catchy nickname.

After taking his wife and infant child to Greenhorn Valley in 1859, Zan is granted water rights (by Colo. Terr. Court) for three old irrigation ditches. Zan builds upon the original John Brown ditches, recreating farm land on the north side of Greenhorn Creek. He farms hay and grain. From one ditch Zan creates a large pond behind his ranch house and barns. The ditches are among the oldest in Colorado; some are still in use.

Zan Hicklin becomes one of the most influential ranchers and farmers of the Valley. He breeds a large herd of cattle and cultivates the rich bottom land along Greenhorn Creek. He sells beef, grain, and vegetables to friends, neighbors, and travelers. Zan is well-known for his jovial wit, generous hospitality, and good business sense.

In 1861 Zan is referring to his settlement as *Greenhorn Ranch* or *Greenhorn Rancho.* The ranch is known to others as simply *Hicklin.* Ovando J. Hollister in his 1867 map of Colorado also labels this location as *Hicklin.* The 1870 Census lists the Hicklins as residents of *Greenhorn* with 380 acres of crop. In December 1871 the *Pueblo Chieftain* reports 35 families settled in and around the town of *Greenhorn.* As the ranch grows into a small business center with post office, general store, and guest rooms, the complex becomes known as *Crow Post Office* at *Crow Village.*

When the Civil War breaks out in 1861, Colorado is still a southern territory (being south of the Arkansas River) but is claimed by the North. Southerners (especially from Georgia who have recently arrived in Colorado Territory as prospectors) organize themselves to seize gold fields for the Confederacy. These Southerners have a training camp in Mace's Hole near Beulah. Mace's Hole is in an isolated valley with limited accessibility 23 miles southwest of Pueblo and 12 miles northwest of Greenhorn. Mace is named after Juan Mace, a Mexican cattle rustler who hides stolen animals in the valley. Some say he was caught and hanged. Others say he was just hanging around. Juan says nothing at all.

Zan Hicklin is a southern sympathizer from Missouri. Through his ranch, 600 Confederates are secretly guided to Mace's Hole for training. Conducting secret meetings at night, Zan supplies Union troops by day.

When Union volunteers take 200 head of Zan's cattle as food for their troops, he cannot protest too loudly because his neighbors already suspect him of aiding the Confederates. When Zan bills Uncle Sam for the loss of his cattle, he receives financial compensation.

While Zan provides the Confederates with information about Union activity, he is successful in persuading visitors he is loyal to the Union. He does this by regularly passing himself off as a silly, dim-witted buffoon. In reality Zan is *"cunning as a fox, brave and resolute."*

At one point Zan Hicklin is arrested by Union officers. When he is about to be shackled and taken to Fort Garland stockade, Zan uses babbling buffoonery to weasel his way out of the grim situation. Part of his ploy is to insist on taking a personal oath of allegiance. After Zan commits a pledge of loyalty to the U.S. Constitution, he is released from bondage.

Although Confederate Rebels near the headwater of San Carlos Creek constitute a serious threat in 1862, they are driven out of the area by Union volunteers. Toward the end, zealous Zan helps Rebel leader Captain D. E. Conner and his recruits escape to Texas.

On March 2 of 1861, just two days after the Territory of Colorado is created, the Overland Mail Bill is enacted, Before long a daily stagecoach and pony express are regular services passing through Greenhorn Rancho.

In 1867 to keep up with the times, Zan prepares a *swing station* at his ranch for the Denver/Trinidad/Santa Fe stage line. This does not mean everyone is messing around at the swing station as some have suggested. Swing stations are public pit stops with basic services located every 8 to 15 miles. Some stations include eating and sleeping facilities.

Eight miles northeast of the Greenhorn swing station, a Muddy Creek

Stage Stop is established at the junction of Greenhorn and Muddy Creeks, half mile east of I-25. Muddy Creek Stage Stop becomes known as *Miller's Stage Station,* and *"It was the best eating place from Denver to Trinidad in 1867."* Miller's Stop has a post office from 1870-1886. The P.O. is moved two miles south to a settlement known as Abbey (1891-1914.)

To the north of Miller's Station and seven miles south of El Pueblo, another stage stop is created near the Taos Trail crossing of St. Charles Creek. This is the same spot where Charles Autobees secured part of the Nolan Land Grant in 1846. He created a farming camp central to the Hispanic community which made up about 25% of Pueblo County.

As a result of these new stage stations, the Hicklins become well-known for sharing their home, food, barn, and bunkhouse with terribly-tired travelers who pass through. A story dating from this period reveals Zan Hicklin's sense of humor: Calvin Jones arrives at the Hicklin Ranch with an antelope slung over his horse and covered with a blanket. While travelers have stopped for the night and are within hearing distance, Zan and Calvin (both practical jokers) decide to have some fun. Zan begins to complain loudly with Jones, saying, *"What did you have to kill one of those tough old Arapahoes for? Why didn't you shoot one of those tender young Utes?"* For supper the antelope roast is presented for eating, and it is promptly refused by the travelers who are certain they sit among mad cannibals. Nonetheless, Zan and Calvin eat a happy, hearty meal while enjoying a little laughter from time to time at their visitors' expense.

On the serious side, three years before his death Zan Hicklin learns about the uncontrolled killing of buffalo on the plains. In the winter of 1872-1873, Bob Wright and Charlie Rath kill 200,000 buffalo. Tom Nickson holds the record for exterminating 140 buffalo in 40 minutes; in total he destroys 2,173 buffalo in 35 days. Colonel Dodge estimates between 1872-1874 four million buffalo are killed, three-fourths of them just for hides. By the end of 1875, the Great Plains are not so great; the mammoth buffalo of the plains are all gone - and so is Zan Hicklin.

Indians and settlers alike must find another way to survive. Until settlers of the plains can determine what kind of crops to grow on the land, they collect bleached buffalo bones in a fight against hard times. It takes 100 skeletons to make a ton of bones worth eight dollars when delivered to a Santa Fe station. From Santa Fe the bones are hauled east and ground into fertilizer. Coloradans survive on basic bone money.

Zan Hicklin had two brothers named Talman and John who live with the Hicklins periodically. Brother Talman dies in January of 1873, one year before Zan. His death results from a poker game at the Ranch House. Talman has great expectations for his hand of playing cards when another gambler (about to put his saddle on the table for collateral) bumps Talman's arm and knocks the promising cards to the floor. Immediately Talman loses the privacy of his winning hand, while saddle man has already lost all of his money during previous play. The accident triggers both men to explosive rage, and a traditional gun duel results. Talman is shot first and dies within minutes. His brother John will later die in Walsenburg, but the circumstance of his death and date are uncertain.

In the final years, Zan is quite prosperous. Along with his prosperity comes celebration; along with celebration comes heavy drinking. Sometimes *"he became so incapacitated in Pueblo that he could not make it back home that night."* When Zan comes down with pneumonia, it combines with the alcohol consumption causing his 55 year old body to collapse. Zan dies rather suddenly on February of 1874.

Just before making his final exit, humor and hospitality emerge from his lips one more time. Zan's final request is to be buried with a flask of whiskey in his coat pocket, so he can party with friends who have passed on before him. For one reason or another his wistful wish is not granted, a fact that takes nearly 100 years to uncover.

In the late 1960s, when Zan's grave site is unearthed as a publicity stunt and transported a half mile west, local citizens comply with his original request. A bottle of Crow Whiskey is carefully placed into Zan's coat pocket at the new grave site. The publicity stunt is promoted on national news as if it were a major historical event. Apparently it was a very slow day for national news.

Near a large rock in an open field on a hill above the old Hicklin Ranch House, a four-foot-high marble stone marks the new resting place of good old Zan. The top half of the white stone has broken off and leans against the white marble base in year 2000.

The Alexander and Estefana Hicklin village has been the continuous site of a small business plaza for 141 years, beginning in 1859 and continuing into the 21st century. Zealous Zan farmed the Greenhorn Valley for 15 years, employing many Mexican peons to work 400 acres of irrigated farm field. At one time he had 175 acres of corn, 75 of oats, 75 of wheat, 40 of beans, 15 of buckwheat, and the rest in wild hay.

After losing Alexander to pneumonia and an eldest son to gunfire. Dona Estefana carried on as best she could for another 17 years. She had to fight the U.S. Government to prove the land was hers, and she had to fight the squatters who invaded the land grant of her murdered father. Thus, there is ample reason to remember the Hicklins as hardworking, well-liked, adventurous people who left behind a legacy of practical jokes, courageous escapades, and fireside folklore.

George Sears

In 1872 George Sears arrives from Kansas and settles on Graneros Creek where he begins ranching Texas Longhorn cattle. A few years later, while squatters invade the Hicklin estate, H. T. Austin, his sons (John and Bush), along with George Sears dig a water well at the side of the road on Sears' property. The well is on the Taos Trail three miles south of Hicklin Ranch and five miles southeast of Rye. The wellhead will become known as the *Old Oaken Bucket* and memorialized in a song by the same name.

In late 1870s (about the time Hicklin Jr. is murdered) a lively little settlement begins to develop around the water well at Graneros Creek. Dr. T. D. Baird (physician), J. H. McDaniel (druggist and notary), and C. C. Stein (attorney at law) establish services. George Sears will emerge as postmaster at the Graneros Post Office from 1889-1925.

George has a young son (Robert W. Sears) who spends much of his life at the Graneros settlement. Robert Sears recalls the following:

"...my father, George Sears, started a miniature department store, catering to the needs of grimy travelers on the Old Santa Fe Trail [It was better known as the Taos Trail] and to the scattered stockmen who had settled on the mountain streams. As Postmasters for thirty years, we passed out mail to an ever-growing patronage."

The miniature department store grows into a blacksmith shop, drug store, general store, grain-grinding mill, lumber yard, Odd Fellows Hall, saloon, and wagon-making business. The little village is now a small frontier town beginning to bubble with action.

General George has something for everyone. His Odd Fellows Hall features quilts, clothing, and blankets. His general store sells black gunpowder, bolts of unbleached muslin (for underwear), bright-colored bandanas, buckshot, calicos and ginghams, cashmere shawls, cheap jewelry, cotton stockings, cowhide boots, cravats, fine-toothed combs, green coffee beans, leather hat bands, red flannel underwear, and thread to keep it all together. The shoe department carries high heel shoes for ladies and copper-toed, hobnailed boots for high-stepping gentlemen. The grocery department is laid out around a pot-bellied stove and displays large bins of rice, coffee, beans, brown sugar, cane sugar, and tea. Next to the bulk bins rest large burlap bags of peanuts and small buckets of stick candy including lemon drops, molasses, and peppermint sticks. The tobacco section contains a variety of cigars, *Star and Climax* chewing tobacco, nickel bags of *Bull Durham*, and rolling paper for do-it-yourself cigarettes. The drug counter displays calomel, camphor, castor oil, Epsom salts, quinine, peppermint, and turpentine. Rope, coiled in the basement, is pulled through openings in the floor and sold by the pound.

With more and more visitors arriving, general George builds a small hotel, and it becomes known as the Thirty-Mile House. It is about 30 miles from Pueblo, 30 miles from Walsenburg, 30 miles from La Veta, and 30 miles from Gardner. Thirty miles is a good day's journey by horse.

The Thirty-Mile House has rooms for a dozen guests, and general George charges one dollar for supper, bed, and breakfast. The dollar fee also includes barn shelter and feed for a team of tired horses.

Visitors come from fairly far distances to attend the unusual oyster suppers put on at the Odd Fellow Hall. The suppers cost $2.50 each and include after-dinner dancing until dawn. As after-dinner dancers become numerous, they are divided into small groups (4-6 couples) and given numbers, because there is limited space to do the popular square dancing.

General George provides a basic bunkhouse for those with meager means. These casual campers put their blankets on bunk beds made of rough boards and sleep in the small shelter for free. Here in the shelter Mexican families make tortillas and coffee before entering the buildings. Later on, the Shady Greenhorn services will be built at this same location.

Local ranchers trade potatoes, bacon, and lard for store merchandise. The ranchers, who establish good credit with general George, pay off their accounts only once a year. Many of the local ranchers leave their property deeds and other valuable papers in George's large steel safe.

The stagecoach is a pleasant means of travel for the time, and Graneros village becomes a stage stop on the Taos Trail. Until train tracks are laid and locomotives arrive, the Barlow & Sanderson Stage Line becomes the most popular means of transportation south of Pueblo. *"The stage provided a safe and convenient way to transport merchant wives, children and well-to-do city folk."*

By 1870 Pueblo has grown to a population of 1,000, and the stage carries citizens between Pueblo and Santa Fe. In addition to the locals, there are homesteaders, gold seekers, and merchants arriving from the East in large numbers. Several relay stations are required for the changing of horses, mail, and passengers. Traveling south out of Pueblo, the first relay station is *St. Charles* on St. Charles Creek. The second station is *Stanley Ranch* located between St. Charles and Greenhorn Creeks, where Stanley will build a school house in 1886. The third stop is *Greenhorn* at the Hicklin Ranch, later to be called Crow Junction and Crow Village. The fare from Pueblo to Greenhorn is $5.00.

In the 1880s the Greenhorn station is moved a few miles south to Sears' settlement on the Graneros. While horse teams are changed on the coaches, passengers enjoy a refreshing drink at the well and buy snacks. *"There, according to Sears, the stage would change the mail at 2 a.m. and sleepy passengers who were traveling on could purchase cheese and crackers, canned salmon and sardines, cigarettes and chewing tobacco."*

After departing Graneros, the stage line heads south to *Beacon* (1865 to 1876), a settlement located on Huerfano River west of Huerfano Butte. Beacon is renamed *St. Mary's* and exists as St. Mary's until 1907. The youngest son of Alexander and Estefana Hicklin, Alfred, will be married at St. Mary's in the 1890s. The stage road will become Hwy 85-87.

When Lewis Barlow dies of pneumonia at the Summit House of Sangre de Cristo Pass in January of 1876, it foreshadows the coming death of his stagecoach service. His associate, Sanderson, continues into the early 1880s with service to Cuchara, Salida, and Lake City. His stage line through Badito and over the Sangre de Cristo Pass is among the last to die in Southern Colorado. Railroads are in place; they offer faster service; and they are more luxurious than the stagecoach.

When the Denver & Rio Grande track is laid a few miles to the east of Graneros village, *Graneros Flats* becomes a small camp built around the train stop. A school is constructed in 1890; Len Pritchard is the school teacher. By 1910 Graneros Flats has grown to become a depot, store, post office, and school with 25 students.

Even though railroad lines are being established to the east of George Sears' village, ox-driven wagons stop to draw water from the Graneros well. Before long, noisy horseless carriages sputter into town, operated by manly motorists with machine mania.

To keep mad motorists on the straight and narrow, imported oak saplings are planted along the main road at Graneros. As these little saplings grow, they will create the new name of *Shady Greenhorn.* The oak trees share the ground cover with cedar, choke cherries, clematis, pinion, wild grape, plums, and wild gourds. These striped gourds are perfectly round (the size of tennis balls) and not edible. They do, however, provide many colorful decorations for homes and businesses in the region.

Ten years after general George moves to California in 1904, the Fossceco family comes to the Graneros and recreates the village with a new restaurant, service garage, tourist cabins, and small zoo.

What Happened to the Indians?

Eight years after Colorado becomes one of the United States (Aug. I, 1876), 700 U.S. soldiers exterminate Cheyennes (Nov. 29, 1884) who are under promise of protection at Sand Creek. Most of the Cheyennes gunned down are women and children. As they lay dying, they are scalped by Colonel John M. Chivington and his soldiers. Chivington brags with exaggeration that he has slaughtered 400-500 Indians, with soldier losses of only *"nine killed and thirty-eight wounded."* The Cheyennes who survive the massacre report 140 family-member deaths.

In Denver Chivington receives a hero's welcome. In turn he exhibits 100 blood-clotted scalps before a cheering crowd. Dick Wootton bestows his own blessing on the Chivington massacre: *"It was the necessity for punishing all the Indians who belonged to the hostile combinations...."*

By 1889 reservations are in place and Indian children are stripped from their parents and taken to boarding schools. Here they are required to dress like whites, speak like whites, and learn wonderful white ways. Up until 1912, Indians are not allowed to leave their reservations without permission. Congress grants citizenship to native Americans (1924), allows tribes to form their own governments (1934), then terminates federal services and benefits (1950), except for schooling. Getting the Indian children to become civilized like whites is a high priority.

It takes the Native Americans awhile to understand the white man's game. Once the natives realize they are in a legal contest, a few become skilled lawyers and win back bits and pieces of their sacred lands. As native lawyers produce great medicine for their people, Indian children dream of becoming lawyers above and beyond any other occupation.

In Colorado Ute attorneys become white-man smart and win 12 million dollars for lands taken from them in Southern Colorado (1951.) It doesn't stop here. Ute lawyers go on to win millions of additional dollars for other sacred lands taken (1960).

Today most Native Americans prefer to stay on their sacred lands and not associate with the U.S. melting pot. When natives see U.S. values reflected on television and in movie videos, their red skins are much amused, but not enough to want whiteness. Most of the family-oriented natives feel rather sorry for the material-minded Americans.

Fossceco Family

About 1915 the Fossceco family acquires what is left of Sears' Graneros village and other farmland along the Graneros. The Fossceco family includes two sisters (Mary and Mellie) and seven brothers (Albert, Alven, Charles, Floyd, Frank, Nick, and Tony.) The Fosscecos farm wheat and ranch cattle. Their estate will grow to 26,000 acres. It will reach to the upper grasslands of Muddy Creek on the north and extending east to the Colorado & Southern and Denver & Rio Grande Western railroads.

"The Fossceco family lived upstairs in the 30 Mile House and changed its name to the Greenhorn Inn. Single rooms rented for $1.75 in the 1920's. In 1934, a new cafe was built and called the Shady Greenhorn Cafe. A dinner of soup, salad, vegetables, drink, desert and choice of meat cost 45 cents."

Where the Taos Trail crosses Graneros Creek and Thirty Mile House once stood, the Fosscecos build homes. The tree-shaded community serves ranchers and travelers with a roadside inn, restaurant, general store, and service station. The garage is equipped to repair any kind of horseless carriage traveling *Old County Road,* as it is now called. Old County Road runs three miles north and crosses Greenhorn Creek a quarter mile east of Meadows Park. The same county trail will be bridged over the creek a mile to the west in 1928. The new path will become *Greenhorn Road.*

As the oak trees grow large and remain rather fixed, the Colorado Highway Department wants to chop down the trees - making for a bigger, better, wider road through *Shady Greenhorn*. The efforts of local property owners and county commissioners stop the highway department. Since the trees themselves have become bigger, better, and wider to create *Shady*, chopping down the trees would have ended significant shade at *Shady*. Had this happened, *Shady* would have simply become - *Sunny.*

Shady Greenhorn in 1949 (Courtesy of Pueblo Library District)

Perhaps the most interesting feature of Shady Greenhorn is the small zoo where the Fosscecos maintain a bear, badger, lynx, porcupine, and bobcat for the tourists. In addition to the zoo animals, deer, antelope, squirrels, and rabbits are often seen in their natural environment along Graneros Creek.

In the mid-1940s the roadside business of Shady Greenhorn experiences a sudden death when the main highway between Pueblo and Walsenburg (U.S. 85-87) is moved two miles east of Shady where I-25 will be constructed. As fewer and fewer travelers use the old road, business slumps, and the cafe closes. The Fossceco family partnership dissolves. Most of the children retire or return to ranching and farming. As the children grown less in number, the survivors divide up the land and sell off their parcels, except for Alven.

Alven, his wife, Josephine, and their two children, Anthony and Marla, remain at Shady Greenhorn. In 1950 they build a new house near Graneros Creek. In 1952 the Greenhorn Inn is torn down. The store and garage soon close. Only Alven's zoo animals remain as reminders of the tourist trade Shady once enjoyed. Daughter Marla recalls her father's business as:

"...a spot, on an otherwise lonely highway, where he can offer a traveler not only the usual services - but more -- a chance to step off the car, feast his or her eyes on a spectacular view, engage in some idle chit chat with the owner and take time out to poke around the animal farm."

About 1965 Josephine Fossceco becomes secretary for Ralph C. Taylor, the Executive vice-President of Colorado City Development Co. As part of her responsibilities, she becomes Colorado City's first postmaster mistress. The final remains of Shady Greenhorn are auctioned off in 1969.

Alven builds a new Graneros Canyon Service Station, souvenir shop, cafe, and zoo. His complex is constructed on the southeast corner of Graneros Gorge interchange at Interstate-25.

Alven's Graneros Canyon Animal Park features two brown bears, three llamas, a burro, a billy goat, and three unusual Siberian deer. He is planning to obtain a buffalo in July of 1976 when a pair of maladjusted gun slingers shoot and kill one of his Siberian deer. More than likely, these goofy gun slingers would have a field day shooting fish in a barrel, or reducing animal populations at the San Diego Zoo.

Alven donates his last bear to a zoo In 1986.

Marion Mine

The neighboring village of Rye is located five miles west of Colorado City on a plateau in the foothills below Greenhorn Mountain. From an elevation of 7,000 feet at Rye, Greenhorn Mountain rises nearly 13,000 feet above sea level to the west.

Along the Greenhorn Mountain Range (or *Wet Mountains*), the foothills of Rye stretch north to Canon City. Early trails along these foothills are used by Indians and mountain men, long before gold is discovered in Colorado. Unlike Cripple Creek and Victor, where mountains are still being carved away by grand gold seekers, an abundance of yellow metal was never found in the Wet Mountains above Greenhorn Valley. Consequently these marvelous mountains remain ungored by the great gold grabbers of the West. Of course without gold there is no yellow jewelry; without yellow jewelry there are no jewelry stores; and without jewelry stores there is very little happiness among certain human populations.

There is only one mining operation to be found on the east side of Greenhorn Mountains. First known as *Greenhorn Mine* and later named the *Marion Mine,* it is located near the source of St. Charles Creek. The mine is ten miles northwest of Rye and three miles west of Isabel Lake. Early on, this location is known as *Fairview.*

In the mid-1870s Zina Fairchilds, whose homestead includes the present San Isabel Village, is prospecting near the source of St. Charles Creek. Zina finds a vein of promising quartz, but he lacks funds to construct a mine. He does nothing until 1879 when he shares his discovery with Hardscrabble cattlemen Jim H. Graves and Saul Wixson. Graves and Wixson agree to dig a tunnel into the mountain to intersect the quartz vein at a lower level. They finance the tunnel construction in exchange for controlling interest of the joint venture.

Ground is broken in June of 1880. Progress is slow because most work is confined to a few summer months of warm weather. Jim Graves, a single man with no family, builds a cabin at the mine and works year around by himself. Five years later the promising vein of quartz is reached. The vein is found to contain zinc, lead, and copper, but only a trace of silver and gold. Zinc sulfide is a major part of the ore.

Fairchilds, Graves, and Wixson do not have the resources to bring in a milling operation, so they search for a buyer. After 1885, they work the mine only enough to maintain a legal right to the claim. Twenty-one years pass before the three men are able to convince Denver miners Frank Buckley and Henry E. McElwain to purchase their miscellaneous mine for $20,000 in 1906. At this time, the name of the mine is changed to *Marion*, in honor of McElwain's wife. Many of Colorado's most productive mines are named after women, but lady Marion will not be among the many mines that produce gobs of glittering gold.

When Buckley and McElwain take over the mine, Henry Gray is hired as superintendent. He supervises the construction of wagon roads to the mine, a boarding house below the mine, a supply store, and an office. Log cabins are built along a steep wagon trail passing through a boulder field. The boulder path leads to the mine entrance, which burrows into the base of the canyon. Here at the mine entrance, steel rails are laid into the tunnel so ore cars can remove rock more efficiently than wheelbarrows.

With a need for power and electricity, a reservoir site is sought and found a mile and a quarter above the mine on Amethyst Creek which runs down through the camp. After assembling a saw mill at the lake site 1,100 feet above the mine, Amethyst Creek is dammed with a rock and timber wall. Water from Marion Lake is then piped to:

"...wheels in 6,600 ft. of pressure pipe...beginning with a diameter of 10 in. and diminishing to 8 in. at the lower end....the pressure at the nozzle is 465 lbs. to the inch....This water pressure ran the mill, a hoist in the mine, and compressor to power the rock drills, and provided electricity for the store and post office, four houses, a bunkhouse and boarding house, and even street lights that were once part of the site."

In addition to Henry Gray, George Kindle is hired as mine engineer. His wife runs a small boarding house for miners. Transporting the ore from mine to smelter is a difficult trip. The operation begins in 1906 as ore is placed in heavy canvas bags. It is loaded on custom built wagons pulled by six horses then hauled down the mountain side to Graneros Flats. The round trip takes four days; the horse drivers are Bill Gammon and Charlie Dusenberry. At Graneros the ore is loaded on Denver & Rio Grande railroad cars heading northwest to a smelter in Florence near Canon City. At Florence the ore is separated and refined into various minerals.

Because of its high elevation, the mining camp is buried in snow for six or seven months each year. While George Kindle and his wife are prepared with sufficient food and firewood for the long winters, operating expenses continue to exceeded the value of the ore. During operations from 1906-1915, one miner is killed and another blinded from an explosion in the mine. By 1915 mining operations have been suspended. Mining engineer George Kindle looks after the Marion camp until 1933 when major machinery is scrapped and hauled away.

Ruins of the Marion Mine are not well marked as of year 2000. One needs a guide, a good map, good directions, or good luck; but the long uphill hike is worthwhile. Furthermore vandals are too lazy to hike three miles uphill, and litter bugs have already stuffed their gullets and discarded their debris before reaching the mysterious mine. Marion remains a clean, beautiful, box canyon of dangerous, but majestic, ruins. The ruins are massive; they hang together precariously. Dark hollows seem to invite those with a death wish.

Zina Fairchilds sells what is left of his ranch to H. T. Ashley who operates a saw mill and mercantile business at Rye. When Ashley builds cabins three miles below the Marion Mine on the St. Charles, the retreat becomes an oasis for summer visitors. Before long, St. Charles Creek will be damned at the San Isabel Village to create Isabel Lake.

Rye Village

While others are hunting, trapping, and trading in 1843, a man called *Simpson* discovers good soil and plants corn west of the John Brown camp. This man is George Simpson who frequents the Valley along with frontier trappers like John Brown, Marcelino Baca, and Archa Metcalf. Simpson has a successful crop of golden-yellow corn, and most of it is sold to Army officers at Fort Garland west of La Veta Pass.

Although the Wet Mountains escape the Gold Rush of 1849, the fertile foothills grow in farming and ranching. Eventually, the vast beauty of Rye will develop into recreational facilities and resort communities.

By the 1860s general knowledge of the Hicklin Ranch, irrigation ditches, Marion Mine, and San Isabel Village attract settlers to the Rye area. Among the first to arrive are Mr. and Mrs. John Williams (1860); John Warner (1866); William and Rush Fisher (1866); and Mr. and Mrs. David Frink (1866). The Williams and Frinks settle a few miles east of Rye. Mrs. Frink, Mrs. Williams, and four-year-old Sara Williams are the first anglo females in the Rye area.

In 1868 Laura Williams is born in a log cabin near the site where

Lake Beckwith will be expanded in 1947. Laura will marry and become Mrs. Halsey. Mrs. Halsey will one day become the ceremonial queen of a new land development (*Colorado City*) surrounding Lake Beckwith.

In 1869 Thomas Medill and William Smith arrive about the same time. They help to build irrigation ditches for the farm fields. William G. Finlay settles north of Rye on Muddy Creek.

In 1870 George Haynes arrives along with David, Thomas, and Joel Nichols. David Nichols establishes the first local post office (1879-80) on Table Mountain two and a half miles northeast of Rye. Charles T. Fisher is appointed the first postmaster. John Pritchard plats the land for a settlement. And Table Mountain residents establish a cemetery.

According to Hazel Atterberry, Table Mountain still has a cemetery with 90 grave sites and a second *"cemetery that contains the remains of what she believes to be those of the Indian chief, Cuerno Verde and five of his warriors."* When asked if she really believes the Comanche chief is buried there, she replies, *"I'm positive."* The two cemeteries are on private land, and the grave markers have been demolished by cattle. Yet the grim ghost of Chief Green Horn can sometimes be seen at dusk.

In 1871 Burton Moore and Joseph B. Doze arrive. Joseph Doze sets out the first orchard of fruit and nut trees. Some of his immediate neighbors begin to behave strangely, and a few even seem to go a bit nuts. Most everyone else, however, looks quite healthy.

Mrs. David Frink and Tim Howard teach school in the homes of their pupils. The first school house and church are built one mile south of Rye, *"on what was known as the Rock Place."*

Circuit riders (traveling missionaries) of various persuasions begin to arrive. Father Clark, *"a dear old white-haired man of God,"* is a Baptist preacher serving the communities of Rye, Beulah, Canon City, La Veta, Rosita, and Silver Cliff.

John Morrow and J. A. Allison organize the Cumberland Presbyterian Church where Reverend Berry labors to save souls. Reverend Berry is also a carpenter and helps build many of the early homes in Rye.

Methodist minister Paul Ray Quillian, like Father Clark, is a circuit rider who travels the Front Range with the word of God. Rev. Paul Ray establishes church groups in Gardner (where he is homesteading), Beulah, La Veta, and Walsenburg. Paul Ray arrives from Gardner once a month on horseback, and services are held in the school house a mile south of Rye. *"We all loved him and his fine wife, who came with him occasionally."*

Some Rye residents now believe there are too many religious

persuasions trying to serve the same area. It's put to a vote, and the Methodist persuasion is elected to serve the entire community, or at least Paul Ray's flock of sheep. In 1872 the Rye Home Church is established by Asbury *"Paul Ray"* Quillian, minister of the Southern Methodist Episcopal Church. Later on, Rev. O. F. Sensebough will serve the Beulah and Rye villages. He will be instrumental in constructing the Southern Methodist parsonage at Rye. Also Reverend Cooper will spend several years in Rye. During his ministry, a Rye Home Church building will be erected in 1889 at the top of Main Street, *"just before the curve that leads up Park Road."*

The first Catholic mass will be celebrated in 1936. Regular masses will be held in the home of Mr. and Mrs. Roley for the first ten years.

Returning to 1872 when the Rye Home Church is being established, Finn Cox, George Sears, and Major Sheets ride into town. George will create his village on Graneros Creek five miles southeast of Rye, and Major Sheets will provide land for the town of Rye.

The 1873 arrivals are John and Joseph Peterson, Calvin Goss, John T. Graybeal, Henry Depp (Deep), and James G. Thomas. Petersons homestead a ranch. Calvin Goss purchases land from the Hicklins and operates a post office at their Ranch. The postal station is named *Crow* after Matthew Crow who is then postmaster in the neighboring town of Pueblo.

John Graybeal has his former Negro slave, Hiram Graybeal, bring one of his horse teams from North Carolina to Rye. The Graybeal house will become known as Don Owens home.

Henry Depp and his wife homestead the entrance to Greenhorn Canon where the creek emerges from the mountains. They turn the Canon into a resort ranch. It will be sold to Pueblo folk and renamed *Cuerno Verde.*

James G. Thomas, also known as Jimmie and a former school teacher, settles on Table Mountain in 1877. He establishes a post office and supply store in 1879. In time Mr. Thomas will do much more.

The 1874 newcomers are Dr. Litterall, Avery Carter, Jesse Marshall, and Captain William Meredith. Dr. Litterall arrives from the South and becomes one of the town builders. He is also a useful doctor to the ill and dying. In the late 1880's Dr. Litterall builds a two story house with four porches and seven exterior doors. For many years the building will be used as the home, switchboard, and office of the Rye telephone operator.

Dr. Litterall's neighbors are the David F. Hunters, Major Sam Sheets, Noah and Charity Dixon, Henry Depp, John Higgins, Jesse Marshall, Henry (Harry) Hardin, and James Porter Ashley. The Hardins and the Ashleys have both come to Colorado from North Carolina.

The ranch lands of Captain William Meredith and Major Sam Sheets come together at the junction of Main and Boulder Streets. Rye village grows out from this intersection. Captain Meredith is believed to have the first piano in southern Colorado.

Old Dr. Beckwith, not to be confused with Lt. Edward Beckwith, arrives about 1876 and locates three miles east of Rye. His land estate will become known as the *William Hunter Place*.

In 1878 Mr. and Mrs. Jacob Sayler settle into town. The Saylers will run a shoe store and own a hotel.

Enoch and Caroline Mead move to Table Mountain in 1880 where they construct a water-powered saw mill.

Two earlier arrivals. Jimmie Thomas and George Sears, become business partners in 1881 and move the post office/supply store from David Nichols' ranch on Table Mountain to Rye, "*next to the big bluff on Captain William Meredith and Major Sheets' place.*" The *Table Mountain* name goes along with the post office. It is not until the 1930s the name *Table Mountain* is changed to *Rye* when the U. S. Department of P.O. insists on a shorter name. *Rye*, a hardy grain of grass growing wild in the fields, is incorporated as a town in 1937.

Thomas and Sears general store is the first business to appear in what will become the town of Rye. Their general store will grown to a larger mercantile business.

In 1881 David Hunter moves to Rye from Bond County, IL, and drops anchor on Little Graneros Creek. Hunter establishes a homestead which will become well-known as *Hayden Ranch*. David opens a post office one mile south of Rye at a location referred to as *Lebanon*. Unfortunately he loses his wife in a fire that destroys their ranch home. One of his sons will be murdered about 1912. Another son named Louis R. Hunter, known as *Uncle Louis*, will operate the Hunter ranch for many years. Uncle Louis will sell the ranch to Hayden, who sells it to Evans, who sells it to "Dick" Clennin, Jr. Mr. Dick Clennin names his ranch *The Diamond Slash*.

In 1882, after the Thomas & Sears post-office and supply store have been erected, Mr. Jimmie Thomas builds a ten-room hotel on the corner of Main and Boulder. It is known as the *Mountain View Hotel* and is a popular stage stop for travelers. First Jacob Sayler and then J. H. McDaniel manage the hotel. Mr. and Mrs. Jacob Sayler will buy the hotel, and Mrs. Sayler will manage it for a number of years after Mr. Sayler dies in 1900. Some years later the Mountain View Hotel will burn to the ground.

In 1883, shortly after the Mountain View Hotel is constructed,

"*Pick*" Smith erects a two-story building. Pick turns the lower level into a drug store. He makes the upper level into a public meeting hall where ballroom dances, amateur plays, and church socials are to be enjoyed. Within the public meeting hall, *Good Templers* assemble to fight against the misuse of alcohol.

In 1884 James and Frances Hardin arrive and establish a farm on Old San Isabel Road north of Rye. In addition to their crops, the Hardins raise nine children in a home to be known as *Mrs. Wirt's Place*.

In 1885 the Southern Methodists construct a parsonage known as the *Oldshaw Home*. The Oldshaw Home is located next to the two story *McKellip Home* which has four porches and seven outside doors.

East from the Mountain View Hotel, Joe Moody builds a skating rink that is enjoyed for about two years until a heavy, spring snow storm collapses the roof. Tiger Thomas replaces the skating rink with another two-story building. The upstairs meeting hall is used as a community center for skating, dances, plays, church socials, and *Woodman of the World* meetings. The W.O.W. will hold meetings in the hall for several years, expressing strong feelings and having striking successes. In front of Jimmie's two-story meeting hall and community center, a large rock is placed. It becomes a playground for several generations of children, and it becomes a popular point for picture taking.

James Bray builds an ice-house and butcher shop. William Hayes manages a livery stable. East of the livery stable, J. A. Trulove puts up a dry goods store. Next door to the dry goods, Jacob Sayler operates a shoe store. On the south side near Greenhorn Creek, a blacksmith shop is established. F. D. Miller creates a barber shop and bachelors' hall on the west side. Also on the west side, John Bagley owns and operates a grist mill (or is it a lumber mill?) Mr. Bagley builds one of the first homes in Rye, to be known as the *Hudson Home*. Across the street from Hudson Home, Bagley builds another dwelling for his family. Mysteriously, John leaves home one day and is never heard from again.

Most of the Rye businesses and homes are made possible by Frank Benham and Finn Cox who create thousands of board feet of lumber from their sawmill. The trees are taken from neighboring forests.

By 1889 Rye is the most populated community in Pueblo County outside the City of Pueblo. Summer tourists are swelling into town. Rye has become known as a resort village with quiet foothills setting, a little babbling brook, and many shade trees.

Another star attraction is Mrs. Jennie Frosst who brings many educational, cultural, and social activities to Rye during the late 1870s to the early 1890s. Having come from a cultural background in Boston, jewel-like Jennie shares numerous talents. First, Jennie teaches in the old school house; later on she teaches third grade at the new Centennial School. Second, she gives singing lessons. Third, she organizes literature and debate societies. Fourth, she raises money for a church organ, then plays the organ for her church services. Finally, she teaches Sunday school classes. Jennie's giving side is alive and well when she marries John Irving who has established a ranch southeast of Rye.

In 1898 a large wood schoolhouse with bell in the steeple is built in Rye. It eliminates the need for various smaller schools in outlying areas. This is the beginning of many long-five-mile-walk-to-school stories frequently told by fathers, grandfathers, and great grandfathers.

To open the 20th century, Rye Telephone Company installs one telephone line departing town in opposite directions. Many residents locate along the line to stay in touch. Good gossip must be passed quickly or it will slip back into the slimy sewer from whence it came.

In 1903 Hamilton *"Ham"* Ashley and his father, James, buy half interest in a mercantile store which is owned by George Sears and Marion Meredith. The store is located on the southwest corner of Main and Boulder. Sears Mercantile is operated by the Ashleys for ten years. Ham will drive the first automobile through the streets of Rye and open his own *Ashley Lumber and Mercantile* in 1925 on the southeast corner of Main and Boulder. He will become the first mayor of Rye in 1937. This hunk of Ham will hog the leadership and remain mayor of Rye for 16 years. He will pass on at age 85, two years after the birth of Colorado City.

At the turn of the century, Dr. W. P. Gillingham is running a quiet retreat center for patients suffering from tuberculosis and other related lung problems. His *Idylwild* camp is hidden among the pines on the west side of Rye. The camp includes: quiet living in *"house-tents,"* medication, diet, and the personal attention of Dr. Gillingham. In 1905 Mr. and Mrs. W. G. Moody purchase the retreat and turn it into a summer resort for tourists. Mrs. Moody manages the attraction until her death in 1947.

Rye is becoming known for its milk, butter, and cheese, some of which is carried in wagons 30 miles to Pueblo. The Rudolph Robach family of Switzerland produces Swiss cheese sold locally and to the distant mining camps of Rosita, Querida, and Florence.

Established in 1918, the Rye Star Route delivers mail. From Rye parcels are carried north into the mountain villages of San Isabel and

Wetmore, east to Cedarwood and Graneros, & south to Lascar and Apache.

When the old creamery, the Mountain View Hotel, and a few other businesses are destroyed by fire, a new creamery, a cabinet-making shop, and the Rye Bank replace the former businesses. The town of Rye now has a public school population of 150 students, and the Home Church boasts a membership of 109. In 1929 the Wilsons open a restaurant and miniature golf course at their hotel.

Resulting from the rapid growth of the automobile, Rye and San Isabel Village become popular summer resorts for Pueblo motorists. In 1936 the citizens of Rye and Pueblo raise $10,000 to purchase land for a lake at San Isabel Village, ten miles northwest of Rye. In order to create the lake, Rye, Pueblo, and the U.S. Forest Service join hands with the Civilian Conservation Corps. CCC is a government program started during the Great Depression for young men who needed jobs.

A sizable dam with a road on top is constructed across St. Charles Creek. The dam stretches 720 ft. long, 117 ft. high, and 578 ft. thick at its base. It is put together by manual labor and costs the U.S. Government $500,000. The CCC workers are sheltered in wooden barracks at the construction site. The new lake is called *St. Charles Lake* but later changed to *Lake Isabel* at San Isabel Village. To stock the lake and neighboring streams with fish, the State of Colorado establishes a fish hatchery one mile east of Rye.

Up until 1945, one-room school buildings serve the neighboring communities of Abbey, Apache, Cedarwood, Graneros, and San Isabel. One-room school houses have been the heart and soul of these villages providing local citizens with church services, town meetings, special elections, club meetings, dances, and other social events. When these schools are consolidated into a single central location at Rye, the small communities begin to disappear. They die from lack of traditional human interaction. Greenhorn Valley becomes known as *Rye Consolidated School District #13*. When the entire Pueblo County is put under one central administration, the Valley becomes known as the south side of *School District #70*. Although neighboring villages fade away, Rye maintains its colorful mix of residents with a small town atmosphere.

The Church of Jesus Christ of Latter Day Saints (LDS) has its first meeting in 1956. A church building is erected in 1963, the same year Colorado City is born five miles to the east. Rye will play a major roll in anchoring the new land development and its arrivals to community facilities and services.

Rebirth of Colorado City

The original *Colorado City* was established on the west side of Colorado Springs and became the first capitol of Colorado Territory. It was annexed to Colorado Springs in 1917 and no longer exists as Colorado City. Most people still refer to the area as *Old Colorado City*. This makes for some confusion when one refers to a new *Colorado City*, 70 miles south of *Old Colorado City* and 25 miles south of Pueblo.

The new Colorado City is believed by some historians to have Colorado's oldest irrigation ditches still in continuous use. Four miles below Rye, the main irrigation ditch comes off the north side of Greenhorn Creek, flows northeast into Lake Beckwith, and descends east through the 27 hole Hollydot golf course. When the irrigation ditch reaches the far end of the golf course, the elevation is about 6,000 feet above sea level.

Colorado City is nearly identical in area to the historical Hicklin Ranch. This early crossroads is designated on older maps as *Hicklands* or *Hickland Station*. In 1870, when the Goss family arrive from Kansas, Calvin Goss acquires 21 acres of the Hicklin Ranch and builds a log cabin. His home becomes the local post office from 1885-1891 and again from 1896-1907. As postmaster, Calvin names the post office after Matthew D. Crow, his friend and postmaster of Pueblo. Calvin's post office becomes known as *Crow Ranch, Crow Village, Crow Station,* and *Crow Junction*. It includes a stage stop, general store, and small hotel. In 1886 Crow has one of the first schools in the valley, located just west of the post office.

After the post office closes in 1907, the Hayden family purchases the entire Hicklin estate, and the land becomes *Hayden Ranch,* and the small lake above becomes known as *Hayden Reservoir*. Most people still refer to the general location as Crow Village with a Mercantile Store.

At the same location a second general merchandising store is built in 1910. The first floor and basement shelve drugs, clothing, hardware, groceries, dry goods, and ranch supplies. The upstairs provides a number of small rooms for weary travelers and party poopers. Ranchers, farmers, and railroad workers gather at the general store for Saturday night dances lasting until dawn. Those who drink too much and are unable to dance the night away have a safe place to hang out, hang in, and hang over.

In 1920 the Campbell Brothers, Elmer and Frank, rent the green, two story, *"Old Crow Building"* from the Hayden family. The Campbells add a service station to the mercantile business. As a young girl growing up in the area, Madeline Thacker remembers how it use to be:

> *"The Campbells sold groceries, dry goods, hardware and gasoline from the pumps in front. In a room attached to the main building they received cream in 5 gallon cans. Selling cream was the nearest thing to a steady income most farm and ranch families had in those days. It bought groceries, clothes and other bare necessities....The Campbell store is remembered fondly by long time residents, for along with the merchandise they sold, they dispensed friendship."*

Elmer Campbell and his wife live in the rear of the store. They have rooms upstairs to rent. Across the road from the store is a small farm house where brother Frank Campbell lives. The Campbells generate a sufficient business, and in 1931 a Colorado magazine describes Crow Village as a *"modern town."*

In 1946 the Campbells sell their operation to Howard Kline who continues the roadside business for another year. When the main highway is moved a few miles east, to where I-25 will evolve, Howard moves east with the road change. He puts up a new store where the Texaco Service Station is currently located. The Old Crow Mercantile, a two-story frame building, will be moved off its basement foundation to the south side of Hwy-165 and Crow Cut-Off. Here the Mercantile building will be used for storage by the California developers of Colorado City.

A year after Howard Kline moves his business to the Texaco site, Mr. and Mrs. Holland Duell Jr. arrive at Greenhorn Valley from New Mexico. The Duells purchase 7,000 acres referred to as *Crowe Ranch.*

The Duells have departed from their native home of New Rochelle, NY, and they have traveled west to become ranchers raising Herefords in Cimmaron, NM. In 1947 the Duells move their cattle operation to Greenhorn Valley where they continue to raise registered Herefords. Using the original irrigation ditch, they enlarge the existing pond to create *Lake Beckwith*. In 1955 the Duells sell their cattle and lease the land.

A year later Holland Duell Jr. and Conyers Stewart form a business arrangement at Littleton, CO, where Stewart is training horses. The two business men intend to establish a thoroughbred farm at Holland Duell's Crowe Ranch on Greenhorn Creek. The Crowe Ranch is an appropriate location for Holland and Conyers to horse around because horse racing has been popular in Greenhorn Valley for well over 100 years. It was a favorite amusement of old timers like William Bent, Kit Carson, Lucien Maxwell, Thomas Boggs, and the late Zan Hicklin. Among friends and associates, Holland and Conyers become known as *Holly* and *Connie*.

Conyers (Connie) Stewart is a native of Biloxi and attends a private school in New York where he first meets Holland Duell. As a runaway boy, Conyers Stewart drifts west and becomes a skilled horseman in Montana where he meets and marries a lady named Grace. Conyers gains a fine reputation and trains horses for local ranchers who race the summer fair circuit. In 1947 he visits a new race track in Raton, NM, where he renews an acquaintance with Holland who now has a ranch near Raton. Conyers follows the race circuit to California, spends a few years training horses, then returns to a new race track in Littleton, CO. While at Denver (1950-1955), he again bumps into Holland who now owns Crowe Ranch in Greenhorn Valley. Impressed by Crowe Ranch's great beauty, Connie forms a partnership with Holly for a breeding, breaking, boarding, farm business.

Holly manages the horse breeding while finishing his nine-hole golf course. In 1960 the nine-hole golf course just east of Lake Beckwith is complete. The golf course and horse farm are first steps to creating a resort community for golfers and horse lovers alike.

Major construction on the Duell-Stewart thoroughbred facilities begins in the fall of 1959. Open for business in 1960, the horse farm accommodates 20 thoroughbreds with complete services. While Holland Duell does the breeding, Conyers Stewart handles the buying, boarding, breaking, and training of horses. As part of the training, a five-eighths mile race track is built to give the horses practice in starting from a gate and running the oval. It takes about six months to train a horse for running the rapid race. Eight years after starting the business, horses-in-training will number about 125. The oval race track, barns, and corrals are still quite visible from Colorado City Interchange at I-25.

In 1962 at age 55, two years after beginning the horse farm business, horseman Holly sells 6,500 acres of his historic ranch to California land developers. Holly reserves 500 prime acres, including the 179-acre thoroughbred farm in the center of the development, for family and friends. Holly wants the new development to be called *Crowton* to avoid confusion with Old Colorado City on the west side of Colorado Springs. He and his supporters are out-voted, and the historical *Crowe Ranch* is buried in a funeral ceremony put on by California developers.

Colorado City Development Co. becomes the local name for *California City Development Co.* headquartered in the RCA Building, Suite

810, 6363 Sunset Blvd, Los Angeles, CA 90028. Nathan K. Mendelsohn is president, and he is the same man who in 1958 started California City, 100 miles northeast of Los Angeles. His company claims to have offices in New York, St. Louis, Hollywood, Honolulu, and the Philippines. During the summer of 1963, new offices are said to open in West Germany, Switzerland, and Italy. Most likely these offices are little more than a single sales broker who agrees to advertise Mendelsohn's real estate.

Holly Duell Jr. is made vice-president and superintendent of Parks and Recreation. John O'Sullivan is designated vice-president of Planning and Development of the Colorado City project.

In 1963, when Colorado City is about to give birth, longtime journalist and respected historian Ralph C. Taylor publishes a brief history of Southern Colorado, entitled *Colorado South of the Border*. Near the end of his book, Ralph Taylor describes a new land development. It will be designed and built as a modern "utopian city":

"Colorado City will be a group of villages surrounded by open country, where every resident will be within walking distance of open spaces that will be preserved in perpetuity....this modern community will have country club living for everybody - golf, horses, hunting, fishing, boating, hiking, flying, and still have all the comforts and conveniences of city life."

Uncle Webster defines *utopian* as "*...an imaginary and indefinitely remote place...having impossibly ideal conditions.*" As it turns out, Ralph Taylor is correct; *an imaginary* town will be created in a *remote place*, and the overall design will reflect *impossibly ideal conditions*.

It is hardly a coincidence Ralph Taylor's Book, *Colorado South of the Border*, appears in 1963. The very same year his book is published, Ralph is hired as an executive with the California City Development Co. about to create the same utopian city. In part Ralph's book is a subtle advertisement for his new employer and their proposed land project called *Colorado City*.

Rainbow Ralph graduated from Central High School the day before Pueblo's 1921 flood. The day after the flood, Ralph was hired as a cub reporter for *The Pueblo Star-Journal*, and he stayed with the newspaper for more than four decades. During the Great Depression, Ralph's wages were cut back, so he sought supplementary work outside the paper. His greatest successes came as publicity director for both Colorado State

Hospital and Colorado Springs Broadmoor Hotel. In 1933 owners of The *Star-Journal* purchased their rival, *The Pueblo Chieftain*. Ten years later Ralph was *"news director"* for both newspapers, and he trained more than 100 reporters. In 1958 Ralph's business ventures outside the newspaper generated more income than his job as news director. With a business partner he bought 1,500 acres of farmland along Beulah Highway on the southwest side of Pueblo. Together they hired a construction company to build homes. *"Ralph's land is now covered by residences, schools and shopping malls."* Ralph is doing exceptionally well.

In May of 1963, after a whopping 42 years of managing news, rainbow Ralph retires from the paper and takes an executive position as director of public relations with the California City Development Company (CCDC.) As a part of his responsibilities, Ralph publishes a small paper on behalf of the new Colorado City development. Since only a small number of of people reside in the immediate area, the little paper is basically an advertisement for the development. It is CCDC's intention to build a city; it is Ralph's job to manage the news and sell it.

In the beginning Ralph's newspaper is titled *Colorado City Call*. After about a year, the name changes to *The Colorado City Sun*. His paper includes information about both California City and Colorado City. Before long, rainbow Ralph will be promoted to a vice-president position in the CCDC organization.

Ralph's publication explains how president and planner of CCDC, Nat K. Mendelsohn, wants to create small communities similar to early New England towns. Each community is to be unique with its own name and lifestyle. Mendelsohn imagines a dozen small communities surrounded by natural beauty of the area with recreational parks and green pathways tying them all together. The parks and pathways are to be designed first on prime real estate, instead of last in undesirable areas. By creating adequate streets, sufficient parks, and open spaces, he hopes to avoid problems like slums plaguing many communities.

President Nat K. Mendelsohn visualizes 10,000 to 12,000 homesites with three or four people in each home, creating a population of 30,000 to 40,000. He estimates the project will cost $130 million and require 12 to 15 years. President Mendelsohn projects the following:

"Let's say it may take 20 years to complete the entire project. The first five years will see the over-all pattern take shape. The second five years probably will be those of greatest expansion."

Mighty Nat K. Mendelsohn was born March 23, 1915, in Prague, Czechoslovakia. At age five, he came to America with his parents at the end of World War I. Like many emigrant family members, Nat worked hard to take advantage of American opportunities. Young Mendelsohn:

"...graduated from the free College of the City of New York in 1935 with high grades and majors in English literature and philosophy. The following year in graduate school at Columbia University was a specialization in 17th Century literature. A master's degree was earned in 1937 after a year's course in education at Teachers' College at Columbia. Mendelsohn completed his work for a PH.D. at Columbia but too many new experiences kept him from writing his required thesis."

It is rather odd mighty Mendelsohn *completed his work for a PH.D.* without *writing his required thesis*. This being so unusual, there is a good chance Nathan did not actually complete his doctorate degree.

With a background in English and philosophy, mighty Mendelsohn studies social economics and becomes a professor of sociology at Columbia University. When Mendelsohn creates California City Development Company (CCDC), his vice-president and general manager, Norman Gross, is both friend and mathematics instructor. Consequently the CCDC leadership will consist of two educators who give up modest incomes in teaching to become wealthy real estate developers.

In 1963 at the birth of Colorado City, mighty Mendelsohn is living in Hollywood Hills, CA, with wife Sylvia and daughter Wendy. A second daughter is attending college in New York. Mendelsohn heads a variety of companies and is constantly developing new challenges. His business interests reach from the Pacific Islands of the West to Europe in the East.

As the Colorado City project gets underway, California architect and community planner, Wayne Williams, spends a year in Pueblo designing:

"...a dozen villages spread over 5,000 acres, but linked together by natural and developed parks, playgrounds and recreational facilities, so that all of the eventual residents will be virtually surrounded with outdoor living and recreation."

After a year of city planning, the first community buildings are designed by William E. Burk Jr. of Albuquerque. The buildings include a variety of community services and recreational facilities for the young, the working, the vacationing, and the retired:

"...the idea was to give those actively working the advantages of retirement living, while retired people could and should enjoy a retirement atmosphere without being separated from younger people."

The mighty Mendelsohn development targets land buyers and home builders who want recreational living at its very best, *"...those who want more out of life."* There will be no need for Colorado City residents to dart off to California and Florida for fine-featured, frivolous fun. His young utopian city will have it all.

Mighty Mendelsohn expects many of his land buyers to come from the neighboring City of Pueblo. He is convinced Puebloans will flee their city for country living and not mind the 25-mile commute to work. Also, among those who regularly vacation in Colorado, a number will visit Greenhorn Valley and buy land for their future retirement.

Central to the development, Lake Beckwith has existed as a small lake for some years. The name *Beckwith* could bare the name of Lt. E. G. Beckwith who accompanied Capt. J. W. Gunnison through the area 110 years earlier. During Lt. Beckwith's visit to the region, he took time to describe the Valley in grand style as he rode along the same old trails where native Indians, Spanish Conquistadors, and French trappers once stopped to rest awhile and trade some goods. With no disrespect to Lt. Beckwith, some locals attribute the name *Beckwith* to a Mr. Beckwith who enlarged the small lake into it current size in the early 1900's.

In August of 1963 work begins on the *"new city"* when contractor Richard Graham of Rye installs a pipeline from the small tower off Lake Beckwith's northeast shoreline to a filtration plant down below the dam. The road on top of the dam, between the tower and the filtration plant, is widened for two-way traffic. A horse path guarded by a rail fence of logs is added alongside the road. This road crossing the dam is named *Cuerno Verde Boulevard*, and it will become a principal street running through the first two neighborhood developments created in C-City.

M. K. Shelman builds a marina on the north side of Lake Beckwith. The marina has the combined purposes of sales office and boat dock. Here at the shores of Lake Beckwith, C-City is officially born on October 6, 1963. Governor John A. Love and Secretary of State Byron Anderson present a king-size birth certificate. It is four feet wide and eight feet

BIRTH CERTIFICATE
OF
COLORADO CITY

This is to certify that this 6th day of Oct. in the year of our lord 1963 and in the 87th year of the sovereign state of Colorado was born

COLORADO CITY

in the valley of Greenhorn, county of Pueblo

Governor of Colorado

Attest

Secretary of State

IN THE PRESENCE OF

The attractive, great grand daughters of Ceran St. Vrain, Gloria St. Vrain (top) and Julie St. Vrain (side), hold the huge birth certificate for Colorado City, celebrated on October 6 of 1963.

(Courtesy of Pueblo Regional Library)

long with plenty of space for 2,000 spectators to sign the silly certificate. As the inception takes place, both mother Mendelsohn and his infant city are doing well at time of delivery. Witnesses to the birth are also doing quite well as they gorge their gullets with a free buffalo and beef barbecue. It is hoped some of the 8,000 guzzlers in attendance will feel content enough to belly up to the bar and buy a little lot, a large lot, or even a whole lot of lots.

Attending the genesis are two great grand daughters of Ceran St. Vrain, the first land owner of Greenhorn Valley. Miss Gloria St. Vrain is a teacher at Corwin Junior High School, and Miss Julie St. Vrain is a junior at Southern Colorado State College.

First Lady Mrs. John A. Love cuts the large, beautiful, multi-colored, birthday cake. The eight-by-eight-foot cake weighs 350-pounds and is designed as a replica of new C-City. As spectators eat the cake city, mighty Mendelsohn gives his captive audience a sales pitch:

"The need is to develop urban communities where man's relationship to nature is not lost, where even the middle and lower income families can go out and recreate themselves in surroundings close by. Developing this better way of life is our business."

The real business of CCDC is to bring people; sell them land; hope they build; then have their hindquarters taxed for all related services. After CCDC sells lots of land and banks the profits, the developers will create local boards to handle public services like water, sanitation, roads, recreation, library, police, and fire protection.

Homesites begin at $990 per lot with monthly payments as low as $17 per month. During the first year, building permits increase from #147 in 1962 upward to #463 in 1963.

A 14,000 square feet community center is planned for the north side of Lake Beckwith near the marina. The center is to provide business offices for sales, accounting, construction, and management. On behalf of the lot owners, there is to be a library, motel, restaurant, cocktail lounge, public lounge, reception area, and outdoor swimming pool. According to vice-president and general manager Norman Gross, the complex is to be finished by the spring of 1964. The center will not materialize.

The first water well at C-City is dug half a mile from Lake Beckwith by Hier & Price of Sedalia. It drops 850 feet deep and produces 150 gallons-per-minute. The water is channeled across grasslands into Lake

Beckwith which will be a backup water storage and supply for the community. A second well, also half mile away, is found to be a good producer. Geologists Peaker and Riess of California are hired to locate sites for a dozen more wells. They proclaim: *"...beneath Colorado City there is a constantly recharging lake that is capable of producing as much as 4 million gallons of water daily, about equal to the total amount of water used in Pueblo."* This will prove to be untrue.

The CCDC development includes some land overhanging the north wall of Graneros Gorge which drops 500 feet down to Graneros Creek. Although this spectacular gorge is only one mile east of I-25, it is not well-known because it is (for the most part) invisible from neighboring roads. Furthermore the gorgeous gorge is privately owned, and a casual stroll along the canyon creek is strictly forbidden by the owners. Trespassers tend to disturb the canyon cattle and deposit trifling trash. The most popular item left behind is an empty beer container with the words "*Irresponsible Juvenile*" written all over.

As the first year of city development draws to a close, mighty Mendelsohn describes himself as a modern pioneer and explains he is attempting to bring people closer to nature, recreation, and relaxation:

"We are preserving the trees, the hills, the natural values - all the things, plus the atmosphere, that always have been in this wonderful natural setting....Although we live in an age of jets and rockets, everybody is not trying to get to the moon. People haven't lost interest in walking, cycling, horseback riding, fishing, boating, golfing and the many other pleasures for relaxation where they can think about their relationship to the earth and sky, <u>and each other.</u>"

Most likely Mendelsohn wanted to say we can *"think about our relationship to the earth and sky, <u>and God;</u>"* but, of course, that would have been politically incorrect in modern secular society. If Nat had spoken the word *God* out loud, members of the American Liberties for Everyone would have taken him on a fast ride down the long legal road to Supreme Justice. Many law lovers believe exposing ourselves, especially the children, to Bible values like *The Ten Commandments* would be extremely dangerous. After all, since the nation has doubled and tripled the number of prisons in recent years, it makes no sense to allow our crime rate to drop any time soon. A drop in crime would put prison employees out of work, and they have their rights, but not as many rights as the criminals.

First Ten Years

1963: John Weeden arrives from Liberal, KS, in the fall of 1963 and begins building roads. By March of 1964, Weeden has laid out 20 miles of dirt road. The engineering of the first two developments (with 2,067 lots on 72 acres) is complete. Units One and Two are located to the east and northeast below Lake Beckwith around the golf course. Two more water wells have been created.

Construction on the first house begins in February by Clifford Sorrell Construction of Liberal, KS. Sorrell's all-electric house is built on Cuerno Verde Blvd. near the west end of the original golf course, called *West Course*. The house faces to the south and is built of stone and brick.

During April, a wide range of construction is taking place. Clifford Sorrell has finished his first house and is building a second. Treasure Chest Homes is in the process of putting up ten more homes. Dick Graham and Gene Spencer are piping water from the main wells to the first developments. San Isabel Electric is adding service lines as needed. Rye Telephone lays 30,000 feet of cable from Rye to C-City. Robert S. Sneddon and his C-City crews are creating a softball field, Hicklin Memorial Park, and Graneros Gorge Park. The softball field on the west side of Hicklin Memorial Park will open Memorial Day weekend. Clyde James, an eight-year resident of Rye, is hired as night security to guard all new construction and building materials. Even a utopian city has its parasitical prowlers of the day and ghastly ghouls of the night.

A small pro shop is established below Lake Beckwith near Little Taylor Fountain at the west end of the golf course. The nine hole course is re-numbered so play can begin and end at the pro shop, which will have a small cafe by late summer.

About this time Greenhorn Valley receives a prominent new resident, Robert O. Anderson, who is one of American's largest and wealthiest land owners. At age 47 Robert Anderson is worth $50 million in oil, uranium, cattle, and land. In New Mexico and Texas alone Anderson owns 1.1 million acres of land with 55,000 cattle, 25,000 sheep, and 500 horses. While his home base is Roswell, NM, he owns eight other homes, including one in Aspen, CO. Living in one single place is frightfully boring and a darn drag.

Ambitious Anderson purchases the Hatchet Cattle Co. for a mere million and a half dollars. The Hatchet Cattle Co. includes 95,000 acres of ranch land northeast of C-City. Hatchet was first settled by the Stanley family in the 1880's. In 1905 Hatchet was acquired by Pueblo cattlemen and bankers Mahlon T. Everhart, John A. Thatcher, and Mahlon D. Thatcher.

Hatchet Ranch has land on both sides of I-25, and it is located midway between the established City of Pueblo to the north and new C-City development to the south. If C-City grows to a population of 30,000-40,000 people as planners expect, Hatchet land will turn to gold. Most likely ambitious Anderson buys Hatchet because he pictures big bucks rolling off Hatchet into his deep pockets. Although Anderson has 50 million dollars in assets, it isn't really enough to be truly successful.

Speaking of big bucks, CCDC enhances Lake Beckwith with eight cycle-powered, pontoon scooters and several unsinkable, aluminum, row boats for both new residences and visitors. The scooters and boats are purchased in preparation for a special sales promotion.

In May of 1964, CCDC hosts a birthday party at Lake Beckwith marina for Mrs. Laura Williams Halsey. Laura Halsey is thought to be the oldest living native of Colorado. She was actually born 96 years earlier in a log cabin near Lake Beckwith. During the birthday celebration, Laura shares a log cabin cake with her younger, 88-year-old sister, Mrs. May McHarg. With friends and spectators on hand, Laura remembers:

"When I was a little girl I waded in this lake....in fact we used to walk over here to take our baths. We would wade out and dry in the sun; we didn't have any towels. The old log cabin is gone, but I guess 96 years is a long time to live, even for a log cabin."

Born in 1868, nine years after the Hicklins came to Greenhorn Valley, loving Laura is only six years old when John Frink, the father-in-law of Thomas Hicklin, is buried in the Hicklin family cemetery:

"He was bitten by a rattlesnake. As the snake slithered into a prairie dog hole, he grabbed its tail intending to snap its head off. He didn't know that rattlers keep their heads at the hole opening and pull their bodies in, so the fangs were there to sink into his hand as he reached for the tail....I guess I was at Mr. Hicklin's funeral, everybody went to the funerals, and everybody cried. We used to have some beautiful funerals. I was only six when he died...."

Mrs. Laura Williams Halsey, Miss Colorado City of 1964, poses with an unidentified Frontier person at left, and Mrs. and Mr. Ralph C. Taylor, executive vice-president of CCDC, at right.

(Courtesy of Pueblo Regional Library)

From the beginning of C-City development, Old Crow Village (where the Hicklins once lived) remains the center for businesses, building sites, and connecting roads. During the building of roads, the Hicklin family cemetery is *suddenly* found to be smack-dab in the *"roadway of progress."* CCDC announces the Hicklin family cemetery will be moved to a different location. Perhaps there are two or three laws against changing a roadway once it is plotted down on official drawing paper.

Amongst much hoopla, a few local residents scratch their heads and suspect moving the Hicklin graveyard is a publicity stunt to market the new development. Surely C-City developers would not stoop so low as to use the dead bodies of historical figures to promote land sales.

Back in the 1930s the Hicklin family cemetery had an iron fence standing guard, but it has since disappeared. As to who was actually buried in the cemetery, there is considerable disagreement. Frenchman Beaubois, who was shot and killed in the Hicklin kitchen, was said to be *"buried behind the Hicklin ranch house."* When Zan Hicklin passed away, the grave site behind the house became the official family cemetery.

Besides Mr. Hicklin and Beaubois, the skeletons of five other persons are discovered and moved off the hillside of old Crow Village to the new *Hicklin Memorial Park*.

All of the original graves are unmarked except the grave of Talman Hicklin, a brother of Zan. The remaining four graves are most likely those of Alex Jr., Zan's son who was shot and killed by a poacher; Thomas, another son who died several years after being shot; Thomas Hicklin's father-in-law, John Frink whose funeral Laura Williams attended; and twin daughters of Alexander Jr. who were buried together. Others believe Sara Jane Sears, the wife of pioneer George Sears; and Ed Tomer, a drifter who had taken ill and died at the Hicklin Ranch are among the bones.

When Zan Hicklin was on his death bed in February of 1874, he asked Estefana to bury him with a bottle of booze in each pocket so he could celebrate with old friends who had passed on before him. For a period of 90 years, friends and relatives assumed Estefana had complied with his final request, but no one knew for certain.

Laura Williams Halsey, who had attended Zan Hicklin's original funeral at age six, is once again attending Zan Hicklin's grave site. The 96-year old lady explains why she is attending his second funeral: *"I was there when they buried him. I wanted to be there when they dug him up; and if there had been any liquor there, I wanted some. Although, I always have been a temperate woman."*

More than 100 curious onlookers watch morticians from Rouse Funeral Home in Pueblo remove Zan Hicklin's remains. When lifted from the earth, Hicklin's old wooden coffin is badly decayed except for the copper handles which have turned green. Inside the coffin, small clusters of red hair, mustache, and beard are still visible on Zan's skull. It is soon discovered he had been buried in leather boots which are still in fair condition. One antique collector at the grave site is seen rubbing his chin and carefully eyeballing what is left of Zan.

Sad to say, when the remains of Mr. Hicklin are exhumed on May 26 of 1964, no booze is found in his pockets. Yet his final wish is ultimately granted when he is moved to another grave site. Before the casket is lowered into the earth, a bottle of Old Crow Whisky is carefully placed on Zan's bones by loving Laura Halsey. As destiny is being fulfilled, Laura proclaims, *"I always wondered if Mrs. Hicklin carried out his wish. Now I am glad to know that it has been done."*

The transplanting of legendary Zan Hicklin, and the fulfillment of his final request by the mature queen of C-City is carried by Associated Press, Central Press, United Press International, and most all TV and radio networks. Lowell Thomas, Paul Harvey, and other *"news"* commentators feature the story so not to be left out in the ratings. CCDC scores a large publicity victory by digging up a local legend and having the mature queen of C-City perform a whisky-bottle burial. No doubt about it, the booze burial was by far the most important national news of the day.

Hicklin Memorial Park was never developed into a park, and today Zan Hicklin's grave is just as forgotten as it was when California developers dug up the remains of Mr. Hicklin. A broken tombstone and a few pine trees highlight some sunken graves in a field of weeds just south of Valverde Road and east of the baseball field. Used and abused, the memorial of Alexander Hicklin is once again slipping into oblivion.

As C-City is taking shape, the memory of Kit Carson (pioneer, Indian Scout, and military commander) and Thomas T. Tobin (brother of Charles Autobees) returns to the Valley. Mrs. Attie Provenzano, great grand daughter of both Carson and Tobin, is one of the first persons to purchase property. Attie Provenzano plans to build an adobe studio, museum, and home in the area. As a result of Mrs. Attie's artistic talent and craft work, she is well-known throughout the West. However instead of trying to commercialize her art, Attie spends most of her time helping others *"slow down and have more fun out of life."* She believes persons of all ages should have at least two hobbies, the more unusual the better. As an

Mrs. Attie Provenzano, great grand daughter of Kit Carson and Thomas Tobin, was among the first to buy property in C-City and well-known for her dried apple heads. No doubt she was ahead of her time.

(Courtesy of Pueblo Regional Library)

example to all, Attie's specializes in creating life-like doll heads from withered apples. She shapes facial features onto the apple skin with her fingers, then works cold cream and facial powder into the skin. When it becomes soft and the wrinkles disappear, she adds raisins, figs, and mashed potatoes for frightful touches. The rotten apple heads are so realistic she is often accused of shrinking human heads. The question of shrinking human heads may never be answered, but some local potato heads have been caught shrinking their own headpieces by attaching withered noodles to the boob-tube for endless periods of time.

In August of 1964, C-City Post Office is officially launched into service by a few hundred citizens including the Boy Scouts of Rye. Once again 96-year-old Laura Williams Halsey of Pueblo is on hand. Loving Laura presents an oversized postcard to Postmaster McMartin. The card is to be the first piece of mail canceled at C-City, and it is addressed to President and Mrs. Lyndon B. Johnson. The message on the card tells about C-City development and invites the Johnsons to visit the first annual celebration coming up in October. The Johnsons, however, do not accept the invitation. Perhaps they missed the national news coverage on Zan's booze burial and the transplanting of his family cemetery.

During the official post office commencement, the wonderfully wise, white-haired queen of Colorado, Mrs. Laura Halsey, addresses the ceremonial audience as follows:

"I am glad to be here because I am looking my best....I was born in this valley (Greenhorn) 96 years ago and I have lived every day of my life in Pueblo County except six years when I taught school in Huerfano County....I think it is beautiful and I love every foot of this country - and I love every one of you people."

Loving Laura is hereby designated the first *"Miss Colorado City."* In appreciation of the honor, Laura presents mighty Mendelsohn (president of CCDC and founder of C-City) with a painting titled *Mount of the Holy Cross*.

Laura had received the painted picture at her wedding 74 years earlier. The painting had been created by the 14-year-old son of a local Methodist minister. The art piece portrays a stream of water winding along rocky shorelines in magnificent mountains where one unusual tree stands tall in the upper right quarter. Laura requests the painting be hung in the new post office so all who come and go can enjoy this wonderful work of art. The audience gives Laura a standing ovation.

Laura Williams Halsey presents her *Mount of the Holy Cross* painting to Nat K. Mendelsohn, president of CCDC and developer of Colorado City.

(Courtesy of Pueblo Regional Library)

Laura's parents, Mr. and Mrs. John Williams, come to Colorado from Joplin, MO, on an oxen-drawn wagon in 1858, ten years before Laura's birth. The Williams drop anchor near Fort Garland and later move to the upper Huerfano Valley. The constant threat of Indians forces them to seek safety among the nearby settlers of Greenhorn Creek.

Loving Laura is born (1868) in a simple, Greenhorn cabin with an earth floor and a dirt roof. Her father establishes the first sawmill in Greenhorn Valley. Laura's mother works as a traveling seamstress. She has the only sewing machine, cook stove, and Holy Bible in the Valley:

"Mother made dresses and wove rugs. We moved in with the families while mother sewed for them. It wasn't much trouble to move, because we didn't have much. We had the only cook stove, sewing machine and Holy Bible in the Valley. We just loaded them into the wagon with our bedding, clothes and utensils....In the summer, when anyone killed a deer he would divide with the neighbors so it would not spoil. People don't do those things anymore - they seem to be getting selfish....

"We always opened school with prayer....I taught the children Gospel songs. Long after those children were grown they told me they went around their homes singing those songs and it meant so much to them. Maybe our new President will let them teach the Bible in schools again."

As a young school teacher, loving Laura brought stability and joy to her students with prayer, Bible values, and gospel song. If Laura were teaching Bible values and gospel songs in the classroom today, she would be severely reprimanded; most likely fired from her teaching position; and possibly banned for life from teaching children. Bible values and morals have been carefully removed from government, schools, and employment.

During the first year of operation, C-City post office processes 51,904 pieces of mail. Postmaster Kenneth D. Barrett reports 31,862 pieces of outgoing mail and 20,042 pieces of incoming mail.

The newly born *Chatauqua* program is sponsored by Rye community and features open air programs of music on summer evenings.

In September Ralph C. Taylor is promoted from executive to vice-president of CCDC by company directors visiting from California and New York. In addition to public relations, Ralph's new responsibilities include assisting president Mendelsohn with planning and development.

On October 3, 1964, while C-City celebrates a second year birthday party, the Stampede Cub Rodeo is held in conjunction with the Rye

Aspencade, which celebrates tree leaves turning brilliant gold in the fall.

In late October a large stone gazebo is erected on the north rim of Graneros Gorge, five hundred feet above Graneros Creek. The gazebo is designed to serve as viewing point, picnic area, and activity shelter. It is dedicated to the memory of Jack O'Sullivan who died a few months earlier. Jack O'Sullivan was vice-president in charge of construction for the new city. One of his last projects was to design the gazebo which is part of a 45 acre development (*Graneros Grove Public Park*) just east of Interstate 25 and the Graneros Gorge Exit.

The Colorado Department of Highways records a whopping 4,450 vehicles (on average) every 24 hours. By early November the Department of Highways has straightened, widened, and paved Hwy-165 between the C-City exit at I-25 and the main entrance to C-City development. During the next few months, Hwy-165 will be paved from the main entrance of C-City five miles up the hill to Rye Village.

1965: According to mighty Mendelsohn, most of the 2,067 home sites in the first three village units are either sold or under contract. Plans are being made so four more villages will to be ready by summer for the CCDC's next major sales promotion.

In March the Mendelsohn corporation deeds 123.5 acres of golf course; 72.0 acres of Lake Beckwith; 52.5 acres set aside for school sites and parks; all wells, water mains, and the entire water distribution system including all of the historic Hicklin irrigation ditches to the Metropolitan Water, Sanitation, and Recreation Districts.

During the same month at I-25 and Hwy-165 exit, Fountain Sand and Gravel Co. from Pueblo builds a concrete plant designed to produce 60 yards of concrete an hour. Southeast of the same interchange, M. C. Kirkland begins construction on a motel and 20-acre trailer park. The motel features 20 units, and the trailer park with bathhouse and office building has space for 50 mobile homes and travel trailers.

In April at Lake Beckwith, construction begins on a marina with sales office. The multi-use building with glass-enclosed corridor is to become a recreation center and assembly hall for local residents.

Governor John Love approves 1.4 million dollars to widen U.S. Hwy 85-87 into four lanes from old Crow Junction to Apache City in Huerfano County eight miles south . The name *Apache City* comes from a local creek where Luisa Brown made her legendary escape from Apaches. In 1854 a Mexican trader from Culebra (known as San Luis) was killed on the creek by Ute Indians. *Apache Creek* first appeared on maps in 1879, and the location had a post office. By 1897 the name changed to *Apache Station*. In time the settlement became *Apache Flats,* then *Apache City.* Farms in the area grew beans, corn, and wheat. Like many small towns of Greenhorn Valley, the schoolhouse served as a center for PTA, church, dance, and club meetings. *"The high school burned in 1942, and what was left of Apache burned to the ground in 1986."* Apache City was never incorporated as a town, much less a city.

In July of 1965, $700,000 in water district bonds are issued, and highway workmen are finishing the new interchange at old Crow Junction. The new junction is designated *Colorado City & Rye Interchange.* Traveling west from the Interchange, Hwy-165 serves C-City, Rye, Lake Isabel, and much of the San Isabel National Forest.

Arriving from the Broadmoor in Colorado Springs, Jacob A. Emrich becomes club manager and resident pro to the C-City Golf Club. Jacob Emrich is known on the pro circuit both nationally and in Europe. Refreshments are served daily at the clubhouse which will someday become a Community Center with Library for the community.

While new executive vice-president of CCDC, Ralph C. Taylor, is vacationing in Hawaii, *Little Taylor Park* is constructed below Lake Beckwith to the northeast. Construction superintendent Robert White and his workmen employ forty tons of native moss rock to erect a waterfall monument in honor of rainbow Ralph. Supplied by a portion of the Hicklin Irrigation Ditch, water cascades down the moss rock monument into a circular foundation pool. The water pool is surrounded by walkways, water ponds, falls, and little rapids. The small stream rejoins the main Hicklin Irrigation Ditch and flows east through the golf course.

Three miles to the southeast of Taylor Park on a hilltop between Greenhorn and Graneros creeks, ground is broken for an electronics business owned and operated by Claude M. Hathaway. Claude Hathaway's Engineering Laboratory is the first business constructed in the official *Industrial Park* located west of Graneros Gorge exit off I-25.

Claude Hathaway has received many national and international awards, including General Electric's prize for outstanding ability and the prestigious *Coffin Award.* Although there is considerable speculation about the Coffin Award, it is generally believed Claude received the award for his battery-operated, burial box, which is designed to keep secular corpses from contaminating good ground water.

Creative Claude opens his laboratories October 25 of 1965 with 24 employees, anticipating another 110 workers as soon as his electronic inventions swell in popularity. Two products produced in Claude's *"Agritronics unit"* are as follows:

"...an optical comparator that projected images of small parts on a screen and made possible accurate measurements to within ten thousandths of an inch. [and] The autonator was a device attached to motor vehicles that converted DC to AC current, making possible use of ordinary power tools and welders...."

C-City's third anniversary is celebrated on October 2. Saddle clubs from around the State come to town and join the Rye Aspencade for a happy horse ride in the mountains. Aspencade is a local tradition of viewing the aspen trees as they turn from green to glittering gold.

Near the end of the year, Mr. and Mrs. Holland Duell Jr. complete their studio and guest house designed with Spanish architecture.

1966: Colorado City Development Co. opens one sales office in Pueblo, a second office in Chicago, and a third is being planned for Wichita, KS. Groups of potential buyers from Pueblo, Colorado Springs, and Denver arrive on chartered buses every weekend. Land speculators from the Chicago area fly into Colorado two or three times a month. Jayhawkers from Kansas are soon to arrive via motor coach. Marketing is in high gear and on a serious roll. Or is it a jelly roll?

C-City now has a resident population of 59 adults and 36 children. Those children of school age are transported to Rye schools in buses from District 70 of Pueblo County.

As guests of CCDC, new property owners can play the golf course and fish the lake free of charge. On the other hand, non-property owners from outside the Metropolitan Recreation District play golf for $2.00 during the week and $2.50 on weekends and holidays. While locals can fish free, non-property owners fish for 50 cents per adult and 25 cents per child, age 12 and under. To keep fisher-persons from having too much fun in one single day, a limit of 15 fish per person is imposed by the Metro Recreation District. Fisher-persons must take, *"no more than two trout, two bass, ten blue gill, ten perch, and ten catfish"* - which adds up to 34 fish. There is something fishy about this math.

In spring of 1966 several miles of horse trails (some lined with trees) are being created to accommodate dozens of horse students arriving

Horse trail and pedestrian path between rows of trees at Colorado City

(Courtesy of Pueblo Regional Library)

at the Duell-Stewart training school. The *horse farm*, as it was called, is considered to be among the finest in the West. It has complete facilities for breeding, foaling, training, and special care for pampered, spoiled-brat horses. The thoroughbred farm produces a handful of speedy steeds that carry C-City to the circle of winners. Some of the hot horses are named *Zip Pocket* (holder of three world records); *Rowdy Fleet* (owned by Holland Duell); *Good Investment; Dun Dancer; Colorado City* (also owned by Holland Duell); and *Barbara Coma* (sometimes called *Barbacoma*.)

Near to the Duell-Stewart training grounds, Louise Ridenour and the Grabers (Morris and Betty) establish the town's first automotive service station at Bent Brothers Dr. and Hwy-165. The Ridenour-Graber Enco Automotive Service Center includes a hardware and cafe. Later on, Graber and Sons will operate a Skelly Service Station at the same location.

On August 20th a crowd of 500 persons inaugurate the new Fire Station, also at Bent Brothers Dr. and Hwy-165. Behind its cornerstone, the Grand Lodge of Colorado Masons places a metal box containing current copies of three newspapers and information on the birth of C-City.

While I-25 is being completed on the west edge of town, the Water and Sanitation District cleans out the main Hicklin Irrigation Ditch channeling Greenhorn Creek water to Lake Beckwith and the golf course.

1967: In January home construction begins on Alpine Village overlooking Lake Beckwith from the foothills of Table Mountain. C-City's eighth subdivision includes 316 building sites between the lake and today's water tank to the west. As a recreational housing area on prime land above the lake, Alpine is designated for summer cottages. After all, permanent residents would hardly want to gaze down on majestic water when they can build elsewhere and study the earth beneath their feet.

Alpine Village features *Alpine, Chalet,* and *Ranch* designs. The Alpine is an A-frame cottage with two-bedrooms, one-bath, and a loft. The Chalet has three dormers facing forward like a Swiss Chalet, a two-car garage on the right side, a master bedroom on the left, and a setback entry up the middle. The Ranch is a two-bedroom, one-car garage rancher with three optional floor plans. Bedrooms, garages, and dens can be added (unit by unit) to suit the needs of the buyer. Butkovich Construction Co. is the builder for these modular-type cabins in Alpine Village.

On January 22 of 1967 a new $600,000, junior-senior high school is dedicated by administrators of School District #70 in Pueblo County. The schoolhouse is large enough to serve the children of both C-City and Rye.

Breaking of ground for the Enco Service Center of Ridenour and Graber at Old Crow Village. Nat Mendelsohn and Holland Duell are in attendance. Silos in upper left corner are no longer standing.

(Courtesy of Pueblo Regional Library)

MERBISC (Most Extraordinary Recreation Bargain In Southern Colorado) is invented from the combined efforts of good old CCDC and the Metropolitan Recreation District, which was organized three years earlier by property owners. MERBISC is an institution designed to provide property owners with luxurious living at bargain-basement prices. In order to do this, the MERBISC organization takes over the operation of all recreational facilities in C-City - including the Golf Course; Lake Beckwith; 14-acre Rodeo Park (with lights and riding trails); campground (with pavilion and restrooms); 62-acre Greenhorn Meadows Park (with baseball fields, outdoor ice skating rink, and picnic areas); and a large stone Gazebo in Graneros Gorge Park above Graneros Gorge.

MERBISC promises local property owners the full use of all the recreational facilities for a ten-year-period at the measly membership cost of $100. Non-property owners (voteless visitors) can use the very same facilities for ten years paying a much larger fee of $500. In today's *Rights Revolution*, law lovers would be well on their way to executing a large, laborious lawsuit against this dastardly discrimination.

MERBISC promises to expand existing facilities so residents and visitors alike can have bigger, better, happier, healthier holidays. There will be a new golf course clubhouse, a junior Olympic-size swimming pool, and a playground with a multi-use concrete slab. The concrete slab will allow all ages to experience a solid footing. During February of the new year, $250,000 bonds will be issued by C-City Metropolitan Recreation District for swimming pool, playgrounds, and parks.

While MERBISC plans for the future, the old Crow Village (at Bent Brothers Blvd. & Hwy-165) is being recreated as a modern pueblo-like complex. As the modern Pueblo is erected, a tired old ranch barn, three silos, and Mercantile Building with hotel will be moved or knocked down. Crow Village has been a business center in Greenhorn Valley for more than a century, and it will continue to exist as a trade center.

The new commercial complex is to be used for the CCDC administration, Duell-Stewart headquarters, Metro Recreation District offices, Water and Sanitation shop, a laundry/dry cleaning business, a barber/beauty shop, and a post office.

By April of 1967, other services surround the commercial complex. Among them are a Fire Station, a telephone building, and the Enco Service Station with fast food Drive-In. Sometimes a small, rural community (with calm life style) needs some fast food to plunge it back into the handsome hubbub of big-city, fast-lane reality.

As fall arrives, three little islands and a 200-feet-long peninsula are created on the west side of Lake Beckwith. The dirt work is performed by large earth-moving equipment. Heavy winter snows fill the lake and bring water up to the Marina.

1968: While San Isabel Electric Association completes a $450,000 substation on the north side of town (near today's middle school), John King builds a $130,000 *Stuckey's* gas station and cafe at the C-City & Rye Interchange off I-25.

Water from the historic Hicklin Ditch is cascading through the stone monument at Little Taylor Park below the lake. A quarter mile east of Taylor Park, MERBISC opens its new swimming pool facility.

The Commercial Plaza is now open for business. It includes apartments, a telephone company, fire department, CCDC offices and shops, Metro office, Water and Sanitation shop, post office, laundry and dry cleaning, notions, and headquarters for the Theresians of American.

The Theresians of America was founded in 1961. Seven years later the organization moves its national headquarters from the sizable City of Pueblo to the small community of C-City. It claims 6,000 members with 150 groups in 30 states. Theresians are *"women dedicated to the Sisterhood Vocation Apostolate,...to develop high ideals and to contribute to the natural and supernatural needs of people."* With a purpose of developing *"high ideals,"* the focus must have been on the Heavenly Father, the Great Physician, and the Principal Provider of healthy human services.

In addition to local C-City's land sales, Colorado City Development Co. claims to have sales offices in Pueblo, Colorado Springs, Denver, Dallas, Honolulu, Hinsdale, Norridge, and Oaklawn. Also Europe, Hong Kong, and the Philippine Islands. From his massive promotional network, mighty Mendelsohn hopes his utopian city will soon become well-dotted with 10,000 happy homes filled with 35,000 taxpaying residences.

On September 27 C-City's anniversary is designated *Greenhorn Rendezvous*. The birthday party is again held in conjunction with Rye's annual Aspencade celebration including three days of contests, prizes, and public tours into the mountains for viewing the golden aspen.

At the end of the year, postmistress Mrs. Bert Houston reports 37,844 pieces of outgoing mail; 68,015 pieces of incoming; and $4,647 in postage sales. There is no mention of the increase in cost of postage.

Looking at the weather records of Howard Billups, Greenhorn Valley receives 16.88 inches of precipitation during 1968, which is significantly more than neighboring areas. Most likely the Wet Mountains have always blessed the Greenhorn Valley with abundant amounts of rain and snow.

From the life-giving mountain moisture, Lions appear at dusk and assemble into a Lions Club for the betterment of the community.

1969: On April 17 the mighty Mendelsohn companies (CCDC) merge with Great Western United (or GWU), 358th largest industrial corporation in the U.S. Among the various companies of Great Western United based in Denver are GW Cities (builder of U.S. cities); the GW Sugar Co. (largest producer of U.S. beet sugar); GW Restaurant Co. (The Prime Time Restaurants); Shakey's Pizza (with 344 parlors in 39 states); GW Foods Co.; GW United Research and Development Center; Colorado Milling & Elevator Co.; Moore's Lime Co.; and Emerald Christmas Tree Co.

The leader of Great Western United is a young man by the name of William M. White Jr. who promises GWU will *"expand and expedite projects in C-City."* Wonderful William White announces CCDC will continue to operate under president Mendelsohn and his current executives.

Mighty Mendelsohn in response to 50 New York analysts declares he will eventually develop cities in all of the Western States including Hawaii. Although he does not say so at the time, Mendelsohn is thinking about the distant moon as a possible city site.

After holler and hoopla, the Water and Sanitation District completes $330,000 in sewer and water lines, budgeting an additional $374,165 for line extensions in 1970. The District establishes a sewage treatment plant near I-25 on the north side of Greenhorn Creek. From this low point, the sewer lines are run upstream to the Commercial Plaza and surrounding apartments. From the apartment complex sewer lines are extended farther west into established residential villages.

Not far from the treatment facility, *Applewood Mobile Home Estates* plans the necessary utilities, lovely landscaping, swimming pool, play area, barbecue pits, and cabanas. The name *Applewood* comes from 1,200 apple trees brought from the tree farm of Mr. and Mrs. Molello and planted in the mobile home park. The Molellos live near Penrose, CO.

The Metro Recreation District completes $60,000 in recreational facilities. The passing of a $250,000 bond issue enables Metro to complete the MERBISC building and swimming pool. The MERBISC building is composed of two wings. One wing contains a large meeting hall for social gatherings. The other is a golfer wing with pro shop, offices, locker rooms, restrooms, showers, and snack bar. Improvements at the

William M. White Jr.
President of Great Western Cities
and Western United Corporation

Nat K. Mendelsohn
Vice-president of GWC and WUC
after merger of CCDC and GWU

(Courtesy of Pueblo Regional Library)

swimming pool include a wading pool, playground, and multi-purpose slab of cement. Metro plans another $50,000 in projects for the coming year.

The $104,200 Commercial Plaza continues to expand with Alpine Liquors, Ester Swift's Beauty Parlor, Hillenbrand's Grocery Market, Sam Jones' Insurance Agency, Vince's Barber Shop, and more office space.

Two miles southeast of the Plaza at the Industrial Park, a large structure is added to creative Claude's Engineering Laboratories. Nearby a sizable warehouse and shop building are under construction.

With 30 miles of road linking units together, lots in 23 villages are plotted, recorded, and available for sale. In September of 1969, Knollwood Village has a grand opening. The public is invited to see the model homes and register for $7,500 in prizes. After registering for prizes and viewing the models, the public is invited for golfing, boating, fishing, and swimming - not to mention buying, buying, and buying some more.

Knollwood is located on a hill immediately southwest of Lake Beckwith and has 115 lots in the hillside village. New homes including the lot are selling from $19,450 to $29,800. Created by Eugene Vincent Conroy and Associates, four home designs are available: the *Yodeler, Retreat, Lakeview,* and *Hideaway.* Conroy's all-electric kitchens please the San Isabel Electric Association to the point of bestowing their electrophilic *"Ben Franklin Award."* Useful Eugene (who has designed 50,000 homes in Calif., Colo., N.M. and Nev.) not only designed Knollwood Village, but Alpine Village, the MERBISC Center, and the Commercial Plaza.

At the Commercial Plaza, the historical Mercantile Building with cafe and service station are removed making way for bigger, better, newer facilities. The Mercantile building itself is moved to the golf course maintenance area and used as a CCDC storage unit.

To help kill the unique history of Greenhorn Valley, civic groups celebrate the death of Old Crow Junction and the birth of a New Holiday Inn. Participating in the death of Crow are the Chamber of Commerce, Lions Club, a former Pueblo County commissioner, and the national director of Theresians. On hand to observe the burial of Crow are two grandchildren of Calvin William Goss. Goss established Crow Post Office near Crow Junction in the 1880's. Since Old Crow Junction is named after Calvin Goss's friend and Postmaster from Pueblo, Mr. Matthew Crow, it makes pretty silly sense to bury a large black bird in memory of Matthew Crow. *"During a mock funeral where a large cut out black bird was laid out in a pine box and buried in a shallow grave, Crow Junction of I-25 became the new Colorado City Interchange."* What are Calvin Goss's two grandchildren thinking about during the burial of this fake bird?

To the west of black bird burial, the Duell-Stewart Thoroughbred Farm is actively training horses. Connie Stewart is the horse trainer; Albert Duell is office manager; and Edward Viulla looks after the farm facilities. Their best horses will win on tracks at Santa Anita in CA; Turf Paradise in Phoenix, AZ; Centennial Track in Littleton, CO; and Arlington, Hawthorne, and Sportsman tracks around Chicago.

By the end of the year, the town has two large water reservoirs. A third water tank is to be set above Alpine Village. C-City has a thirsty population of 207. There are 85 adults and 122 children school age or younger. Most of the new residents are from out-of-state areas.

Drifting up Hwy-165 just beyond Lake Isabel, James R. Bishop and his family members lay the first stones for their Bishop Castle.

1970: In January commercial wood worker Lew Allee and wife Jane arrive from Hutchinson, KS. Lew studies real estate and begins selling home sites for C-City Realty Company. Within ten years Lew will have his own *Concept 80 Realty*. He will become well-known in the community.

In February Rye Fire Protection purchases a new fire truck for $45,000 and stations it with two other fire fighting vehicles and a four-wheel-drive rescue unit on the west side of Commercial Plaza. Volunteer firemen install the truck hoses, nozzles, and required accessories.

Industrial Park expands with two more businesses. Moorelite Concrete Co. produces premix concrete and concrete products including concrete septic tanks and water meter boxes. Maxwell Haus begins an operation making aluminum caps and camper tops for pickup trucks. Maxwell has worked 23 years for Fisher Body as a tool designer, and his son, John, assists him in the new business located in the old Palisades Lumber Building, a quarter mile west of Hathaway.

By spring the number of new businesses exceeds the number of ground level compartments at Commercial Plaza. In total, 237 persons are reported to be employed at C-City, many commuting from nearby Rye, Walsenburg, Pueblo, and Colorado Springs. A small number of roadrunners come from far away places like La Junta, Denver, and Boulder.

A second 62-passenger school bus is purchased by School District #70 to transport children to and from Rye educational facilities, K-12. Overcrowding at the Rye schools is becoming a problem.

In August the town scores two first places. The First Baptist Church establishes a congregation, and Robert Moore opens Conoco's first service station in the State of Colorado.

When CCDC and associates merge with GWU of Denver and associates, they come up with three low priced, vacation home designs to stimulate house construction. The models are *Highland, Scenic,* and *Leisure,* priced from $11,250 to $12,400 including a small lot.

1971: In January CCDC/GWU begins an FHA subdivision near C-City Junction at I-25. Sixty-eight homes are being planned each with a curb, gutter, sidewalk, and paving. One can have three or four bedrooms, single or double car garages, and one or two baths. The homes are priced from $19,600 to $22,100. This community will become known as *The Village.*

By February the Industrial Park has a variety of businesses including construction, distribution, electronics, manufacture, storage, painting, plumbing and heating. Ray Askew of Rocky Ford has recently arrived with his three sons and a small fleet of trucks for the plumbing and heating.

For several months Pastor and Mrs. Clyde Jones have been conducting church services in their home. A building site on the north side of Hwy-165 and a quarter mile east of Commercial Center Plaza is donated by CCDC/GWU. A church building is needed, and congregation members rise to the occasion. In February ground is broken for the beginning of what will become Colorado City Community Church. The non-denominational Community Church will be built by its members and dedicated in September of 1972. The parking area provides space for 75 automobiles; the sanctuary provides seating for 175 persons. Pastor and Mrs. Clyde Jones both graduated from Bible College in St. Paul, MN. They have previously ministered for 16 years in Kansas, Wisconsin, and South Africa.

Immediately to the east of C-City Community Church, *Hollydot Park* is being planned on a 600 acre estate for high income rollers. The name *Hollydot* combines the names of Mr. *Holly* and Mrs. *Dot* Duell. This 15-million-dollar project is being created on both sides of Hwy-165. On the north side, the plans show an administration building, a private golf course with club house, and 55 building sites from half an acre to an acre with all underground utilities. The Administration Building is designed as a 6,200-square-foot structure backing up to Duell Lake, which is more like a pond. It faces the new golf course, of course. On the south side, the plans show 182 homesites starting at a modest sum of $15,000 per lot. Also 320 condominiums are available from $38,000 to 68,000 per unit. They will be divided into seven complexes. To keep high income folks happy, there will be a four-acre, private swim & tennis club; a horse park;

four ponds; picnic areas; nature trails; and a partridge-in-a-pear-tree. The swim & tennis club is scheduled to open in the spring of 1973.

Two of four Duell children, Albert and Holland III, play important roles in marketing Hollydot Park. The selling of Hollydot is handled by Ken Richardson and Albert C. Duell. Ken is the broker. Albert is treasurer and vice-president of Hollydot Park Co. from 1970-1975. Albert's name is given to the agency,*"Ab" Duell Realty, Inc.* Brother Holland Duell #3 is a Hollydot board member along with Ronald Higgins and Don Henry. Holland *"Chub"* III will spend 32 years of his life learning to rope at Hollydot Turf Club. Chub will become one of the better rodeo calf ropers in the nation.

While Hollydot Park is in the planning stage, CCDC/GWU donates two acres to the First Baptist Church. In April ground is broken for a church building located northeast of Lake Beckwith at the corner of Kaneache and Cuerno Verde Blvd. The two-story structure is made of masonry, 32 by 70 feet, sided with moss rock veneer, and windowed with stained glass. The early work is destroyed by a strong gust of wind blasting *"the partially constructed two-story walls collapsing them and breaking $1,300 worth of windows."* Construction continues, and first services will be held in November. Reverend Irven Johnson and his family arrive to succeed Dr. Floyd Crenshaw, the head of Southern Colorado State College Department of Philosophy, who ministers during the early months.

The CCDC/GWU land development undergoes a change in leadership. Richard L. Maher of Littleton, CO, is appointed vice-president and project manager by chairman and president of Great Western Cities. GWC is the *"community development"* subsidiary of Great Western United (GWU.)

On July 24 C-City has a birthday party known as *Rendezvous Days*. The annual party is three months earlier than normal and includes a fast-draw competition. Good gunslingers need to draw fast and kill first.

In August a $600,000 Holiday Inn is ready for public service. Erected on the southwest corner of C-City and Rye Interchange, Holiday Inn has two levels, 60 rooms, a restaurant, outside gardens, and swimming pool. Holiday begins with 51 employees serving 60 motel rooms furnished with the latest in *"color televisions!"* The Inn's La Fiesta Restaurant and El Palacio Lounge feature Mediterranean decor. The motel itself is southwestern in design. The Inn and cafe are convenient for prospective buyers who arrive each week from out of town. Second to the C-City development operation, Holiday Inn is the largest employer in the area.

To the west of Holiday Inn, Applewood Estates is being composed of 251 mobile home sites ranging in size from 5,000 to 8,000 square feet.

The 83-acre plan designates 25 acres for recreational areas, green belts, and commercial facilities. One recreational area is complete and includes an outdoor swimming pool, playground for children, and picnic area for families. New arrivals can bring their own mobile home to the park or buy one from local dealers. So far, Applewood Estates has 41 residents.

Mr. and Mrs. Chester Aggen purchase the Graber Drive-In, double the size, and name it *The Bit*. Mrs. Aggen has served her city library in Morton Grove, IL, for 17 years as the head librarian.

In the fall Rye Schools are over-crowded with 190 C-City students. GWC is looking at options such as renting houses for classrooms, buying mobile units, or building its own facilities to lease School District #70.

C-City now has a population of 750 residents. Electric, gas, and telephone companies are keeping up with the growth. San Isabel Electric and Pueblo Gas & Fuel companies spend $150,000 during 1971. Rye Telephone Co. installs more than $150,000 in equipment and lines.

1972: A $30,000 air-supported bubble is placed over the Junior-Olympics-size, outdoor, swimming pool so residents can swim year-round. The dome is to be removed in summer for open-air swimming. Mother nature with her wild winds decides to remove the plastic bubble six weeks after it has been installed. There is no possibility for repair.

County Commissioners grant Gail K. Naumann zoning for a public airport east of I-25 near C-City Junction. Naumann estimates there will be five aircraft stationed at the airport and a monthly usage of 50 flights. The zoning is contested by residents of Applewood mobile home park. Moritz Kirkland, operator of the campground east of I-25, joins in the protest. All efforts are unsuccessful to stop the fast flying machines.

Construction begins on a new golf clubhouse between the West Course and Santa Fe Dr. The building is T-shape in design; has 3,700 square feet; costs $116,000, and will become a community center in time.

On July 22 and 23 of 1972, Rendezvous Days celebrate another anniversary with antique autos, magic show, melodrama, a rodeo, a street dance, and nationwide Fast Draw Championships.

By late summer a three million-gallon water tank is finished. The tank is 56 feet high, 90 feet in diameter, and costs $300,000. Water and Sanitation workers establish a labor union. Administrator E. O. Cady is fired from his leadership position by the board of directors.

The Duell-Stewart horse farm is becoming one of the best in the West. Race horses from across the country are receiving kind care and restful refuge at Hollydot Park during the off season. Holland Duell's own 7-year-old gelding named *Colorado City* has track earnings of $123,000.

Mr. Holland Duell Jr. is not only the owner of a horse named *Colorado City*, but he is the true father of Colorado City. How did this come about? At the tender age of seven, Holly begins serious music studies. Upon graduating from Hotchkiss Prep School, Holly attends the prestigious Julliard School of Music in New York and Switzerland. As a violin soloist, he joins a string quartet and plays with Benny Goodman. After touring France and Italy as a violin virtuoso, Holly in 1934 *"...trades in his violin for cowboy boots and goes to work on a dude ranch in Birney, Montana."* Here he meets and marries Dorothy Curry. Following a brief insurance career back East, Holly and Dot buy a 2,500 acre ranch in Vermejo River Valley, NM. Here they breed commercial cattle and raise children: Dorothy, Ab, Susan, and Chub. Holly campaigns for a senate seat but is defeated in the Roosevelt landslide of 1940. Seven years later the Duells move their cattle business to Greenhorn Valley. During 15 years in the Valley, the Duells have improved Lake Beckwith, created a nine-hole golf course, and joined wallets with California developers. Together they plan a dream village for horse lovers, golfers, and fisher-persons. Within this utopian community Holly and Dot create a personal paradise by combining their first names into *Hollydot Park*. Without Holly and Dot there would not have been a new Colorado City built on the old Hicklin Ranch.

By the fall of 1972, Hollydot Park includes a new golf course, a Turf Club, an indoor swimming pool, outdoor tennis courts, 235 home sites (with a few new homes), four condominium sites, and three townhouses on the banks of Greenhorn Creek. Hollydot is rapidly becoming a pretty, private paradise. The executive-type estate has very strict regulations for building, landscaping, and property use. Uncommon, wealthy folk generally like having plenty of rules to distance themselves from the riffraff of common, low income folk.

The new private golf course spreads out east of the old public course and features two separate tee placements giving players an 18-hole round of golf. The course is nearly complete and scheduled to open in spring.

In addition to golf, Hollydot features a Turf Club for horse lovers. Finished in September, the $200,000, 185-acre, equestrian center is a private affair and open only to property owners. With an annual membership fee of $500, the Duells hope the Hollydot Turf Club will bring locals into owning and racing horses. Member facilities provide all necessary horse services for breeding, boarding, and breaking - including tack rooms, a veterinarian room with laboratory, a 20-stall horse barn, automatic horse walkers, and training rings. One training ring has an English-styled jumping course with judging stand at the infield.

Between Hollydot Park and I-25 on Hwy-165, Tri Enterprises, Inc. breaks ground for the *Golden Wheels Drive-in.* A 24 x 32 feet building is constructed with a drive-up window and a small dining area inside.

At the close of 1972, a complaint is registered with the Federal Trade Commission charging that CCDC/GWU, when advertising for real estate trainees, is actually trying to recruit prospective buyers for their Colorado City real estate. In a consent order GWU agrees to stop their alleged, deceptive, sales practices.

1973: For nearly a year C-City Chamber of Commerce has been planning a ten-year anniversary celebration. On June 23rd and 24th the organizers of Rendezvous Days sponsor a muzzle loaders contest, carnival, barbecue, and sailboat races at Lake Beckwith.

Shortly after Rendezvous Days, MERBISC members hold a grand opening for the Hollydot Golf Clubhouse. The Clubhouse has 41,000 square feet of space, a Spanish-styled entrance opening into a lounge, and a large club room with fireplace. The club room and pro shop are walled with large windows to the golf course. The private club includes locker rooms with saunas, dining facilities, snack area, game room, and booze bar.

As part of the grand celebration, visiting golf professional Patty Berg puts on a trick-shot exhibition. Pros and amateurs pair off for tournament play the following day. Resident golf professional, Dave Ruff, is preparing to manage the Hollydot Golf Course and Clubhouse.

During the summer, Metro Recreational District improves Greenhorn Meadows Park. The campground gets new showers and potty facilities. Additional picnic tables and tent spaces are planned.

Just east of the Park, *Commercial Center Plaza*, originally known as *Crow Village*, is renamed *Fountain Square of Colorado City,* Each name change brings more letters to a longer title. Perhaps the new five-word designation will stimulate longer business hours at the plaza.

C-City Lions Club, founded five years earlier, is composed of 35 area businessmen. Among their fund-raisers to serve the community, the Lions originate the publication of a local newspaper. *The Greenhorn Valley News* will change hands many times, but it will serve the region indefinitely.

The *Greenhorn Valley News* will be the primary source of information for the remainder of this epistle.

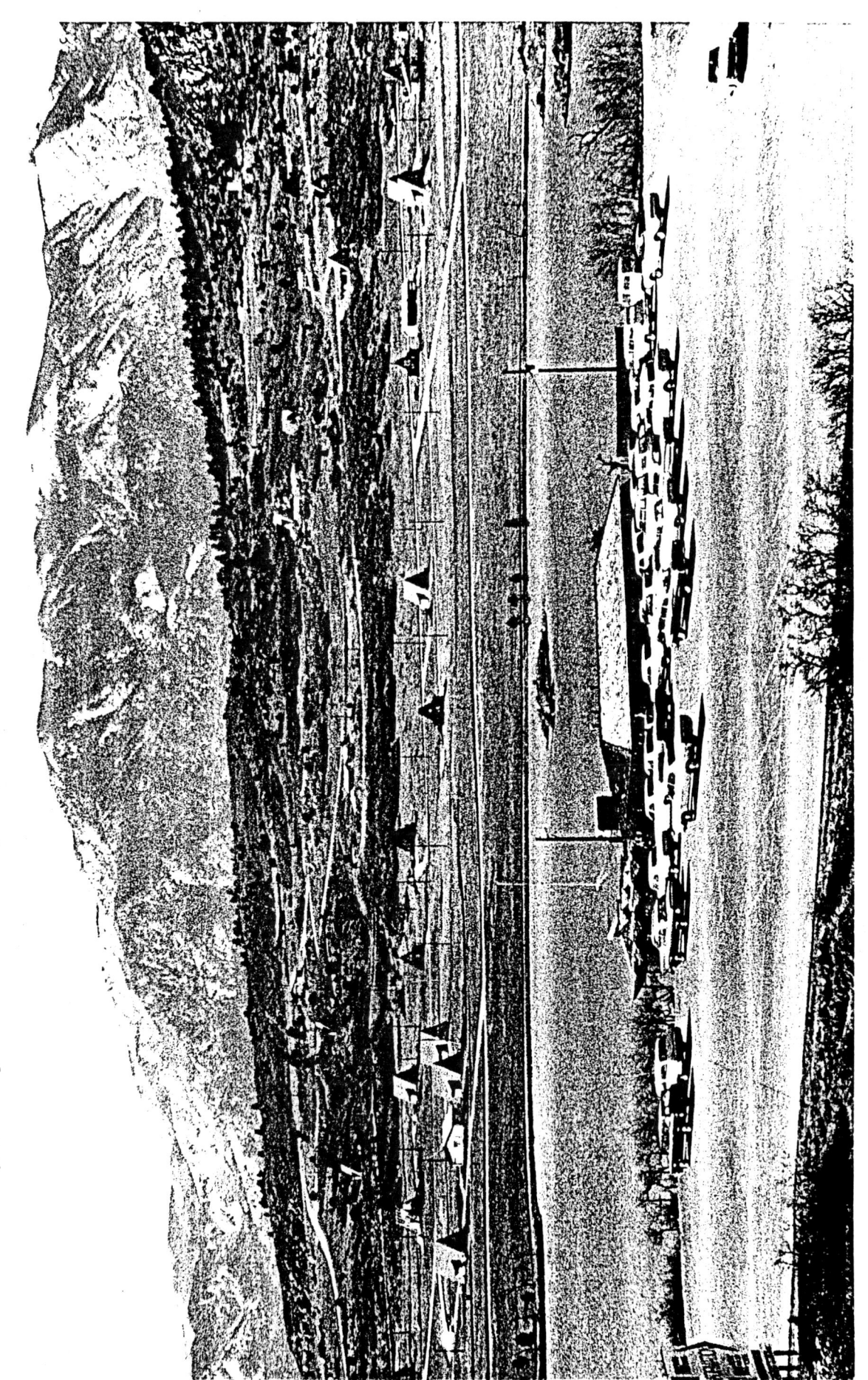

This photograph is taken from the northeast side of Lake Beckwith, looking across the marina parking lot southwest to the Wet Mountains. Taken in the late 1960s or early 1970s, the A-frame summer cottages in Alpine Village (across the lake) appear somewhat like an Indian camp.

(Courtesy of Pueblo Library District)

Not long after The *Greenhorn Valley News* is born, tables, chairs, and several hundred books are added to the MERBISC Center Library. More than a few citizens of the Valley remain indifferent to their televisions.

In October Greenhorn Valley Airport opens across from Holiday Inn, east of C-City Interchange. The 3,900-feet-long airstrip has been paved at the cost of $60,000. While the aircraft tie-downs are in place, charter services, flight instruction, and hanger rental are in the planning stage.

While the airport prepares for sky visitors, new apartments are completed on the north side of the newly-named *Fountain Square of Colorado City*. Condominiums are being constructed on the east side. Centerline Inc. is building with a southwestern look, red tile, and masonry walls. Centerline uses an innovative structural material known as *blockbond*. Some locals are convinced the material, blockbond, will bring the neighborhood closer together.

In 1973 the Metro Recreation District reports C-City Golf Course has accommodated 7,716 golfers. In addition to local MERBISC members (who play for free), the course generated a non-member income of $10,503 - with an operating cost of $33,147. The number of swimming pool visitors was 9,696, generating non-member income of $2,352 - with operating costs of $20,333. MERBISC Center activities attracted 13,603 persons, generating a non-member income of $1,228 - with operating costs of $19,255. Greenhorn Meadows Park had 53 large picnics and 676 happy campers, generating non-member fees of $1,644 - with operating costs of $7,531. Activities at Lake Beckwith lured 4,638 people, generating non-member income of only $125 - with operating costs of $2,548. What is wrong with this picture? MERBISC is providing great recreational facilities to many people while running rapidly in to the reek of red ink.

1974 to 1990

During the next 26 years at Colorado City; oodles of new services, manufactures, doctors, dealers, builders, brokers, and realtors arrive. Also cafes, clubs, churches, and celebrations show up in Greenhorn Valley. As many come, many go; and there is neither time nor space to tell all. What follows is a small number of odd, interesting, or vital events.

The small communities of *Applewood* and *The Village* just west of C-City Interchange report neighborhood events and good gossip in *The Greenhorn Valley News*.

Fountain Square of Colorado City is refered to by residents as simply *Fountain Square*. Most of the locals already know where they live.

By 1974 Hollydot Park is nearly finished, and the Metro swimming pool receives an all-weather cover. The number of C-City businesses has expanded to 65 with 247 employees full-time and part-time. Rye maintains 70 business operations with 280 workers.

In 1975 CCDC/GWC is instrumental in bringing DO-RAY from Chicago to C-City's Industrial Park. Started in 1916 by Sam Dover, the DO-RAY Lamp Company is one of the oldest automotive lighting businesses in the country. Sam Dover's son, David J. Dover, arrives with his father's business and creates a very positive influence on local growth by becoming the largest employer in Greenhorn Valley. With 120 workers DO-RAY manufactures vehicle lighting, engine heaters, and truck mirrors.

Holiday Inn becomes the *Greenhorn Inn of Colorado City.* Before long the inn will become *Best Western,* a franchise with 1,300 motels.

In June of 1975 contractors start building a Middle School. It will be dedicated for school use in the fall of 1976.

While the new school goes up, CCDC/GWC undergoes various changes in ownership and management. Bruce Ducker is named president of GWC, The parent company (GWU of Denver) is acquired by Nelson Bunker Hunt and William Herbert Hunt of Dallas. Bill Botts is appointed president of GWC. CCDC announces the resignations of its Resident Project Manager and its Manager of Construction and Maintenance. Larry Knopf takes over as Project Manager but is soon transferred to another GWC community project in California. These rapid changes will have an unsettling effect on the future development of C-City.

A non-profit research organization named *Inform* publishes a book entitled *Promised Lands*. The critical publication:

"...praises the site location of Colorado City as being very well suited for such a development. The report questions the availability of adequate water supply, the availability of adequate capital and the lack of coherent and continuous planning."

On January 10 of 1977, Brian Haskins, executive vice-president of GWC (parent company of CCDC) addresses the criticisms of *Promised Lands* at a local Lions Club meeting. There are 58 residents in attendance:

"Mr. Haskins told his audience that Great Western Cities has been

involved in reconstruction of its debt and has reached an agreement in principal with a great number of banks led by a major New York bank and the Company is currently in the process in negotiation terms....Mr. Haskins stated that the planning for Colorado City had, in the past, lacked continuity because of changes in ownership and management....In the future, the company will place emphasis on community development and property management, rather than on land sales."

Pleasant J. Craver Middle School is dedicated in April of 1977. Mr. Pleasant J. Craver began teaching at Rye schools in 1951. Four years later he was principal and remained 18 years until 1973. For the next three years, until his death in July of 1976, he served as elementary and middle school principals. Mr. Craver's wife and teacher at the middle school, Mrs. "Pete" Craver, plays an important part in the Middle School dedication.

While the new Middle School built on Crow Cut-Off Rd. in C-City moves forward, the town itself continues to have expansion problems. Jack Price, who will later become chairman of C-City Metro, blames the Metro District and Pueblo County for poor management:

"Originally, the subdivision of Colorado City was set up to include the property that drained into the Greenhorn Valley, which is essentially the core area. A bad decision by the district and county to allow the premature expansion of the size of the subdivision, before the subdivision was sold out, resulted in an excess of 2,200 lots in the core area and 1,500 lots out of the core. A water and sewer availability contract is sold with each lot purchased to defray the cost of running lines to the lots. However, running the water and sewer lines past unsold lots created a burden to the district of approximately $5 million."

The CCDC/GWC companies are slow in following through on their promises, and peripheral lot owners (along with local residents and new business operators) become rather angry. The Colorado Real Estate Commission is invited to look into alleged wrongful practices. Also Pueblo County Commissioners debate whether to spend $40,000 for their District Attorney to investigate possible wrong-doings. Seven of the Commissioners are in favor of the investigation; ten are against.

Late in 1977, CCDC/GWC and the Federal Trade Commission enter into a *"consent agreement."* This first agreement is expanded upon in 1978 by a second agreement reached by four powerful entities: the CCDC/GWC, the Colorado State Real Estate Commission, the Colorado Attorney General, and the Pueblo District Attorney.

Between November of 1977 and June of 1979, the Metro District (water and sanitation) completes 9.69 miles of water lines and 15.25 miles of sewer. The sewage treatment facility is designed to accommodate 5,500 people. The plant is currently serving a population of 1,100, and according to the Zorich-Erker Water Engineering report of June 1978, the average daily water consumption of these 1,100 people is 139 gallons of water per person per day. Surely everyone is getting their eight glasses of water. A few folks are said to be wasted in waterlog.

With an abundance of water and sewer on hand, the local Historical Society invites Ralph C. Taylor to speak at its 4th of July celebration. Although rainbow Ralph is no longer a CCDC vice-president, he remains under contract to write a history of Pueblo schools for School District #60. The celebration marks 200 years since Colonel de Anza defeated Chief Green Horn, an event naming the Greenhorn Valley.

It is now the goal of Metro administrator Bill Hambric to provide water and sewer to all basic core areas by the end of 1979. Of the 11,509 lots planned in the core area, 10,251 (or 89%) are sold. Of the 15,692 lots in the entire Metro District, 13,055 (or 83%) are sold. Developers appear to be doing well in the selling of lots of lots. But is the development itself actually turning into a serious city of 30,000-40,000 residents?

Although developers have sold 83% of their planned building sites, they have generated a home-owning, tax-paying population of only 1,100 residents. These 1,100 residents, including many children, are now paying the tab for services to accommodate a sizable city. Most of the out-of-state land speculators purchased C-City lots for investment purposes, or for down-the-road retirement which may or may not come.

Illinois lot owners are especially unhappy with their investments and complain to their Illinois Attorney General, William Scott, who files suit in Chicago. Attorney Scott alleges fraud in the purchases of property at C-City. He wants $20 million dollars in compensation for his voters:

"Scott charges that more than 3,500 persons lost between $2,000 and $20,000 each on land purchases since 1967 when Colorado City was promoted as a planned community with a projected increase in land value. The suit claims the buyers were misled, that the land was declining in value and that improvements could not be made because of inadequate water and sewage lines....

"Defendants named in the suit are the Hunt International Resources Corp. of Dallas; one of its subsidiaries, Great Western United Corp. of Los Angeles, and Nelson Bunker Hunt and W. H. Hunt. Also named as corporate defendants in the suit are Great Western United Properties, Inc., Great Western Cities Inc., Great Western Cities Realty Co., Inc., all of Los Angeles; the Colorado City Development Co., Inc., and Colorado City Realty Co., Inc., both of Colorado City. Other defendants named are Thomas Maney, top administrative official for Great Western Cities and William J. White and Nathan Mendelsohn, Colorado City early developers."

Great Western Cities of North Hollywood, CA, responds to the allegations raised in the complaint by scalding Scott:

"...Certain of the allegations are so grossly inaccurate that they suggest the total absence of a good faith, independent investigation of the facts by the Illinois Attorney General's office. The timing of the lawsuit and the inclusion of certain of the individual defendants suggest that Mr. Scott is seeking publicity value to improve his political image at a time when he is under criminal indictment. Great Western Cities is confident that further investigation of the project will establish that the development is in fact an attractive and viable community and any allegations of wrongdoing on the part of Great Western Cities are unfounded."

In yet another lawsuit the Colorado City Lot Owners and Taxpayers Association seeks recovery action through investigator Mark P. Binstein, who is controversial. U.S. District Judge S. Hugh Dillin of Indianapolis, IN, is quoted in the *Pueblo Chieftain* as saying, *"This man (Binstein) in the name of saving your property is ripping you off, in my opinion, and I so find that he has done so to the tune of all these hundreds of thousands of dollars."* Judge Dillin gives some evidence to his opinion by stating Mark P. Binstein has been convicted on a securities fraud case, and he has *"...misused and misappropriated over $180,000 that had been collected from those Pueblo West landowners in several states."*

In reply Binstein files suit against CCDC/GWC and parent companies. He also launches libel suits against the local Chamber of Commerce and *The Greenhorn Valley News*. Binstein alleges his *"...reputation was defamed by written and oral statements made by the defendants regarding his conduct and research for the Lot Owners Association."*

Because of law suits, counter suits, and suffering succotash, C-City receives adverse publicity which leads to a slowing in land sales, home construction, and business development. A large number of existing land owners stop paying their property taxes. As a result of $22,500 in delinquent taxes, the Pueblo County Treasure puts 450 land parcels up for sale, but only 50 of the lots sell. Things get so bad, a rumor circulates suggesting C-City has become a ghost town. But the only ghost to be found in Greenhorn Valley is that of Chief Cuerno Verde, himself, who is still restless 200 years after his dastardly defeat.

As the ghoulish ghost of Cuerno Verde haunts law lovers low in the Valley, Bishop's Castle high in the mountains is in its tenth year of construction. It has *no blueprint, no definite design, no construction formula, and no building permits.* So much for perfect planning. The 35-year-old James R. Bishop dreams to have a moat, a drawbridge, and a stone wall around the family castle.

Like Jim Bishop, Albert C. Duell, son of Connie and Dot, is a person of creative vision. After graduating from Rye High School in 1956, Ab earns an A.A. Degree from Pueblo College and a B.S. in Agri-Business from Arizona State. Following his schooling, Ab purchases land from the granddaughter of Calvin Goss and builds a home on the historical Crow Post Office site. He becomes a real estate agent, opens *Ab Duell Realty, Inc.* and helps sell Hollydot Park. Near his 21-acre home site, Ab breaks ground for his *Greenhorn Valley Regional Shopping Center* featuring a 5,000-square-feet True Value Hardware. His *Greenhorn Valley Regional Shopping Center* is not to be confused with the *Commercial Center Plaza of Greenhorn Valley,* a mile to the west. The longer the name or title, the better the chance for sizzling success.

Ab and wife Mary host a grand opening for their True Value Hardware on March I of 1980. Parents Holly and Dot Duell, along with 500 other persons, attend the official opening of their son's new hardware store.

Just west of True Value Hardware, the illustrious *Hollydot Park* is renamed *Meadowcreek.* In the spirit of keep-it-fresh, the annual July celebration is changed from *Rendezvous Days* to *Heritage Day.* In 1980 Heritage Day activities are put on by the Chamber of Commerce. Events include a six-mile foot-race, a 16 mile pack-burro race, horseshoe pitching contest, antique auto parade, art show, and softball tournament.

CCDC/GWC donates their storage building (which is the historical

The historical Crow Mercantile Building is being placed on 72 feet beams for removal to land just east of the True Value Hardware about 1980. The old Mercantile is to be used for a Masonic Lodge Hall and Historical Society Museum, but wind and hail will collapse the building.

(Courtesy of the Pueblo Library District)

Crow Mercantile) to the *Masons* who may be embarrassed by their short name. The Masons become the *Cuerno Verde Square and Compass Club* and move the Mercantile Building to a lot site provided by Ab and Mary Duell. The new location is 1/4 mile east of their True Value Hardware store.

Some 12,000 work hours go into the huge task of moving and restoring the two-story Mercantile. The building is being transformed into a Masonic Lodge Hall and Historical Society Museum. Nearly a year after the project begins, *"a freak windstorm accompanied by hail completely demolished the structure leaving the group heart broken."*

The Historical Society is planning to write the history of Greenhorn Valley when the museum building collapses from wind and hail. Their history of Greenhorn collapses with the two-story Mercantile.

Upon examining the 1980 census, 2,702 permanent residents are living in the C-City/Rye area. During summer months, the number nearly doubles with recreational visitors vacationing in the Valley.

In March of 1981, Rye Post Office celebrates its 100-year-old birthday. Rye's first post office was on Table Mountain somewhat south of Roy Christenson's house at a location known as the *W. I. Gray Place.*

In April real estate agent Lewis V. Allee assumes the position of Property Manager for CCDC/GWC, in addition to maintaining his own business as broker for Concept 80 Real Estate, Ltd.

Hollydot Park Turf Club is purchased by the Dixit Corporation, and Dixit changes the name to *Meadowcreek Turf Club.* Besides changing the name, Dixit wants to move some of its *"commercial property"* to *"residential property"* status in order to create 117 more building sites. Pueblo County Commissioners unanimously deny the request. When Dixit attempts to sell Meadowcreek to Apex Oil Co. of St. Louis, Meadowcreek homeowners file suite against Dixit for alleged defaults. As *"a gesture of good will,"* Apex Oil releases liens placed on several properties.

In February of 1982, the Cuerno Verde Square and Compass Club becomes an authorized *Masonic Lodge.* Also known as *Greenhorn Valley Lodge #196,* the local Masonic Lodge reports 200 paid memberships.

On March 26 CCDC/GWC is legally obligated by the court system to implement a *lot trade program* bringing landowners from peripheral areas into the core area. The agreement requires all land, which is left over after completion of the trade program, to be delivered to the Metro District. After stalling around and trading only 80 lots in two years, CCDC/GWC takes a Chapter 7 bankruptcy.

Tired of expensive legal defenses, CCDC/GWC wants out from its

Colorado City development obligations. The developers promise to leave behind 3,000 lots totaling about 2,000 acres and $600,000 to $700,000 in cash receivables. Following a full year of negotiations, the Metro District, development companies, Illinois Attorney General (representing 4,700 lot owners), and residents of C-City are seemingly in agreement. More than half (61%) of 350 local property owners approve a contract in which CCDC/GWC must turn over millions of dollars in property and equipment within a ten year period. After ten years, property owners will control their own destiny - good, bad, or indifferent.

In the meantime, one very basic conflict continues. The Metro is spending about one million dollars a year for extended water and sewer lines, but not everyone is happy about it. Members of Colorado City Residents for Progress are against spending big bucks to run water and sewer lines into areas where there are no homes. On the other hand, persons who have purchased land in undeveloped areas can not build a home until Metro provides the water and sewer which has been promised.

By the year's end C-City will have 441 residential homes containing about 1,300 residents requiring water and sewer. Metro will make a nervous projection of a 6% annual growth rate to the year 2,000, at which time the local population is expected to reach 3,711 residents.

As Metro District and local residents lock horns over this issue, other legal allegations grow old and begin to fade away in May of 1982:

"Mark Binstein, associated with the Colorado City Lot Owners and Taxpayers Association's activities against Colorado City developer Great Western Cities, Inc., agreed to dismiss Robert Nicholson, President of the Colorado City Chamber of Commerce, the Greenhorn Valley News and its editor, Henry Blackburn from his pending lawsuit in Chicago, Illinois, against, among others, GWC and various local persons and entities."

In July Ab and Mary Duell sell their Greenhorn Valley True Value Hardware to Willard and Betty Klipfel. The Duells will continue to operate the Variety Store in their Greenhorn Valley Shopping Center.

The annual Rye Chautauqua program, born in 1966, continues to present professional and amateur musicians for Valley residents and summer visitors. Heritage Day becomes another annual celebration featuring displays, rides, performers, and a wide variety of other events. Also the MERBISC Center is still around recreating its facilities with fresh paint and new furnishings for use by local clubs and individuals.

Senior citizens perform most of the renovation work.

In September of 1983, city developers pack up and close their doors. Colorado City Development Company of California relocates to their nice, new, utopian development in New Mexico.

The following month a second grocery store opens under the name of *Greenhorn Valley Grocery and Market in Colorado City*. The long title guarantees success, if local folks can remember it.

For those citizens who no longer needed groceries, C-City's own fresh-built cemetery is dedicated northeast of town near Interstate-25.

The *Greenhorn Valley News* was started by the Lions Club in 1973. The Alcorns purchased the paper in 1974; the Blackburns in 1976. In April, 1984, the Blackburns sell the paper back to eight Lions. After 11 years, the *Greenhorn Valley News* has come home to the Lions Club, but not for long. The paper will be sold again and again.

New publishers adopt the slogan "*Watch Us Grow*" and promise to:

"...actively support all programs and organizations which are dedicated to community betterment and economic development....The new owners of the Greenhorn Valley News intend to help to correct false rumors and keep you all better informed about what is happening so that you can make intelligent decisions regarding your role in elections, community activities, and especially in the positive programs which will result in general community good rather than self-interest for a few."

In February of 1984, the Rye Woman's Club celebrates its 50th anniversary with a program reflecting on its history. The Greenhorn Valley Baptist Church heralds its 20th year of local services.

While C-City organizations celebrate, CCDC/GWC files Chapter 7 bankruptcy in Dallas. *"The conglomerate lists $27,000,000 in liabilities and only $6,000,000 in assets."* Because the developers are slow to complete a list of assets, the bankruptcy court can not proceed. Fortunately some of the assets were transferred to Metro months earlier. Other major properties, like Fountain Square, have not been transferred creating uncertainty for city managers.

To be on the safe side, Metro develops a plan to liquidate C-City assets in order to satisfy the legal agreement between itself, CCDC/GWC, and the Illinois Attorney General. In a move to save money, the Recreation District is dissolved. The Metro hopes local organizations will pick up the slack in preserving community recreation.

In May Heritage Day participants reenacted the bloody killing of Chief Cuerno Verde at Greenhorn Meadows Park. Three members of the *Board of Directors of the Heritage Days Committee* resign for personal reasons, *"but also cited lack of community support."* Perhaps the original massacre contained enough bloody murder, and a graphic reminder of the killings was not needed. Besides, anyone (including the youngest of children) can saturate one's selves with death each and every day from TV.

Good fortune smiles on C-City the following summer, and Heritage Day takes place as a *"Crafts and Fine Arts Festival,"* featuring children's events, western displays, live entertainment, skydiving performance, street dance, softball tournament, 10-K and two mile runs. From here on, Heritage Day will promote crafts, fine arts, and healthy recreation.

On another positive note, *Colorado City Residents for Progress* and the *Sportsman's Club* join hands for a spring cleanup. There is more than just a bit of trash around town.

One month after C-City celebrates its 21st birthday, the original developer and president of CCDC, Nathan K. Mendelsohn, dies in Texas. After selling his business interests in Colorado and California, Mendelsohn had supervised land developments in New Mexico and Texas.

By the end of the year, a modern concrete liner has been laid for the historic Hicklin Ditch which controls the water level at Lake Beckwith and provides a backup water supply for C-City. Approximately 8,000 feet in length, the liner is designed to stop water loss from the original, hand-dug, dirt ditch, first used for irrigating grain fields. Wild grains still flourishes along both sides of the narrow waterway.

About 1,500 lots in the core area of Metro District are set aside for trading purposes. Those who have purchased land in peripheral areas, where water and sewer was promised but now unlikely, can trade their nearly worthless lot for a more valuable piece of land inside the core where water and sewer exist. This land trade is to satisfy an agreement signed three years ago by Metro, CCDC/GWC, and the Illinois Attorney General. But to complicate matters, 770 lots to be used in the trade owe back taxes as of December 1984.

Pueblo County Treasure is wanting $250,000 in back taxes. In addition to facing a delinquent tax burden, Metro is dealing with an old insurance issue and expensive legal fees resulting from the Dallas Bankruptcy Court. American justice is determined by those having the most money to buy the best attorneys for *due process of law*. Due process is like *cleaning house*. Both require costly cleaning agents.

The Dallas Bankruptcy Court tells Metro District to allocate $526,000 for the payment of back taxes on lots to be used in the land exchange program. With large fishy debts hunched on the horizon, Metro places 200 carp in Lake Beckwith to reduce the growth of weeds.

By March, 1985, DO-RAY is manufacturing 2,000 different lights for automotive, marine, RV, truck, and trailer industries. In September C-City's largest employer (approaching 200) celebrates its 10th anniversary.

Three new businesses at Fountain Square coordinate grand openings: *Petal Cellar* (featuring floral items and a wire service); *Gnomes Attic* (specializing in handmade items); and the *Stylish Pet Parlor* (grooming cats and dogs). *Charlotte's Web Restaurant* moves up to full speed, and *Ol" Zan's* cafe changes ownership.

Meadowcreek (originally Hollydot) is annexed to the Metro District, but will keep its Homeowner Assoc. and maintain its affluent identity.

While CCDC/GWC and Metro District are negotiating in the Dallas Bankruptcy Court, William Michael Furman of the Liberty Trust Investment Company in Odessa, TX, makes an offer to buy 4,676 lots still titled to CCDC/GWC. Metro lawyers put together a better offer and submit it to the Bankruptcy Court. On July 25 of 1985, the Court awards all properties (4,676 lots for $250,000 in back taxes) to C-City Metro District for the Lot Trade Program which is required *"by the Illinois Attorney General in the Illinois Class Action suite and mandated by the Illinois Consent Decree."* All properties are deeded to Metro.

Metro now has 3,000 lots in the core area with essential utilities. When Metro mails out 1,400 letters to lot owners in the peripheral areas, 170 of those owners accept the opportunity to exchange lots. The peripheral areas affected are Units 30, 31, 45, and portions of 23 and 24. Once traded, Metro hopes to consolidate the 1,400 peripheral lots into larger tracts which can be sold to help finance the Lot Trade Program.

Near the end of 1985, Metro board members and Pueblo County officials clash over the issue of back taxes. They have opposite views as to how the Lot Trade Program should be administrated. Pueblo County Treasurer refuses to sell or exchange 1,000 lots delinquent from back taxes. Nine hundred are in the core area. Metro interprets the Treasurer's refusal as a stall tactic to benefit the County Treasury rather than allowing Metro to move forward. Metro points out the 1,000 lots (owing back taxes) are only accruing hypothetical taxes and not putting monies into the County Treasury. Jack Price, chairman of the Metro Board, makes a solemn declaration:

"All we have received from the county via the newspapers are exaggerated accounts of what this would supposedly cost the county and intimations that Colorado City taxes would be raised in an attempt to split the community. The allegations are untrue...It is apparent that the delaying tactics of the county treasurer has cost the Metro District a minimum of $325,000, plus attorney fees....In summary, if the county would leave us alone and let the Colorado City Metropolitan District guide its community through this workable six to nine-month plan, both Colorado City and Pueblo County would benefit. Colorado City would reduce its area, eliminating a $5 million construction cost, and...satisfy some 1,000 taxpayers at no sacrifice to the residents and minimal overall affects to Pueblo County. The Pueblo County treasurer would realize more real dollars as compared to accrued dollars, and also would reduce the amount of lots on tax-sale rolls by having taxpayers who will pay their taxes. This would result in more real dollars in the county coffers, and allow Colorado City to continue its economic growth and become a more viable community."

Although Metro District received $2.2 million from the Illinois Attorney General in a lawsuit settled 3 years earlier to perform the Lot Trade Program, chairman Price complains: Pueblo County is bleeding the Metro $20,000 per month with stall tactics. Price claims his Metro District has offered to pay Pueblo County $500,000 for property taxes covering a two-year period, but County has refused the offer. Not only does County refuse the half million dollars, but *"they have taken the lots that have been listed for tax sale away from the market."* Price says his Metro would have completed the exchange program a year earlier had Pueblo County not caused needless delays.

No longer content to sit and wait, the *Colorado City Economic Development Group* attempts to bolster community image by printing 20,000 brochures costing about $9,000. The brochure stresses clean air, adequate water, beautiful scenery, and recreation opportunities. They hope the advertising will *"increase lot values, as well as the houses."*

At the beginning of 1986, Metro has 503 water meters in use with a three-residents-per-house population of about 1,509. These core customers are consuming four million gallons of water each month.

Remember William Michael Furman of Liberty Trust Investment Company in Odessa, TX, who tried (but failed) to purchase 4,676

CCDC/GWC lots at the Dallas Bankruptcy Court? The same Michael Furman, also owning *Liberty Federal Saving Bank in Raton, NM,* is not a person to give up easily. In January of 1986, he tries to buy the 260-acre Meadowcreek subdivision from Dixit Corporation for $500,000. Affluent Meadowcreek contains 100 platted lots, townhouse sites, tennis courts, clubhouse, swimming pool, and equipment storage. With money to spare, Furman offers another $500,000 for 100 lots in the core area of Metro District and 700 outside the core. Money Mike is attempting to become the largest property owner in C-City. His savings and investment businesses are apparently doing rather well.

Another prominent figure around town is Albert C. Duell who appears regularly in the *Greenhorn Valley News* because of his leasing operations: shopping center, post office, and liquor store. Able Ab offers to donate half an acre on the northeast corner of his property to C-City Chamber of Commerce. The donation has some restrictions. When the Chamber is unable to meet the conditions, Ab withdraws his offer.

Four months later, after Ab is an unsuccessful candidate for Metro Board, he offers to donate the same half acre for a Greenhorn Valley museum. Ab says, *"The Greenhorn Valley has a lot of history and we need to preserve that....[and] I am willing to donate a site to any non-profit club or organization in the community that will construct a museum on the site."* Ab wants to preserve the local history while attracting visitors.

The *Greenhorn Valley Historical Society* reorganizes itself, and Imogene Hastings becomes the president. The Historical Society accepts Duell's land offer and plans to create a *Hicklin Memorial Museum.* Ralph C. Taylor donates six manuscripts and 197 photographs regarding the origins and early development of C-City. Since a *Hicklin Memorial Museum* was never established, one might wonder: What ever happened to Ralph Taylor's valuable manuscripts and photographs?

By April of 1986 Metro has traded 510 lots, promised 27, and still negotiating on another 71. Five property owners flatly refuse to exchange their lots, and 28 owners can not be located. In the process of trading property, 116 lots will be repossessed for non-payment.

In September Ab and Mary Duell sell their Valley Grocery Store with gas pumps to Mr. and Mrs. Gary Miller of Rye. During the same month, money Mike Furman promises $300,000 to bring Meadowcreek Golf Course into top playing condition, after which he will donate the course and clubhouse to Metro District. Not stopping here, Mike promises to create a third nine-hole course that will connect the Meadowcreek golf links to the original West Course. This will cost him another $525,000, but Mike is convinced a large 27-hole golf course will be the answer to generating new sales and development for his real estate holdings at C-City.

Joyful Jack Price, chairman of the Metro Board, is convinced money Mike is the answer to their financial future. Jack says, *"The 27-hole golf course would make Colorado City one of the leading golf facilities in the State."* Despite chairman Jack's optimism, Mike Furman will soon be buried in his large real estate holdings.

While money Mike is creating a 27-hole golf course, the town's one major industry closes shop and departs. DO-RAY Lamp Co. cites *"poor business conditions in the market place and foreign competition"* as reasons for closing. When DO-Ray leaves, the lights go out.

Metro leases (with option to buy) the 75,000-square-foot DO-RAY building to money Mike. Mr. Furman wants the facility occupied with wage-earners who can buy some of his 2,000 real estate lots.

In January of 1988, the Metro Shop is burglarized resulting in an estimated loss of $20,000 to $30,000. According to an independent audit presented to the board six months later, *"Colorado City Metropolitan District is one of the most financially sound districts in the state."* It appears the backseat burglars were one step ahead of the auditors in seeing Colorado City become *"most financially sound."*

Since the city is found to be financially sound, Lake Beckwith receives $48,000 in upgrades to include a walking/jogging/bicycle trail around the lake, bathroom facility, more trees and shrubs, new parking lots, nine picnic tables, and a few cooking grills.

In the fall of 1988, residents celebrate the town's 25th birthday. Early vice-president of CCDC and long-time friend of the Historical Society, Ralph Taylor, is among the guest speakers.

During the year, a high-tech toy company named *Phonetica One* tries to establish itself in the C-City Industrial Park. Eager to have new businesses, Metro okays a $100,000 loan to Phonetica while officials work on a State Funding Package. The funding is not only turned down by Governor Roy Romer, but the Governor orders an investigation of Phonetica One. In angry response, Phonetica files a $38 million dollar law suit against the State of Colorado and local agencies. Phonetica claims breach of contact is causing their business to fail. Phonetica One is charged with nine felony counts, including failure to pay taxes and attempting to influence a public official. During a government approved foreclosure sale, Metro purchases the Phonetica Building and property for $881,000 with high hopes to put a viable company into the building facility.

At year's end, C-City is made up of 84% married couples, most (79%) of whom own homes. Half the population is under age 50, and half is over 50. Only 51% of C-City residents are employed, and half the employed are commuting to Pueblo. A surprising 43% of residents are retired.

1989 is a big year for local businesses. Norm and Pam Smith from Modesto, CA, purchase the Greenhorn Valley True Value Hardware after vacationing in Rye with Pam's parents, Lee and Pat Mason. At the same Shopping Center, Bill Graham opens a Farmers Insurance. In the same building, Valley Grocery Store (closed for a year) reopens with owners Dan and Tammy Sheppard. Joe Diamond moves his 12-year-old barber shop, *Joe's Clip Joint*, from Pueblo to the lower level of the Medical Center. Across the road at Fountain Square, Mark McDonnell opens *Signs and Upholstery*. Mary Lou Gallegos moves her cafe, *Pat's Place*, from the golf clubhouse to a spot across from the Texaco at I-25. Also at I-25, Sharon Carlson expands her pet supply and grooming center, *The Doghouse*.

Ron and Adele Smith from central Iowa establish a mini-museum of collectibles at their Intermountain Welding Shop in Rye. Close by, the families of Gary Kravig, Gene Baxter, and Keith Baxter open *The Shivers* cafe featuring soups, sandwiches, and ice cream treats. Also in Rye, Jim Henderson opens *Henderson's Auto Shop*. Midway between Rye and C-City, Leo Switzer and Tommy Burkes open *Taco Rock Lounge*.

Taco Rock was originally a VFW Post Building. The VFW turned into the *Rimrock Lounge*, which became the *El Rancho Alegre*. Since there are few Hispanics in Greenhorn Valley, the locals have trouble remembering *El Rancho Alegre*. So they call the place *Taco Rock* in honor of the popular Mexican treat, the taco. After other owners and new names, the Taco Rock location becomes *Taco Rock Lounge* in 1989. By year 2000 Taco Rock will host a new Century 21 Real Estate building, but not for long.

Although C-City is booming with business, it continues to have a problem with unpaid taxes. Between 1,500 and 1,700 acres are in tax delinquent status, and more than seven percent of local land is at least three years behind in taxes. Some of the new developers have fallen on hard times and are unable to pay taxes on their undeveloped tracts.

Tax delinquent lots go to *limbo land,* or are held for a mandatory five-year-period before new buyers can purchase the properties for back taxes, penalties, and handling fees. If no one wants to buy the land after five years, Pueblo County Treasure takes possession of the property. In time, limbo land will be reduced to a three-year-period by the State.

During the next ten years (1990-2000) the C-City/Rye area becomes the second fastest growing region in Pueblo County with 1,395 new residents. The fastest grower is Pueblo West near Lake Pueblo.

Many services, manufactures, doctors, dealers, builders, brokers, realtors (including cafes, clubs, churches, and celebrations) come and go in Greenhorn Valley. A few need mentioning.

In 1991 Columbia House, a national cassette and video distribution company, purchases the vacant DO-RAY manufacturing facility from Metro for $500,000. The arrival of Columbia House to Industrial Park is a major factor in producing local growth. Thanks in part to Dr. Robert L. Campbell.

Doctor Campbell and wife Evelyn move to C-City in 1975. Dr. Bob not only plays a major role in bringing Columbia House to the Industrial Park, but he builds the Medical Building where he doctors from 1975 to 1997. He serves as Medical Consultant for the Fire Department (1975-2000); passes the rodeo arena from Metro to members of the Saddle Club; keeps the Children's Center from collapse; plays doctor at sporting events; and personally designs and erects a 100-foot steel walkway across Greenhorn creek at Meadows Park. In May of 1992, Dr. Robert Campbell retires from the Metro Board after six years of service and is honored by Valley residents with *Dr. Bob Campbell Appreciation Day.*

In addition to his many accomplishments, Dr. Bob writes thoughtful poetry. His favorite theme is *Appreciating Life*. In the following poem, *"I'll Do My Best,"* he creates an exquisite prayer for all to consider:

> *"Each day I live to be nearer to Thee.*
> *I feel the comforts of a man that's free.*
> *I lift my eyes and asked to be blessed,*
> *And tomorrow, Dear Lord, I'll Do My Best."*

In an effort to do their best, volunteers renovate an old building in Rye, and the Greenhorn Valley Theater opens on Main Street in June of 1992. The first performance is an original musical written by Pat Graves and titled *Music on the Greenhorn*. The production features characters like Chief Cuerno Verde, Juan Bautista de Anza, Alexander and Estefana Hicklin.

While the music plays at the Greenhorn Valley Theater, C-City struggles with its own drama of unsold properties. In July *Greenhorn Valley News* reports the following:

"After two and one half years of study and conversation in reference

to how and when to sell lots held by the Colorado City Metro District; the recent lot sale appears to have fallen well short of its expectations. While 162 lots were purchased by 32 buyers, there are still 203 lots available....Pueblo County is currently making a public offering for seven days of 326 Colorado City lots. Any of these lots that are not sold for back taxes and liens during this time will be offered for free under the Pueblo County Housing Mortgage Revenue Bond Program."

The Pueblo County Housing Mortgage Revenue Bond Program is important because it has 48 letters in its name, a sizable accomplishment seldom achieved by simple folk. The program intends to get C-City properties back on tax rolls, where it can collect new monies in the shortest possible time. This then is the long and the short of TPCHMRBP.

In 1993 *Peaks Auto Supply, Re-Do-It Upholstery, Circle S Firearms, Inc.,* and Lou Guzzo's laundromat make clean starts. The Masonic Lodge celebrates its 10-year anniversary and makes plans for a permanent home. After forty-one seniors graduate from Rye High School in June, a farewell picnic is given in honor of Mr. and Mrs. Holland Duell Jr. in July.

Jim and Janet Cook of Rye acquire the Oscar Hadwiger collection of hand carved wood. They place it in their *Western Museum of the Pueblo Saddle Makers* located a block south of Main Street. The collection is a great addition to the Cooks' other western exhibits which include saddles, spurs, guns, cowboy gear, Indian artifacts, and historical documents.

Next door to the Cooks' museum, Ken and Joyce Shollenbarger are hosting an open house at their historical log cabin. Behind the log cabin, the Shollenbargers have created a trading post with gun shop, bunk house, and Indian village. As part of the late summer celebration, they host a Chicagoan cookout, entertainment, and free tours next door to the Cooks' Museum. Although Jim Cook's collections will depart from Rye shortly after the year 2000, he will maintain a museum at the Pueblo State Fair.

The most remarkable event of 1993 is the downfall of William Michael Furman. By November money Mike is serving time in the Federal Penitentiary east of Canon City as a result of his failed saving and investment businesses. The *Greenhorn Valley News* reports:

"...Prior to his incarceration, he attempted to purchase 6,000 lots in Colorado City for development. The land deal apparently never transpired and Furman...held Colorado City and Pueblo County to blame.

"In November of 1993, from prison, Furman filed a seventeen page

affidavit with Pueblo County for $85. The Affidavit of Identity and Imposition of Construction Trust tied up some 6,000 lots in Colorado City with bogus liens....The companies and trust listed on the lien were either out of business or were no longer allowed to conduct business in Colorado. The lot owner would have to apply for a title to his or her own land. Attorney fees, court costs, and the cost of legal ads could run up to thousands of dollars.

"The State Attorney General's office is to be commended for forcing Furman to sign a document removing the liens. It is unknown how many thousands of dollars were lost by property owners seeking clear titles to their properties."

In 1994 *Impressionist Printing* and *Travel Travel* come to Greenhorn Valley. *Peaks Auto Supply* departs Fountain Square moving to the Conoco Station at I-25. Next to Conoco, Greenhorn Inn changes hands. While *C-City Post Office* returns to Fountain Square, *Pizza Stop* and *Mountain High Balloons* (HPS) arrive as new businesses. Across the street, *Alternative Rehab* opens in the Medical Center. *Lil Store* country cafe opens in Rye, and *Circle S Firearms* moves from Rye to Greenhorn Valley Shopping Center.

While local services play musical chairs, Metro's new *"no growth"* policy is challenged by *Colorado City Property Owners Association, Inc.*

In contrast to *no growth*, Jim Bishop turns 50 and celebrates his 25th continuous year of castle building in the mountains near Lake Isabel.

The mountain air gives life to local author Sue Harmon who publishes her second novel, *Spirit of a Bear*. Although a few people in the Valley do read, most everyone can see real good. As the word gets out, *Country Cablevision and Digital Satellite TV* rush in. This is very exciting because everybody enjoys looking at pretty pictures in a box.

While satellite and cable TV come to the Valley, CDs and DVDs are taking over the planet. Consequently Columbia House (provider of records, cassettes, and videos) is under heavy fire from rapid change.

Columbia House was hatched in 1955, and one division came to C-City Industrial Park in 1990. Starting with 120 employees and a small warehouse, Columbia expands to 700 employees with a quarter million square feet of warehouse and office space. By March of 1996 Columbia is handling 120,000 product mailings per day, which fill seven or eight semi trucks departing for major cities around the country. Within five years, Columbia House will die a painful death and disappear from the Valley.

As a foreshadowing of Columbia's demise, Lake Beckwith goes out of balance and the fish begin to die. As early as 1990, Metro decides there is too much vegetation in the lake. City managers spend $10,000 for 3,000 Grass Carp fish to eat the vegetation. The 3,000 Grass Carp are a bit much for the lake. When the Grass Carp eat all the vegetation, the bass and bluegill die, other fish stopped growing, and the yellow perch take over the lake. As the dead bass and bluegill create a foul smell around the lake in 1994, Metro contracts the Department of Wildlife (DOW) to correct their situation. After 18 months, DOW has improved the water quality, and in August of 1996 Metro signs a 20 year contract with DOW to manage Lake Beckwith. City manager Calvin Hamler explains:

"There will be better water storage with an improved wildlife habitat. We will conserve and improve the natural resource of the lake since the DOW will spend money for many capital improvements such as new docks, restrooms, handicapped accessible docks and boat ramps. None of these improvements will cost Colorado City one penny....We can't expect the Division of Wildlife to come in and make lots of capital improvements without a 20 year agreement. In 20 years we will still be drinking water, and will need a healthy, well-managed lake."

The Department of Wildlife promises to stock the lake every year with 7,000-10,000, 10-inch or larger, catchable Trout. They also agreed to assist in picking up trash and enforcing the lake use with citations.

In 1995, while Lake Beckwith is recovering, realtor and resident Jim Butcher is creating a mobile home development west above the lake. When Butcher allows double-wide mobiles onto his hilltop development, he disregards local covenants, Architectural Control Committee approval, and neighborhood outcry. Unlike modular homes that have deeds and are set on permanent foundations, double-wides come with vehicle identification numbers (VIN), titles, and are generally set on concrete blocks so they can be moved (if necessary) to another location. Once in place, the modular and double-wide (both manufactured homes) appear much the same.

In September a 3.5-million-dollar rest stop replaces the old *Brantzell Rest Area* at I-25 and Hwy-165 junction. The modern facility is named *Cuerno Verde Rest Area* by local residents. It features extensive landscaping, hiking trails, and information markers. There is *"a touch screen computer, the first of its kind at a Colorado rest area,"* to provide travelers with current information about weather and road conditions.

The dedication includes everyone who is someone. On hand are the

Chamber of Commerce, Lions Club, VFW Chapter, Rye High School Band, a senator, Regional Director of the Federal Highway Administration, State Transportation Commissioner, Chairman of Frontier Pathway Scenic and Historic Byway, and Chairman of the Comanche Nation from Lawton, OK.

Comanche Chairman Wallace Coffee speaks on heritage, tradition, and children. The Chairman explains how legendary war chief Cuerno Verde (named by the Spanish) was actually called *Kuhtsooehkuh*, meaning *Dangerous Man*, by the Comanches. In lieu of this new fact, the rest area should have been designated as *Dangerous Man Rest Area*.

A mile west of *Dangerous Man Rest Area*, the name of *Greenhorn Valley Shopping Center* is downsized. The gas pump isle and underground tanks are replaced with a hand carved wooden sign reading *Valley Center*.

In 1996 Total Petroleum Inc. reopens its service station featuring a Taco Bell Express and catering to truckers on the move.

A few miles north of Total truck stop, the 21,000 acre Hatchet Ranch is sold to Red Creek Ranch, Inc. During the next two years, Red Creek developers sell 275 land parcels ranging in size from 40 to 200 acres. The smaller 40-acre parcels begin at about $26,000. No double-wide mobiles or modulars are permitted, and a 1,500 square-foot, minimum-size house is required. According to Joe O'Brien, vice-president and partner, *"The reason for the covenants is to keep open space and keep the homes nice, mainly for aesthetic reasons."* One third of new buyers become full-time residents, a second third become part-time dwellers, and a third third remain investors. Seventy percent of these 275 buyers are from Colorado. Two years later, Red Creek will purchase an additional 8,300 acres to become a bigger, better, happier Hatchet.

On January 29, 1997, Ralph C. Taylor passes in Pueblo at age 92. Five months later, Mr. Holland Duell Jr. dies in Poughkeepsie, NY, at age 88.

Still alive, Rye Home United Methodist Church celebrates its 125th birthday. Greenhorn Valley Chamber of Commerce boasts 60 members and ten years of service. During those ten years, the Chamber created three publications: a *Scenic Byways* promotion, a *Greenhorn Valley* brochure, and the *Business Directory and Map* for local residents and new visitors.

G. Kin Snyder, M. D., a native of North Carolina, moves to Rye in 1987 and begins practicing family medicine in the Valley Shopping Center about 1995. Mary Hund-Snyder, certified nurse and midwife, assists Kin Snyder with much of women's health care. The Snyder practice remains in the Valley Center until shortly after year 2000 when Dr. Kin Snyder will move next to Jeff's Valley Pharmacy in the Medical Center Building.

By year 2000 Ab and Mary Duell are living in Wickenburg, AZ, where Ab is broker of his own real estate firm titled *Way Out West*, or *WOW*. When Ab is not locating ranches for his clients, he and Mary spend much of their time *"riding, roping and enjoying life."* Ab's sister, Susan, is the only Duell still residing in Greenhorn Valley

While most of the Duells have moved on to new lifestyles, the C-City/Rye area has grown 55% during the 1990-2000 decade. The U.S. Census reports a regional population figure of 3,908 in year 2000.

YEAR 2000

Year 2000 approaches and many uptown experts cry gloom and doom over the anticipated Y2K computer bug. C-City appears indifferent, uncomplicated, and unmoving. Denver, Colorado Springs, and Pueblo grow bigger, faster, and noisier while Colorado City settles down to a smaller, slower, quieter village with normal community events.

The C-City Post Office, where all residents pick up their mail, claims about 2,000 citizens. Including Rye, the region has a population of about 4,000. The Valley flourishes with Canadian geese in the winter and swells with American vacationers in the summer.

Two to three hundred Canadian geese make semi-annual visits to local lakes, ponds, lawns, parks, and the Hollydot Golf Course - their favorite playground. Both male and female Canadian geese are similar in appearance, span 22 to 48 inches in length, weigh up to 24 pounds, mate for life, and protect each other. They can *"pine to death at the loss of their mate,"* which makes them more humane than most humans. When it comes to raising children, *"Canada geese are devoted parents and never leave their goslings unguarded."* Goose families migrate together, and stay together at their wintering grounds. In spring they return to the same nesting area time and again. In all fairness, these semi-annual visitors of Canadian ancestry must be counted as semi-permanent residents.

In April of 2000, before American tourists arrive, drama grips the sleepy Valley. Before anyone can be certain what is happening, *Greenhorn Valley Players of Rye* perform a comedy called *The Three Jims*. In a more serious morality play, Colorado City Community Church performs a spiritual dramatization of Leonardo da Vinci's *The Last Supper*.

In May at the end of the school year, 62 students graduate from Rye High School, and construction begins on a computer lab, media center, and office space. Across the road at Rye Elementary, ground is broken for more classrooms and a new gym.

In June the Lions Club joins *Aerospace Good Sams RV Club of Colorado Springs* for their third annual cleanup day. Each year Good Sams RV Club comes to town because, *"we enjoy the Greenhorn Valley and its beautiful, cool and peaceful setting."* The two clubs tidy up along Hwy-165 through Colorado City. After several hours, a large pickup truck is filled with trash, including a toilet found in the median. Those at the scene believe the toilet to be a good luck charm left behind by the *Funky Father of Trash,* who habitually lays waste to the roadsides of America.

On July 7th Jim Stewart (son of Conyers Stewart, the co-creator of Stewart-Duell Thoroughbred Farm) opens Valley Auto Sales next to Moore's Valley Auto Repair. Jim Stewart is currently the sole member of the Stewart family still residing in Greenhorn Valley.

Jim graduated from high school in 1963, worked on a ranch in SE Colorado, and spent three years in the Army before attending Ft. Lewis College in Durango. From 1972 Jim managed the Stewart Thoroughbred farm for a number of years. He worked at auto sales in Pueblo for a decade before opening his own Valley Auto Sales in Colorado City.

Year 2000 ends with a bang! On the morning of December 21, a young Mule Deer, feeding on the golf course, is shot several times with a small caliber firearm and left to die near its mother. A $1,000 reward is offered for information leading to arrest and conviction of the gutless gunslinger.

Closing Comments

Most cities, large and small, historically spring up around some dominating influence such as a large industrial complex or a strategic geographical location along an important river or highway. Colorado City did not spring up; it was invented by idealistic California developers.

Nat Mendelsohn, president of CCDC and original developer, knew Colorado was one of the fastest growing states in the nation. It was increasing approximately twice as fast as the rest of the country. The Front Range itself (called the *Emerald Strip*) was growing third fastest in the nation. People were attracted to Colorado because of excellent job opportunities, as well as tremendous scenic and recreational resources.

Consequently Colorado City was well-planned geographically. It had a scenic rural environment, many recreational opportunities, and existed only 25 miles from urban facilities. The development provided living choices for the upper-class, middle-class, and summer visitors. Each village featured a unique design with connecting spaces for walking, cycling, and horse riding.

Built into the heart of the community were recreational and social facilities, such as three 9-hole golf courses, ball parks, camp grounds, a 70-acre lake, thoroughbred horse farm, rodeo grounds, community center, swimming pool, child care, and two small shopping centers.

The original development consisted of 16,000 lots divided in to several small villages surrounding the Commercial Center Plaza at Hwy-165 and Bent Brothers Blvd. About 12,000 of the original 16,000 lots sold, and most were purchased prior to 1972. Seven hundred of the 12,000 lots sold now have dwellings. These 700 homes shelter about 2,000 men, women, and children. These residents make up Colorado City.

With such careful planning, why did C-City fail to thrive and not become a real city? There are reasons. First and foremost, the California developers (CCDC) were interested in making huge profits. Obviously if you cut one large pie into many small pieces, you can sell the many pieces and become wealthy. CCDC divided their large land pie into 16,000 small pieces and sold the vast majority. Although the developers had some larger lots, most of the pie pieces were small, city-sized lots of 1/6, 1/5, and 1/4 of an acre. The 12,000 lots were sold with a promise of basic water and sewer. When CCDC failed to provide these basic services to peripheral villages, it eliminated all possibility of peripheral growth.

Second, most of the lots were sold to land speculators and out-of-state buyers who had little or no intention of becoming a resident any time soon. The small number of buyers who became residents inherited the burden of maintaining a city for 12,000 land owners.

Third, bad publicity resulted from law suits over the serious problem of running water and sewer to outlying areas at the cost of millions of dollars in labor and material. Huge profits had been realized, but the basic services had not. Further land sales and home construction came to a halt. Out of frustration, some property owners filed law suits, others tried to resell, and more than a few stopped paying their taxes.

Fourth, with only a handful of local employers, half the working residents were commuting to Pueblo for jobs. These commuters found it convenient (and less expensive in some cases) to purchase food and household items in urban Pueblo. Since local businesses were disregarded, they found it difficult to survive. Many did not survive.

Fifth, a sizable number of retired residents were on fixed incomes and did not have much spendable income to invest in the local economy. When Colorado City did not become a city, some seniors missed the hubbub of urban living and either moved back to Pueblo or visited the Pueblo regularly to spend what money they had.

Sixth, among those seniors who had extra cash, some were not sports-minded. Consequently they were not participating in local leisure activities like horse riding, golfing, swimming, fishing, boating, hiking, and camping. Over time, they felt isolated and returned to urban places.

Seventh, for the many residents who had jobs in Pueblo, commuting expenses became much larger than first anticipated. In addition to the cost of travel, the round trip added at least an hour to the work day.

Along side these seven reasons, there are probably various other influences which played a part in keeping C-City from materializing in to a city of 30,000 to 40,000. On the other hand, during the last decade, growth has become rather rapid in C-City at 55%. If this growth trend continues, the area will have 6,057 people in year 2010; 9,388 in year 2020; 14,552 in 2030; 22,556 in 2040; and 34,963 in 2050.

For many local residents, the slow-moving pace of life is still utopian. Locals not only pick up mail at the local post office, but they can stop at the gas station, grocery store, hardware, bank, and pharmacy all in a single hour. Rarely does one have to stand in any line, and cashiers know their patrons by name. C-City has no heavy industry, no air pollution, no traffic congestion, not even a traffic light to threaten motorists.

In year 2000 the cost of land and home construction in Greenhorn Valley is a *best buy.* There are still many lots for re-sale (by original owners) in the core area still connected to water and sewer. These lots range in price from $3,000 to $10,000. A piece of land above the lake or on the golf course will be priced on the high end.

There are currently two dozens homes under construction. A brand new ranch-styled house (of average quality) with 1,300 square feet up and 1,300 down (unfinished basement) sells for about $125,000. Although real estate is still a bargain in C-City, property taxes are rather high. This ranch-styled home owner will pay $1,200 in annual property tax.

Greenhorn Valley has several basic services. To nourish the soul, there are six church groups: Methodist, Later Day Saints, Colorado City Community, Catholic, Baptist, and Assembly of God. To stimulate the young mind, there are three schools: an elementary and high school in Rye; a middle school in C-City. All three schools provide high-quality bus transportation. To feed the body, there are seven eating establishments: Cafe Cuerno Verde, Colella's Italian and American, Espey's BBQ, Garden of Eatin' Coffee and Sandwich Shop, Ol' Zan's Place, Prairie Flower Deli, and Subway sandwiches for those who burrow underground. Max's cafe, named after the family dog, will arrive in 2001.

Greenhorn Valley has numerous other businesses and services, many of which are virtually unknown to local residents. They include towing, window replacement, welding supplies & services, well drilling, two video rentals, a veterinarian, upholstery shop, typewriter service, truck hauling, truck rentals, telephone services, a surveyor, small engine repair, siding contractor, shoe store, self storage, saw sharpening & repair, roofing contractor, four real estate companies (including an inspector, appraiser, & property manager), pump service & repair, a psychologist, two propane gas companies, two plumbing & heating contractors, two physicians, a pharmacy, pet grooming, paintball games & supplies, flower nursery, novelty store, newspaper, motel, massage & tanning, mason contractor, log home sales, locksmith, liquor store, light & power company, live theater in summer, two libraries, lawn mower repair & sales, internet services, two insurance agents, insulation & air conditioning, house painting, house cleaning, horse dealer, home repair & maintenance, several home builders, a hardware, grocery store, three gift shops, garden & lawn center, foundation contractor, two florists, fence contractor, feed dealer, fax service, two excavating contractors, two electric contractors, dry wall repair, driveway builder, door/window/siding specialist, disposal service, distribution, a dentist, day care, community credit union, three convenience stores, concrete-ready mix, concrete contractor, computer & communication services, a chiropractor, chimney builder, Chamber of Commerce, two cemeteries, carpet/rug/upholstery cleaner, two camp grounds, cable & satellite services, business consultant, book store, three barber and beauty salons, a bank, auto repair, auto sales, appliance sales, antiques and collectibles, an accountant and two CPAs.

Local residents need to become aware of these many services, because most Valley businesses sell their products and services at competitive prices, *or less than* found in urban Pueblo. Supporting local businesses will ensure the future of Colorado City.

At this turn-of-the-century time, Greenhorn Valley continues to give birth to fresh air, exquisite scenery, and recreative opportunities. Consequently, we residents are blessed with quiet, joyful living.

In the midst of joyous living, we see a number of new sojourners now coming to lodge in our cheerful village. How will this rapid influx of human beings influence our easy-paced community?

Let us not be *greenhorn* inhabitants who reflect *raw, simple, young, inexperienced* behavior like Chief Cuerno Verde. Rather, let us reflect the wisdom and experience of the Valley's history and distinguished characters. Let us now and forever remember the philosophicotheological words of loving Laura Williams Halsey, our own Miss. Colorado City:

"...when anyone killed a deer he would divide with the neighbors so it would not spoil. People don't do those things anymore - they seem to be getting selfish...."

Fare ye well, so long, and Godspeed. Until we meet again, have a pleasant journey, and be good for something or to someone.

Straight from the bootmaker,

Gerald W. Crispin
P.O. Box 19583
Colorado City, CO 81019

Postscript

Apologies are due to those legendary Indian fighters, trappers, traders, and government scouts on the new frontier who are not mentioned (or mentioned briefly), such as: Joseph Barnoy, Carlos Beaubien, Charles Beaubien, Albert G. Boone, Jimmy Boyer, Elton T. and Edwin F. Beckwith, Charles Bent, Senator Beckwith, Kit Carson, Jean-Baptiste Charlefou, Peter Dotson, Joseph B. Doyle, Chat Dubray, Felipe Nerio and Vivian Espinosa, Charles Goodnight, William Kroenig, Antoine Laforet, LeBlanc, Miguel Antonio Leon, Charles Nadeau, Dick McCoy, George Simpson, Tom Tobin, Simeon Turley, Richens (Uncle Dick) Wootton, and the many others. These characters all have stories in need of another time and more space.

Further apologies are offered to those influential people and significant events which have been accidentally or ignorantly omitted from this brief historical sketch.

INDEX

Ab Duell Reality, 149, 159.
Abbey settlement, 116.
Aerospace Good Sams RV Club (Colo. Spgs), 176.
Albert, John, 62-64.
Alcorns, 163.
Allee, Lewis (Lew) & Jane, 147, 161.
Allison, J. A., 111.
Alpine Liquors, 146.
Alpine Village, 140, 146-147.
Alternative Rehab, 172.
American Fur Company, 30.
Anderson, Robert O., 127.
Anderson, Sec. of State Byron, 123.
Anza, Gov. Juan Baptista de, 6, 11, 17-25, 157, 170.
Apache City (Flats, Station), 136-137.
Apache Creek, 7, 9, 43-44, 52, 77-79, 88, 116.
Apache Indians, 7, 13, 16, 20, 33, 43-44, 52, 61.
Apex Oil, 161.
Applewood Mobile Home Estates, 140, 144, 149-150, 154.
Aragon, Juan, 81.
Arapahoe Indians, 13, 16, 32-33, 40, 79, 82.
Architectural Control Committee, 173.
Armijo, Gov. Manuel, 35, 95.
Arroyo Hondo, 82.
Ashley, General William H., 46.
Ashley, Hamilton (Ham) T., 110.
Ashley, James Porter, 112.
Ashley Lumber & Mercantile, 115.
Askew, Ray, 148.
Aspencade, 136-137, 143.
Assembly of God (Christian Chapel), 178.
Astor's Fur Company, 33.
Atterberry, Hazel, 111.
Auston, H. T., 101.
Autobee (s), Charles, 34, 49, 64, 76, 79-86, 99.
Autobee (s), Mariano, 83-84.
Avila, Salvador, 83.
Aztecs and Toltecs, 11-12.
Baca, Benito, 81.
Baca, Elena, 83-84.
Baca, Marcelino, 37, 40, 49, 66, 75-84, 89-90, 110.
Badito (Cone & Village), 14, 11, 15, 103.
Bagley, John, 114.
Baird, Doctor T. D., 101.
Barbara Coma (Barbacoma), 140.
Barclay, Alexander, 34, 37, 41, 44, 59, 65, 83.
Barela, 80.
Barlow & Sanderson Stage Line, 102.
Barlow, Lewis, 103.
Barnoy, Joseph, 83.
Bartlett, Postmaster Kenneth B., 135.
Baxter, Gene & Keith (The Shivers), 169.
Beacon, 103.
Beaubien, Charles, 35.
Beaubien, Narciso, 41.
Beaubois, Mr., 93, 95, 130.
Becknell, William, 30, 37, 83.
Beckwith, Doctor, 113.
Beckwith, Lt. Edward G., 86-90, 113, 123.
Beckwourth, James Pierson, 6, 7, 37, 45, 58, 86.
Beer, Henry, 58.
Benham, Frank, 114.
Bent, Alfredo, 90.
Bent Brothers Drive (Blvd), 140-142, 177.
Bent, Charles, 28-37, 41, 62, 83, 90-93, 96-97.
Bent, George, 33-35, 41.
Bent, Maria Ignacio Jaramillo, 90, 97.
Bent, Robert, 34-35.
Bent, Teresina, 90.
Bent, William, 15, 28-37, 79, 119.
Bents (Old) Fort, 15, 30, 34-35, 37, 41, 47, 49, 87.
Berg, Patty, 152.

Best Western, 155.
Big Nigger, 37.
Big Timbers, 32, 79.
Billups, Howard, 143.
Binstein, Mark P., 158-159, 162.
Bishop, James R. (Castle), 147, 159, 172.
Blackburn, Henry, 162-163.
Blackfoot Indians, 46-47.
Blackhawk (Pascual Riviere), 7, 43, 52, 59.
Boggs, Thomas Oliver, 95, 119.
Bonner, Thomas (Squire) D., 50.
Botts, Bill, 155.
Boy Scouts of Rye, 133.
Brantzel Rest Area, 173.
Bray, James, 114.
Briggs, Calvin T., 37, 58, 65.
Brown, John, 7, 11, 37, 40, 43, 50-53, 55-77, 83, 91, 95, 97, 110.
Brown, John Henry, 55.
Brown, John, Jr., 7, 43-44, 51-55.
Brown, John M., 55.
Brown, Luisa, 6, 7, 43-45, 47, 49, 51-53, 55, 58-59, 65, 95, 136.
Buckley, Frank, 108.
Burk, William E., 122.
Burks, Tommy (Taco Rock Lounge), 169.
Burroughs, John, 37, 58, 65.
Business Directory & Map, 174.
Butcher, Jim, 173.
Butkovich Construction, 140.
Byways (promotion), 174.
Cachupin, Governor, 17.
Cafe Cuerno Verde, 179.
Calhoun, Superintendent James, 81.
California City Development Co., 119-120, 163, 176-177.
Campbell, Dr. Robert L. & Evelyn, 170.
Campbell, Elmer & Frank, 117-118.
Canadian geese, 175.
Candelara, 58, 65.
Carlson, Sharon (The Doghouse), 169.
Carson, Kit, 37, 44, 55, 64-65, 77-78, 90-91, 97, 119, 131.
Carter, Avery, 112.
Cedarwood (Canyon & settlement), 9, 116.
Centerline, Inc., 154.
Chalauqua, 135.
Chamber of Commerce, 146, 152, 159, 174, 179.
Charlefou, Jean-Baptiste, 64.
Charlotte's Web Restaurant, 165.
Charno, 61.
Chavez, Antonio, 83.
Cheyenne Indians, 113, 16, 32-34, 79, 82, 104.
Chief Blanco, 80.
Chief Green Horn (Cuerno Verde), 6, 8, 11, 17-25, 111.
Children's Center, 170.
Chiquito, Juan, 83-84.
Chivington, Col. John M., 86, 104.
Christenson, Roy, 161.
Church of Jesus Christ Of Latter-Day Saints, 178.
Circle of Firearms, Inc., 171-172.
Civilian Conservation Corps (CCC), 16.
Clennin, Dick, 113.
Clyman, James, 46.
Cody, Administrator E. O., 150.
Coffee, Chairman Wallace, 174.
Coffin Award, 137.
Colella's Italian & American Restaurant, 179.
Colorado City & Rye Interchange (I-25), 137, 143, 148-150, 154.
Colorado City Call (newspaper), 121.
Colorado City Community Church, 148, 175, 178.
Colorado City Development Co. (CCDC), 119-147.
Colorado City Development Co. (CCDC/GWC), 155-167, 176-177.
Colorado City Development Co. (CCDC/GWU), 149-152.
Colorado City Economic Development Group, 166.
Colorado City Lot Owners & Taxpayers Assoc, 158, 162.
Colorado City Post Office, 172, 175.
Colorado City Property Owner Assoc., Inc., 172.
Colorado City (race horse), 140, 151.
Colorado City Reality Co., 147.
Colorado City Residents for Progress, 161, 164.
Colorado City Sun (newspaper), 121.
Colorado State Real Estate Commission,

156-157.
Colorado Territory, 98, 117.
Columbia House, 170-172.
Comanche Indians, 8, 11, 13, 16-25, 33, 111, 174.
Commercial (Center) Plaza, 142-148, 152, 159, 177.
Concept 80 Real Estate, Ltd., 161.
Confederacy, 91, 98.
Conn, W. A., 66.
Conner, Captain D. E., 98.
Conoco Service Station, 147.
Conroy, Eugene Vincent & Assoc., 146.
Cook, Jim & Janet, 171.
Cooper, Reverend, 112.
Country Cablevision, 172.
Cox, Finn, 112, 114.
Craver, Pleasant J. & Mrs., 156.
Crenshaw, Dr. Floyd, 149.
Creutzfeldt, F., 90.
Crouix, Senior Governor, 23.
Crow Cut-Off Rd., 146, 156.
Crow Indians, 46-47.
Crow Junction, 8, 12, 103, 117, 136-137, 146.
Crow, Matthew, 146.
Crow (Ranch, Village, Station, P.O.), 12, 96-97, 103, 117-119, 130, 142, 146, 152, 159.
Crowton, 119.
Cuerno Verde Boulevard, 123, 127, 149.
Cuerno Verde (Comanche Chief Green Horn), 6, 8, 11, 17-25, 111, 157, 159, 164, 170, 174.
Cuerno Verde (resort), 112.
Cuerno Verde Rest Area, 173.
Dallas Bankruptcy Court, 164-165.
Dennis, Joe, 66.
Denver Rio Grand Railroad, 103, 109.
Department of Wildlife (DOW), 173.
Depp (Deep), Henry, 112.
Diamond, Joe (Clip Joint), 169.
Diamond Slash, The, 113.
Dickey, Jim, 37, 66.
Digital Satellite TV, 172.
Dillon, U.S. Dist. Judge S. Hugh, 158.
Dixit Corporation, 161, 167.
Dixon, Charity, 112.

Dodge, Colonel, 99.
DO-RAY Lamp Co., 155, 165, 168-170.
Dover, Sam & David J., 155.
Doyle, Joseph Brainbridge, 59, 81, 83-85.
Doze, Joseph B., 111.
Ducker, Bruce, 155.
Duell, Albert (Ab) C. & Mary, 147-149, 159-162, 167, 175.
Duell, Holland (Holly) Jr., 12, 96, 118-120, 151, 159, 171, 174.
Duell, Holland Jr. III (3rd), 149.
Duell Lake, 148.
Duell, Mrs. Dorothy Curry Holland, 96, 151.
Duell-Stewart Thoroughbred Farm, 12, 119, 140, 142, 147, 150.
Duell, Susan, 174.
Dun Dancer, 140.
Dusenberry, Charlie, 109.
El Rancho Alegre, 169.
Emerald Strip, 176.
Emrich, Jacob A., 137.
Espey's BBQ, 179.
Ester Swift's Beauty Parlor, 146.
Estes, Asa, 37, 42, 56, 64.
Everhart, Mahlon T., 128.
Fairchild, Zina, 108, 110.
Fairview (San Isabel), 108.
Father Clark, 111.
Federal Trade Commission, 152, 156.
First Baptist Church of Greenhorn Valley, 147-149, 163, 178.
Fisher, Charles, T., 111.
Fisher, Robert, 49, 64.
Flathead Indians, 82.
Fort William, 32.
Fosscceo, Alven, 107.
Fosscceo (family), 11-12, 105-107.
Fosscceo, Josephine, 107.
Fosscceo, Marla, 107.
Fountain Creek (River), 21, 40, 65, 80.
Fountain Sand & Gravel Co., 136.
Fountain Square of Colorado City, 152-155, 165, 169, 172.
Fowler, Jacob, 28.
Freemont, Lt. John C., 28, 55, 86.
French (France), 13, 15, 30, 35, 37, 61, 93, 123.
Frink, Janie, 96.

Frink, John, 128, 130.
Frink, Mr. & Mrs. David, 110-111.
Frosset, Jennie, 114.
Furman, William Michael, 165-168, 171-172.
Gallegos, Mary Lou (Pat's Place), 169.
Galvez, George, 43.
Gammon, Bill, 109.
Garden of Eatin' Coffee & Sandwich Shop, 179.
Garey (Guerrier), Bill, 49.
Garrard, Lewis, 42.
Gass, Texan H. M., 97.
Geologist Peaker & Riess of CA, 126.
Gillingham, Dr. W. P., 115.
Gnomes Attic, 165.
Gody, 68.
Gold Rush of 1849, 110.
Golden Wheels Drive-in, 152.
Good Investment, 140.
Good Templers, 114.
Goodale, (Goodall & Goodell), 56-59, 77.
Goss, Calvin, 112, 117.
Graber, Morris & Betty, 140, 150.
Graham, Bill (Farmers Insurance), 169.
Graham, Richard (Dick), 123, 127.
Grand Lodge of Colorado Masons, 140.
Graneros Canyon Animal Park, 107.
Graneros Canyon Service Station, 107.
Graneros Creek, 11, 88, 101-106, 112-113, 116, 137.
Graneros Flats, 103, 109.
Graneros Gorge (public park), 12, 103, 107, 126-127, 136, 142.
Graneros Village, 105.
Graves, Jim, 108.
Graves, Pat, 170.
Gray, Henry, 109.
Graybeal, Hiram and John T., 112.
Great Western Cities (GWC), 149.
Great Western United (GWU), 144-147.
Greenhorn Canon, 112.
Greenhorn D&RGW Railroad Station, 12.
Greenhorn Inn, 105.
Greenhorn Inn of Colorado City, 155.
Greenhorn Meadows Park, 152-154, 164, 170.
Greenhorn Mine, 108.

Greenhorn Mountains, 8- 9, 30, 37, 43, 59, 108.
Greenhorn Post Office, 12.
Greenhorn Rancho (Hicklin Ranch), 97.
Greenhorn Road, 11, 59.
Greenhorn Stage Stop, 11, 12.
Greenhorn Valley Airport, 154.
Greenhorn Valley (brochure), 174.
Greenhorn Valley Grocery & Market, 163, 167-169.
Greenhorn Valley News, 152-154, 158-163, 167, 170-171.
Greenhorn Valley Shopping Center, 159, 162, 172, 174.
Greenhorn Valley Theater, 170, 175.
Groaner Flats, 9.
Gross, Norman, 121, 125.
Guerrier, William, 66.
Gunnison, Captain J. W., 80, 86-90, 123.
Guzzo, Lou, 171.
Halsey, Mrs. Laura Williams, 110-111, 128-134.
Hambric, Bill, 157.
Hamler, Calvin, 173.
Hardin, Henry (Harry), 112.
Hardin, James & Frances, 114.
Harmon, Sue, 172.
Haskins, Brian, 155-156.
Hatcher, John L., 64.
Hatchet Cattle Co. (Ranch), 128, 174.
Hathaway, Claude, M., 137-138, 146.
Haus, Maxwell, 147.
Hawkins, John, 37.
Hayden Ranch, 113, 117.
Hayes, William, 114.
Haynes, George, 111.
Henderson, Jim (Auto Shop), 169.
Henry, Don, 149.
Heritage Day (s), 159.
Herold, Doctor, 66.
Herring, Rube, 37, 58, 65.
Hicklin, Alex (Alec), 95-96, 101, 130.
Hicklin, Alexander (Zan), 11, 91, 94-103, 119, 130-131, 170.
Hicklin, Alfred, 96, 103.
Hicklin, Dona Estefana Bent, 37, 90-97, 100-103, 130-131, 170.
Hicklin Irrigation Ditches, 136-137,

140-142, 164.
Hicklin, John, 99-100.
Hicklin Memorial Museum, 167.
Hicklin Memorial Park, 127, 130-131.
Hicklin Ranch (Hicklins, Crow), 11, 12,
    101, 110, 117, 151.
Hicklin, Talman, 99-100, 130.
Hicklin, Thomas (Tom), 95-96, 128, 130.
Hier & Price of Sedalia, 125.
Higgens, John, 112.
Higgens, Ronald, 149.
Hillenbrand's Grocery Store, 146.
Historical Society (Greenhorn Valley), 24,
    157, 161, 167-168.
Holiday Inn, 149, 154-155.
Hollydot Golf Course, 117, 175.
Hollydot Park (Co.), 148-152, 155, 159.
Hollydot Park Turf Club, 149-151.
Houston, Mrs. Bert, 143.
Howard, Tim, 111.
Hudson Home, 114.
Huerfano Butte, 14, 103.
Huerfano (County, Valley),
    15, 30, 112-113, 135-136.
Huerfano River, 9, 16, 79-87, 103.
Hunt, Nelson B. & William H., 155.
Hunter, David F., 112-113.
Hunter, Lewis (Uncle Lewis) R., 113.
Illinois Attorney General (William Scott),
    157-158, 162-166.
Impressionist Printing, 172.
Indian George, 7.
Industrial Park, 137, 146-148, 155,
    168-172.
Irving, John, 115.
James, Clyde, 127.
Jaramillo, Josefa (Josephana), 90.
Jaramillo, Maria Ignacia, 90.
Jaramillo, Pablo, 41.
Jeff's Valley Pharmacy, 174.
Johnson, Pres. & Mrs. Lyndon B., 133.
Johnson, Rev. Irven, 149.
Jones, Calvin, 64, 66, 99.
Jones, Pastor & Mrs. Clyde, 148.
Jose the Fiddler, 51.
Kern, Richard, 90.
Kerney, Gen. Stephen W., 90.
Kindel, George, 109.

Kinney, Charles, 66, 77-80.
Kiowa Indians, 13, 32, 33, 44.
Kirkland, Moritz, 150.
Kline, Howard, 118.
Klipfel, Willard & Betty, 162.
Knollwood Village, 146.
Knopf, Larry, 155.
Kravig, Gary (The Shivers), 169.
Kroenig, William, 49, 83, 85.
Lake Beckwith, 110, 117-118, 123-128,
    133, 136-137, 140, 142, 146,
    149-153, 172-173.
Lake Isabel, 116, 137, 147, 172.
Lascar settlement, 116.
Last Supper, The, 175.
Leal, James White, 41.
Lebanon, 113.
Le Blanc, William Antoine, 62-64, 79.
Ledoux, Abraham, 44.
Ledoux, Felipe, 44.
Ledoux, Mrs. Felipe, 7, 51, 59.
LeDuc (la Duc), Maurice, 37, 61.
Lee, Steve, 41.
Lil Store, 172.
Lime settlement, 82-83.
Lion's Club, 144-146, 152, 174-176.
Litterall, Doctor, 112.
Little Beaver, 37.
Livesey Ranch, 27.
Long, Stephen H., 28.
Lot Trade Program, 165-166.
Love, Gov. & Mrs. John A., 123-125, 136.
Loveland, J. S., 66.
Lucero, Manuel, 81.
Luna, Tanislado de, 81.
Lupton, Landcaster, 65.
M. C. Kirkland, 136.
McDaniel, J. H., 101.
McDonnell, Mark, (Signs & Upholstery),169.
McElwain, Henry E., 109.
Mace's Hole (Beulah), 98.
McHarg, Mrs. May, 128.
McKellip Home, 114.
McMartin, Postmaster, 133.
Maher, Richard L., 149.
Malachite settlement, 11.
Malagres, Gov. Don Facundo, 15.
Marion Mine, 108-110.

Marshall, Jesse, 112.
Martin, Juan Blas, 81.
Mason, Lee & Pat, 169.
Masons (Cuerno Verde Square & Compass Club, Lodge #196), 161, 171.
Maxwell, Lucien Bonaparte, 7, 43, 52, 55, 64, 77, 119.
Mead, Enoch & Caroline, 113.
Meadowcreek, 159-161, 165-170.
Medical Center (Building), 169-174.
Medill, Thomas, 111.
Medina, Juan Rafael, 80.
Meis, Jose, 58.
Mendelsohn, Mrs. Sylvia & Wendy, 122.
Mendelsohn, Nathan K., 120-126, 133, 136, 143-145, 158, 164, 176.
MERBISC (Most Extraordinary Recreation Bargain in Southern Colorado), 142-143, 146, 152-154, 162.
Mercantile (building, store, hotel), 12, 117-118, 142, 146, 160-162.
Meredith, Capt. William, 112-115.
Mestas, Francisco, 81.
Metcalf, Charles (Archa) Archibald, 40-44, 49, 51-55, 66, 110.
Metcalf, Maria de la Luz Trujillo, 44, 51-52, 55, 64.
Metropolitan Recreation District, 138, 142-146, 152-154, 163.
Metropolitan Water & Sewer (Metro), 140, 142-146, 152-157, 161-173.
Miera, Felix, 81.
Miller, F. D., 114.
Miller, Mr. & Mrs. Gary, 167.
Miller's Stage Station, 99.
Mitchell, Levin (Colorado), 37, 83.
Molello, Mr. & Mrs., 144.
Montoya, 79.
Moody, Joe, 114.
Moody, Mr. & Mrs. W. G., 115.
Moore, Burton, 111.
Moore, Robert (Conoco), 147.
Moore's Valley Auto Repair, 176.
Moorlite Concrete Co., 147.
Mora, NM, 83.
Mormon Town, 28, 62.
Morrow, John, 111.
Mount of the Holy Cross, 133-134.

Mountain Branch of Sante Fe Trail, 15, 59.
Mountain High Balloons, 172.
Mountain View Hotel, 113-116.
Muddy Creek, 9, 11, 111.
Muddy Creek Station, 11, 98-99, 105.
Music on the Greenhorn, 170.
Nambe Pueblo, 17.
Naumann, Gail K., 150.
Navajo Indians, 13, 33, 79, 82.
Nelson, Jesse Hodges, 64.
New, William (Bill), 37, 40, 64, 66, 77.
Nichols, David, Joel, & Thomas, 111.
Nicholson, Robert, 162.
Nickson, Tom, 99.
Nicolasa, 58-59, 65.
Noland Land Grant, 99.
O'Brien, Joe, 174.
Odd Fellows Hall (Graneros), 101-102.
Old Colorado City, 117.
Old Oaken Bucket (song), 101.
Oldshaw Home (Southern Methodist parsonage), 112-114.
Oliver, Doctor, 66.
Ol' Zan's (cafe), 165, 179.
Oscar Hadwiger (collection), 171.
O'Sullivan, Jack (John), 120.
Overland Mail Bill, 98.
Owens, Dick, 58-59, 66.
Paiute Indians, 90.
Palisades Lumber, 147.
Pawnee Indians, 13, 15, 33, 76.
Peacock, Doctor, 66.
Peaks Auto Supply, 171-172.
Pecos Pueblo, 17.
Petal Cellar, 165.
Peterson, John & Joseph, 112.
Phillips, Richard L., 95-96.
Phonetica One, 168-169.
Picuris Pueblo, 17.
Pike, Captain Zebulon, 8, 25-28.
Pikes Peak, 8, 9, 20.
Pineda, Juan, 84.
Pizza Shop, 172.
Prairie Flower Deli, 179.
Price, Colonel Sterling, 37, 42.
Price, Jack, 156, 165-168.
Pritchard, John, 111.
Promised Lands, 155.

Provenzano, Mrs. Attie, 131-133.
Pueblo City (County), 123, 143, 156, 159-172, 176-177.
Pueblo County Housing Mortgage Bond Program, 171.
Pueblo School District#70, 140, 147, 150.
Pueblo Trading Post (The Pueblo, El Pueblo), 30, 40-41, 49, 51, 56, 58-59, 80, 99, 102-103.
Quillian, Asbury (Paul Ray), 111-112.
Rath, Charlie, 99.
Rayado, 79.
Red Creek Ranch, 174.
Re-Do-It Upholstery, 171.
Rendezvous Days, 149-152, 159.
Reverend Barry, 111.

Rice, Julia, 96.
Richardson, Ken, 149.
Ridenour-Graber Enco, 140-142.
Ridenour, Louise, 140.
Rimrock Lounge, 169.

Rio Colorado, NM, 79, 83-84.
Robach, Rudolph, 115.
Robidoux's Fort Uncompahgre, 42.
Rock Place, 111.
Roley, Mr. & Mrs., 112.
Romer, Gov. Roy, 168.
Rouse Funeral Home, 131.
Rowdy Fleet, 140.
Ruff, Dave, 152.
Rye Consolidated School District #13, 116.
Rye Fire Protection, 147, 170.
Rye Home United Methodist Church, 174, 178.
Rye Post Office, 161.
Rye settlement, 110-116.
Rye Star Route (mail), 115-116.
Rye Telephone Co., 150.
Rye Women's Club, 163.
St. Aloysius Catholic Church, 112.
St. Charles Creek (settlement), 14, 16, 28, 65, 79-83, 99, 103, 108-110, 116.
St. Charles Lake, 116.
St. John Hotel, 68.
St. Mary's (settlement), 103.
St. Vrain, Ceran, 8, 28-39, 80, 83-84, 90-91, 95, 125.

St. Vrain, Gloria & Julia, 125.
St. Vrain, Vicente, 43.
Sam Jones Insurance Agency, 146.
San Bernardino, CA, 69, 72.
San Carlos Creek (settlement), 14, 16, 28, 65, 79, 81-83, 99.
San Fernando de Taos, 41-42, 90.
San Isabel Electric Assoc., 143, 146, 150.
San Isabel (settlement), 110, 116.
San Juan Bautista, 68.
Sand Creek, 86.
Sandoval, Benito, 81.
Sandoval, Juan Isidro, 81.
Sandoval, Luisa Beckwourth Brown, 6, 7, 43, 45, 47, 49, 51-55.
Sandoval, Maria Natividad, 40, 42.
Santa Cruz da la Canada, 17.
Sarafina (Autobee), 84.
Sayer, Mr. & Mrs. Jacob, 113-114.
Scapoolar, 61.
Sears, George, 96, 105, 112-115.
Sears, Robert, 101.
Sears, Sarah Jane, 130.
Sensebough, Rev. O. F., 112.
Settlement of Meadows, 27.
Shady Greenhorn, 11, 103-107.
Shallenbarger, Ken & Joyce, 171.
Shaw, Emma, 95.
Sheets, Major Sam, 112-113.
Shelman, M. K., 123.
Sheppard, Dan & Tammy, 169.
Siccamo (Sycamore), 82-84.
Simpson, George, 49, 59, 81, 83, 110.
Sioux Indians, 82.
Skelly Service Station, 140.
Smith, Doctor M., 69.
Smith, Jedediah, 46.
Smith, Norm & Pam, 169.
Smith, Rick, 114.
Smith, Ron & Adele, 169.
Smith, William, 111.
Sneddon, Robert S., 127.
Snyder, Dr. Kin & Mary Hund, 174.
Sorrell, Clifford, 127.
South Oak Creek, 89.
Spalding, David, 49.
Spanish Peaks, 9.
Spanish (Spain), 13-28, 51, 61, 123, 174.

Spensor, Gene, 127.
Spirit of a Bear, 172.
Sportsman's Club, 164.
Stamped Club Rodeo, 135.
Stanley (ranch & family), 103, 128.
Stein, C. C., 101.
Stewart, Conyers, 118-119, 147, 176.
Stewart, Jim, 176.
Stone, 56.
Stuckey's (cafe & gas), 143.
Stylish Pet Parlor, 165.
Suaso, Teresita, 49.
Sublette, William L., 46.
Subway (sandwiches), 179.
Swanock, Jim, 37, 66.
Switzer, Leo (Taco Rock Lounge), 169.
Table Mountain, 111-113, 140, 161.
Taco Bell Express, 174.
Taco Rock (location), 169.
Taos Indians, 37, 42.
Taos Pueblo, 37.
Taos Rebellion, 37, 41-43, 50, 62-64, 90.
Taos Trail, 15-16.
Taylor Fountain (Little), 127, 137, 143.
Taylor, Ralph C., 120-121, 129, 135, 157, 167-168, 174.
Tesson, 66.
Texaco Service Station, 118, 169.
Thacker, Madeline, 117.
Tharp, Bill, 49, 58, 65.
Thatcher, Mahlon & John, A., 128.
Theresians of America, 143, 146.
Thirty-Mile House, 102, 105.
Three Jims, The, 175.
Tobin (Autobee), Tom, 58, 62, 64, 83, 131.
Tomasa (Tomacita), 76, 82.
Total Petroleum, 174.
Town, Charles, 7, 43, 52, 64.
Trappers Trail, 15, 59.
Travel Travel, 172.
Treasure Chest Homes, 127.
True Value Hardware, 159-162, 169.
Trujillo, Francisco, 40-42.
Trujillo, Maria de la Luz, 40-44.
Trulove, J. A., 114.
Tucksender, 61.
Turley, Simeon, 34, 43, 49, 62-64, 82-83.
Ulibarri, General Juan, 14.

Union soldiers, 98.
U.S. Census (1990-2000), 175.
Ute Indians, 13, 16, 20, 42-43, 52, 79-81, 83, 93, 104, 137.
Valencia, Jose Ignacio, 80.
Valley Auto Sales, 176.
Valley Center, 174.
VFW Post Building, 169.
Vigil, Cornelio (Cornellio), 35, 41, 84, 95.
Vigil, Guadalupe, 81.
Vilasur, Lt. Don Pedro di, 14.
Vince's Barber Shop, 146.
Viulla, Edward, 147.
W. I. Gray Place, 161.
Ward, Seth, 66.
Warner, John, 96, 110.
Waters, James (Jim), 37, 58, 65-72.
Way Out West (WOW), 175.
Weeden, John, 127.
West Course (golf), 127, 150, 168.
Western Museum of the Pueblo Saddle Makers, 171.
Wet Mountain Valley, 14, 37, 52, 59.
Wet Mountains (Sierra Mojada), 15, 87-88, 108, 110.
Wetmore, 116.
White, Charles, 65.
White, Robert, 137.
White, William M. Jr., 144-145, 158.
Whittlesey, Lt. Joseph H., 44.
William Hunter Place, 113.
Williams, Laura, 110.
Williams, Mr. & Mrs. John, 96, 110, 135.
Williams, Sara, 110.
Williams, Wayne, 122.
Wirt's Place, Mrs., 114.
Wixson, Saul, 108.
Woodmen of the World (WOW), 114.
Wootten, Uncle Dick, 49, 61, 81, 83.
Wright, Bob, 99.
Zip Pocket, 140.
Zorich-Erken Water Engineering, 157.

ORDER FORM

Send to: Benchmark Book Craft   Date_____
         P. O. Box 19583
         Colorado City, CO 81019

Please ship <u>Colorado's Greenhorn Valley, Fact and Folklore, 1700-2000</u> by Gerald W. Crispin

Quantity	Unit Price	Shipping	Total Amount
1	$21.95	$3.00	$24.95
#_____	_____	_____	_____

                Sold to: Shipped to:

Customer   _____   _____
Street   _____   _____
City, State   _____   _____
Zip   _____   _____

         Received _____   Check Number _____

Graneros Gorge from Park Ruins

Little Taylor Park in 2000

Hicklin Ditch off Greenhorn Ck.

Author Gerald in 2000

Shady Greenhorn in 2000

Lake Beckwith in 2000

ISBN 0-9744015-0-1